Competitiveness of CEE Economies and Businesses

To
Professor Arnold Schuh, with our sincere thanks for your valuable contributions to the completion of this work and with hope for future collaboration with our AIB-CEE Chapter

Piotr Trąpczyński
Łukasz Puślecki
Jarosław Grobau

Prague, 1.10.2016

Piotr Trąpczyński • Łukasz Puślecki •
Mirosław Jarosiński
Editors

Competitiveness of CEE Economies and Businesses

Multidisciplinary Perspectives on Challenges and Opportunities

Springer

Editors
Piotr Trąpczyński
Poznań University of Economics
   and Business
Poznań
Poland

Łukasz Puślecki
Poznań University of Economics
   and Business
Poznań
Poland

Mirosław Jarosiński
SGH Warsaw School of Economics
Warsaw
Poland

Reviewed by Arnold Schuh, Vienna University of Economics and Business, Vienna, Austria

ISBN 978-3-319-39653-8   ISBN 978-3-319-39654-5   (eBook)
DOI 10.1007/978-3-319-39654-5

Library of Congress Control Number: 2016947049

© Springer International Publishing Switzerland 2016
This work is subject to copyright. All rights are reserved by the Publisher, whether the whole or part of the material is concerned, specifically the rights of translation, reprinting, reuse of illustrations, recitation, broadcasting, reproduction on microfilms or in any other physical way, and transmission or information storage and retrieval, electronic adaptation, computer software, or by similar or dissimilar methodology now known or hereafter developed.
The use of general descriptive names, registered names, trademarks, service marks, etc. in this publication does not imply, even in the absence of a specific statement, that such names are exempt from the relevant protective laws and regulations and therefore free for general use.
The publisher, the authors and the editors are safe to assume that the advice and information in this book are believed to be true and accurate at the date of publication. Neither the publisher nor the authors or the editors give a warranty, express or implied, with respect to the material contained herein or for any errors or omissions that may have been made.

Printed on acid-free paper

This Springer imprint is published by Springer Nature
The registered company is Springer International Publishing AG Switzerland

Foreword

The discussion of competitiveness of the countries and firms in Central and Eastern Europe is a timely issue. In the last 25 years since the fall of the Iron Curtain, these former socialist countries have undergone a fundamental and remarkable transformation of their economies and societies. They have reached 50–80 % of the EU average in GDP per head and are growing 1–2.5 percentage points faster again than the EU average today. This successful economic development was based on a quick economic and political integration into the EU including access to EU regional funds and the Single Market as well as major internal efforts to adapt the institutional framework, modernise and privatise former state-owned firms, liberalise access to markets and foster entrepreneurship. Strong capital, technology and knowledge transfer via foreign direct investments from the West to CEE and the integration of CEE firms into European or even global value chains contributed to this economic catching-up process too.

To analyse competitiveness, this book relies on both the country and the firm perspective. Firms are operating within the institutional and economic structures of a country, which may facilitate or hinder business success. Governments determine the level of productivity and finally prosperity by how they design institutions, economic policy and production factors. Identifying (traditional) national industry clusters and developing them further—such as the furniture industry in Poland, engineering in Czech Republic, tourism in Croatia or agriculture in Romania, Ukraine and Serbia—is a good example for the close interplay between national economic policy and firms' development of competitive advantage. Similarly, building up new industries such as the automotive industry in Slovakia and Hungary, information technology in Romania, aviation industry in Poland and business process outsourcing in Central Europe in general proves that governments have room to manoeuvre when steering the development of their economies.

Looking at the reforming countries in CEE reveals differences in their comparative advantages. The global financial and economic crisis of 2008–2009 highlighted the strengths and weaknesses of each economy. While Central

European economies such as the Czech Republic, Poland and Slovakia bet more on a qualified workforce and product quality, Southeast European countries such as Romania, Bulgaria and Serbia still rely on low labour costs and low taxes. Overall, we can observe a divergent development in competitiveness. On the one hand, some of the early reformers from Central Europe—Hungary, Slovakia and Slovenia—have been steadily losing in competitiveness since their accession to the EU, dropping more than 20 ranks in the Global Competitiveness Index in the period from 2004 to 2015. On the other hand, Poland, Romania and the Czech Republic have been improving continuously their positions in the same period. Despite these differences, CEE economies face a "sandwich position" in their global competitive positioning. Other emerging economies, particularly from Asia, challenge them in terms of cost and efficiency, while West European economies, Japan and the USA are still ahead in terms of innovation and product quality. Most of the CEE economies are in a transition from an efficiency- to an innovation-driven economy. The task now is not to get stuck as a nearby low-cost producer for Western multinationals but to upgrade existing strengths in industrial production and expand into more knowledge-intensive manufacturing. Encouraging investments in agriculture and food processing and capturing more value in outsourcing are other suggested directions of development.

Here, the firm perspective comes into play. Firms compete on international markets, and the success of a nation is ultimately the result of the competitiveness of its firms. Given the smallness of most of the CEE economies, higher levels of prosperity can only be achieved via business expansion abroad. So far the subsidiaries of foreign multinationals drive the export of CEE economies. The majority of exports stem from the production sites of VW Group, Hyundai, Samsung, Foxconn, General Electrics and Siemens, which service European markets from CEE. Leading domestically owned and internationally active firms are often state-owned or state-controlled ones in the energy and commodity sector, diversified business groups and niche specialists. State-owned firms, publicly listed firms and large business groups are mostly spearheading internationalisation as they have the critical mass of resources to bear the costs and risks of going international. Although size matters, a large potential lies in promoting mid-sized firms that follow smart specialisation strategies. The "hidden champions" and "local heroes" that concentrate on market niches and expand their business internationally are great role models. This type of firm seems to fit the conditions in CEE countries perfectly, namely a well-educated workforce, strong engineering tradition and high affinity to ICT. Add a good dose of entrepreneurship (and seed capital) and you have a formula that could ignite a wave of internationally successful firms originating from CEE.

It is not surprising that these entrepreneur run firms increasingly attract the attention of business researchers and policymakers. This overview of the competitive assets of CEE countries, their specific economic structures and potential development paths is a good starting point for deeper research. In this sense, this book provides a valuable contribution to the understanding of the mechanisms of competitiveness in the region of Central and Eastern Europe.

Competence Center for Emerging Markets & CEE　　　　　　　　Arnold Schuh
Vienna University of Economics and Business
Vienna, Austria

Contents

Part I Country-Level Developments

The Competitiveness of EU Member States from Central and Eastern Europe in 2007–2014 3
Marzenna Anna Weresa

Competitiveness, Entrepreneurship and Economic Growth 25
Romana Korez-Vide and Polona Tominc

Facilitating Outward Foreign Direct Investment (OFDI): The Perspective of Support Providers in Poland in the Aftermath of 2008+ Economic Crisis 45
Marta Götz and Barbara Jankowska

Attracting FDI to the New EU Member States 65
Tomasz Dorożyński and Anetta Kuna-Marszałek

Policies to Promote Eco-innovation: Results for Selected CEE Countries and Germany 89
Małgorzata Stefania Lewandowska

CEE Countries as a Business Process Outsourcing Destination 115
Patryk Dziurski

Part II Firm-Level Developments

Contrasting Methods: An Explorative Investigation on Firm-Level Export Competitiveness Based on Qualitative and Quantitative Research Findings 133
Erzsébet Czakó, Péter Juhász, and László Reszegi

Emerging CEE Multinationals in the Electronics Industry 149
Magdolna Sass

Human Capital and HRM as a Source of Competitive Advantage and Effectiveness: Evidence from Poland 175
Anna Jawor-Joniewicz and Łukasz Sienkiewicz

Examination of Central and Eastern European Professional Football Clubs' Sport Success, Financial Position and Business Strategy in International Environment 197
Krisztina András and Zsolt Havran

Local Heroes in Hungary 211
Miklós Stocker

About the Editors and Authors

Editors

Mirosław Jarosiński, PhD, is an Associate Professor in the Institute of Management at the SGH Warsaw School of Economics, Poland. Besides graduate studies at SGH, he has been teaching in the Canadian Executive MBA Programme, Master's in International Business and CEMS Master's in International Management, all of them at the Warsaw School of Economics.

Mirosław Jarosiński is a CEMS Academic Director at the Warsaw School of Economics. In the period of 2006–2011, he was a Programme Director of Master Studies in International Business at SGH. In the period 2008–2010, he was the EU Project Leader of the INTERPARSE Programme (International Trade Education in Partnership with Small and Medium Sized Enterprises) co-financed by the Government of Canada and the European Commission. Mirosław Jarosiński is a member of several international organisations. Since 2014, he has been active in the Academy of International Business Central and Eastern Europe Chapter.

Mirosław Jarosiński obtained his PhD degree in Management from the Warsaw School of Economics, Poland. He specialises in Strategic Management and International Management. His research focuses on International New Ventures and Born Globals from emerging markets.

Łukasz Puślecki, PhD, is an Assistant Professor at the Department of International Management, Faculty of International Business and Economics, Poznań University of Economics and Business (PUEB), Poland. He is also Director of Joint MSc in International Business and Management (JMScIBM) Programme between Poznań University of Economics and Business and Nottingham Trent University, Nottingham Business School (UK). Dr. Puślecki holds positions in several professional and academic institutions. He is the Chair of the Academy of International Business Central and Eastern Europe (AIB-CEE) Chapter, Vice-Chair of Assessing Committee of Youth Award Foundation, Germany, member of Hessen Academy of

Research and Planning on Rural Areas (HAL), Germany, and member of the board of the Faculty of International Business and Economics, PUEB, Poland. He is an expert in Knowledge and Innovation Institute, Warsaw, Poland, as well as expert on youth policy in ECCP (European Centre of Citizens' Partnership) and ERY NETWORK (European Regions for Youth) on behalf of Memorandum of Understanding signed by 10 European Regions and expert in Vocational Training and Education in EREI-VET Network of 14 European Regions (European Regions Enhancing Internationalization of Vocational Education and Training). He is the member of the Academy of International Business (AIB) and the Association of Strategic Alliance Professionals (ASAP).

Łukasz Puślecki obtained his PhD in international economics from the Poznań University of Economics and Business. His research focuses on technological cooperation, strategic alliances (SA) and strategic technology alliances (STA), open innovation alliances (OIA) as well as on innovation, technological competitiveness and knowledge-based economies.

Piotr Trąpczyński, PhD, is an Assistant Professor at the Department of International Competitiveness, Poznań University of Economics and Business (PUEB), Poland. He is also an MBA and Master lecturer with specialisation in international business strategy and international marketing, as well as head of the research project "The determinants of foreign direct investment performance in the internationalisation process of Polish companies", financed by the National Science Centre of Poland (for the period 2013–2015).

Prior to these positions, Piotr worked as Research Assistant at the Berlin Campus of ESCP Europe, where he completed a European Doctoral Programme in International Business, and he is lecturer in international business at the Academy of Business and Economics (VWA) in Berlin. He had also gained business experience through several positions in the IT industry, strategic management consulting and brand management in the FMCG sector. He gained his PhD degree at the Poznań University of Economics and Business, as well as MSc from the City University of London, Dipl.-Kfm and Master degrees of the ESCP Europe in Berlin and Paris.

His research interests include internationalisation into and from emerging and transition economies (with focus on the CEE), FDI performance, firm competitiveness as well as mixed-method research.

Dr. Piotr Trąpczyński is also supported by the Foundation for Polish Science (FNP).

Authors

Krisztina András, PhD, is Associate Professor at the Institute of Business Economics, the Corvinus Business School. She is the director of the Sport Business Research Centre in the Corvinus University of Budapest (Hungary). Her major research topics are professional sports, sport and competitiveness and effects of sport mega events. She is often interviewed in sport management issues by the media. She has served as the vice-president of the Guardian of Budapest 2024 Olympic Games and the Sport Management Committee of the Hungarian Society of Sport Science.

Erzsébet Czakó, PhD, is Professor at the Department of Business Studies, Institute of Business Economics, Faculty of Business Administration, Corvinus University of Budapest (Hungary), where she has worked since her graduation and where she obtained her PhD and Habilitation degrees in Business and Management. Her research interests pertain to the contents of and approaches to competitiveness at national, industry and firm levels. Her lastly adopted research and teaching field is international business (IB). Her particular research interest relates to theories of IB and international strategies. She has been a member of the board of the Academy of International Business Central and Eastern European (AIB-CEE) Chapter since 2013.

Tomasz Dorożyński, PhD, is Assistant Professor at the Department of International Trade, Faculty of Economics and Sociology, University of Łódź (Poland). He is a member to several organisations of researchers in economics and international business, such as European International Business Academy, European Economics and Finance Society. His research achievements include ca. 90 publications. He has been involved in many research projects, also as project manager. The results of his studies have been presented at numerous domestic and international conferences, e.g. in the UK, Sweden, Germany, France and Brazil. His research work focuses, *inter alia*, on FDI and regional development.

Patryk Dziurski, MA, economist and a PhD Candidate at the SGH Warsaw School of Economics (Poland). He has published papers on managing organisations in creative industries, crisis management as well as business process outsourcing. His research focuses on the specificity of management in organisations operating in creative industries in Poland, especially in the design sector.

Marta Götz, PhD, is Associate Professor at Vistula University in Warsaw (Poland) since February 2016. Previously, she has been research fellow at the Institute for Western Affairs (Instytut Zachodni) in Poznań, a research centre under the auspices of the Ministry of Foreign Affairs and the Ministry of Science and Higher Education, as well as teaching assistant at the Department of International Economics, at Warsaw School of Economics in Warsaw. She has conducted individual and team projects granted by the National Science Centre and the Visegrad Fund. She is a member of the Academy of International Business (AIB), European International Business Academy (EIBA) and the Brussels-based Finance Watch association. Her areas of expertise include foreign direct investment, macroeconomics of the EU or economic transformations in reunified Germany.

Zsolt Havran is PhD candidate at the Corvinus University of Budapest (Hungary) and Assistant Professor at the Institute of Business Economics, the Corvinus Business School. His key research area is the examination of the human resource management in terms of professional sport. His research interests include transfer market of professional football, valuation of professional players and football markets of the Central and Eastern European region. He is a member of the Sport Business Research Centre in the Corvinus University of Budapest and the Hungarian Society of Sport Science.

Barbara Jankowska, PhD, is Associate Professor at the Poznań University of Economics and Business (PUEB), Poland, Faculty of International Business and Economics, Head of the Department of International Competitiveness, Chair of the Program Council at the Poznan-Atlanta MBA Program, National Representative of Poland in the European International Business Academy, member of the Polish Economic Society and member of the Academy of International Business. Her main research areas include international business (international competitiveness of firms and industries, strategy of the firm in international business, foreign direct investment), strategic management, industrial organisation and business clustering. She is the author or co-author of more than 100 publications, among them 6 books in her area of expertise.

Anna Jawor-Joniewicz, PhD, is Assistant Professor at the Department of Human Resources Management of the Institute for Labour and Social Affairs (Poland). She has over 15 years of working experience as researcher and analyst. She specialises in the analysis of human resources management (motivating, organisational culture, diversity management), labour market as well as equal opportunities for men and women. She actively cooperates with non-government organisations focusing on the prevention of gender-based discrimination.

Péter Juhász, PhD, is Associate Professor of the Department of Finance at Corvinus University of Budapest (CUB) (Hungary). He holds a PhD from CUB and his research topics include business valuation, appraisal of off-balance sheet assets, financial modelling and competitiveness and performance analysis of companies.

Romana Korez-Vide, PhD, is Assistant Professor at the Faculty of Economics and Business, University of Maribor (Slovenia). Her teaching and research area is International Economics and Business. So far she has explored globalisation of economies, institutional mechanisms for promotion of international trade and investment, trade costs and international trade flows, intercultural differences and stereotypes in international business and national competitiveness and economic growth. She is author and co-author of scientific and professional articles, chapters and conference papers and reviewer of papers in several international journals. She is a member of the Academy of International Business.

Anetta Kuna-Marszałek, PhD, is Senior Lecturer at the Department of International Trade, Faculty of Economics and Sociology, University of Łódź (Poland). For the last 10 years, her primary research interests have been focused on various aspects of contemporary economics, including research on links between trade liberalisation and environmental policies. She is currently working on internationalisation of business activities, foreign direct investment and support instruments for exporters. She is an author and co-author of over 50 papers, chapters and articles, including the award-winning book about anti-dumping investigations as an instrument of protection. She participated in several research projects, including projects co-financed by the EU.

Małgorzata Stefania Lewandowska, PhD, is Researcher and Lecturer at the Institute of International Management and Marketing, SGH Warsaw School of Economics (Poland). She holds a PhD degree from the Collegium of the World Economy SGH (2006) and MBA from Université du Québec à Montréal, Canada (2002). She is the author of several papers, mainly on international business and international cooperation issues. Her main research interest is innovation determinants, innovation cooperation at the firms' level as well as eco-innovation. She is lecturer of International Business, International Business Transactions and Strategies of Polish Enterprises in SGH and guest speaker on CEMS Blocked Seminars in Vienna, Wirtschaftuniversitat and Vysoka Skola Ekonomicka v Praze. She is involved in several research projects on international cooperation of enterprises in innovation processes, trends in marketing environment of Polish enterprises and business models of Polish firms. She is active in projects financed by the European Union, such as Global SGH, Lifelong Learning Programme (Leonardo da Vinci: Transfer of Innovation, Stimulating Learning for Idea-to-Market) and Horizon 2020: Investigating the Impact of the Innovation Union (I3U).

László Reszegi, PhD, is Honorary Professor of the Department of Business Studies at Corvinus University of Budapest (CUB) (Hungary) and Chair of Business Development Research Centre. He has lectured and taught business valuation, managerial accounting and performance analysis at CUB for several decades and has extensive experience in business consulting.

Magdolna Sass, PhD, is Senior Research Fellow at Hungarian Academy of Sciences CERS Institute of Economics since 1996. Her areas of expertise are foreign direct investment and internationalisation of firms. She has been involved in several research projects on European, national and regional levels. She has published more than 150 papers, including in Eastern European Economics, Post-Communist Economies, European Planning Studies, European Urban and Regional Studies, Review of Managerial Science and Acta Oeconomica. She is member of the editorial board of Post-Communist Economies and Croatian Economic Survey.

Łukasz Sienkiewicz, PhD, is Assistant Professor at the Institute of Human Capital of the SGH Warsaw School of Economics (Poland). He specialises in human capital management and labour market issues. His research interests include (but are not limited to) human capital development, competency-based HRM, wage research and analysis, labour market intelligence, skills surveying and forecasting, functioning of public employment services and self-employment. He currently holds expert roles in the area of labour market, human capital and skills with the European Commission and CEDEFOP.

Miklós Stocker, PhD, is Senior Assistant Professor of Corvinus University of Budapest (Hungary), Faculty of Business Administration, Department of Business Studies. His teaching and research interests are Strategic Management, International Strategy, Knowledge Management and Sports Management. He is regularly teaching Business Economics and Strategy related courses and Case solving courses in English and Hungarian. He conducted several research projects; he was Project manager for the Hungarian chapter of Hidden Champions in CEE and Turkey (full project by CEEMAN and IEDC Bled). He is member of Academy of International Business and Hungarian Society of Sport Sciences and member of the public body of Hungarian Academy of Sciences. He is Curator of Foundation for Business Economics Research and Education and General Secretary of the Hungarian Table Tennis Association.

Polona Tominc, PhD, is Full Professor in the Department of Quantitative Economic Analysis at the Faculty of Economics and Business, University of Maribor (Slovenia). Her research is focused on statistical methods in economics, especially in the field of entrepreneurship and gender differences. She teaches statistics and quantitative methods in entrepreneurial research. She participated in more than 30 scientific and professional conferences and is author of books and chapters in books and articles in scientific and professional journals, published in Slovenia and abroad. She actively participates in the DIANA network analysing female entrepreneurship and is a team member of GEM Slovenia and Slovenian entrepreneurship observatory research team.

Marzenna Anna Weresa, PhD, is Full Professor of Economics at the World Economy Research Institute, SGH Warsaw School of Economics (Poland). She holds a PhD degree in Economics (1995) and habilitation (DSc) in Economics (2002) from the Warsaw School of Economics. Her research focuses on international economics, in particular, issues relating to FDI, technology transfer, innovation and competitiveness. She has authored and co-authored over 100 books and scientific articles. In 2012–2015, she was a member of the High Level Economic Policy Expert Group (I4G and RISE), providing advice to the European Commission on policies for research and innovation.

Introduction

The main objective of this book is to present the challenges and opportunities related to the competitiveness of countries and firms in the region of Central and Eastern Europe (CEE). While the unprecedented scale of transformation in the region of Central and Eastern Europe since the early 1990s has provided a distinct research setting for international business and economics scholars for more than two decades, there have also been recent discussions about the extent to which the region still constitutes a unique business environment. The region's economies have reached different levels of market development and of modern business practice adoption, some of them being frequently classified as advanced economies. Consequently, the same level of heterogeneity among CEE countries can also be observed at the level of different sectors and business.

The internationalisation of countries and firms has played a crucial role in the catch-up process of the region. Attractive privatisation opportunities, lower costs and overall market size have attracted a significant number of internationally operating firms to this region. More importantly, however, the CEE region is gradually becoming home to firms undertaking foreign expansion and significantly contributing to the growth of international trade and investment. Traditionally, these local firms have been found to suffer from a competitiveness gap compared with their counterparts from developed countries. In both aforesaid situations of inward and outward business operations in the CEE region, the question as to the drivers and directions of competitiveness shifts at country and firm levels gains particular importance. Thus, this volume contains state-of-the-art conceptual and empirical papers devoted to changes in the international competitive position of the CEE region, its countries and firms alike. The contributions point to possible sources of competitive advantage of CEE countries and firms, given the recent intensive debates about the danger of middle-income trap and the potential solutions to it.

This book is a collection of contributions submitted to the international conference focused around international business in the CEE region entitled "*International Business and Research in the CEE Region. Why is it worth doing*", organised by the CEE Chapter of the Academy of International Business (AIB-CEE) and SGH

Warsaw School of Economics in Warsaw on 17–19 September 2015. The papers belong to two parts. The first part devoted to country-level developments revolves around determinants of outward and inward FDI from and into the CEE region, whereby these contributions link the internationalisation of local firms or the inflow of foreign investment into the region to firm and regional competitiveness, respectively. The second part is devoted to firm-level developments and related to firm-level export competitiveness, as well as business strategies in international environment. Given the recent surge of publications from the CEE region in the discipline of management and economics, this book which increases the visibility of CEE-based research within the international community deserves particular attention.

The first contribution entitled *"The Competitiveness of EU Member States from Central and Eastern Europe in 2007–2014"* is authored by Marzenna Anna Weresa and aims to examine changes in the competitiveness of 11 European Union member states in Central and Eastern Europe (CEE11) from 2007 to 2014. The empirical research builds on a synthesis of key theories that explain the concept of competitiveness and expand it to include sustainable competitiveness, a new notion that takes into account social and environmental factors determining the quality of life. The subsequent chapter titled *"Competitiveness, Entrepreneurship and Economic Growth"* prepared by Romana Korez-Vide and Polona Tominc explores country competitiveness and entrepreneurship as drivers of economic growth. The research was carried out on a sample of Central and Eastern European (CEE) member states of the European Union (EU).

The third chapter titled *"Facilitating Outward Foreign Direct Investment (OFDI): The Perspective of Support Providers in Poland in the Aftermath of 2008+ Economic Crisis"* written by Marta Götz and Barbara Jankowska focuses on the role of formal institutions and in particular the home country government and their policies towards outward foreign direct investments after the crisis years of 2008 and 2009. As the post-crisis decrease of OFDI flows was not that significant in the case of Poland, the authors examine measures taken by the Polish government and other public institutions to encourage Polish firms to invest abroad. The fourth chapter *"Attracting FDI to the New EU Member States"* devised by Tomasz Dorożyński and Anetta Kuna-Marszałek identifies factors determining the investment attractiveness of the 13 new EU Member States having an impact upon the scale of foreign direct investment in these countries. The authors first assess the investment attractiveness of the chosen Member States on the basis of selected international rankings and then establish relationships between selected investment attractiveness' determinants and FDI inflows.

The following fifth chapter entitled *"Policies to Promote Eco-Innovation. Results for Selected CEE Countries and Germany"* developed by Małgorzata Stefania Lewandowska concentrates on a comparative cross-country analysis of the relationship between eco-innovation and its main drivers for firms coming from selected CEE countries. The empirical research has been carried out on data from Bulgaria, Czech Republic, Romania and Germany. The sixth and last chapter of the first part of the book titled *"CEE Countries as a Business Process Outsourcing*

Destination" by Patryk Dziurski provides the analysis of business process outsourcing destinations identifying the four major ones: Asia Pacific, Central and Eastern Europe, Latin America as well as the Middle East and North Africa. Then he indicates key challenges which BPO providers face in CEE.

The text by Erzsébet Czakó, Péter Juhász and László Reszegi entitled *"Contrasting Methods: An Explorative Investigation on Firm-Level Export Competitiveness Based on Qualitative and Quantitative Research Findings"* begins the second part of the book. It serves as a bridge between the two parts since the authors draw conclusions at both firm and national levels. Their research concentrates on Hungarian small- and medium-sized enterprises' performance and shows that export-intensive SMEs are amongst the financially high performing firms. The next chapter authored by Magdolna Sass titled *"Emerging CEE Multinationals in the Electronics Industry"* analyses and characterises indigenous CEE electronics multinational companies from Hungary, Poland and Slovenia having significant outward FDI in electronics.

The third chapter of the second part written by Anna Jawor-Joniewicz and Łukasz Sienkiewicz titled *"Human Capital and HRM as a Source of Competitive Advantage and Effectiveness: Evidence from Poland"* explores the interrelations between human capital and human resources management of a company and their influence on the competitive advantage and company effectiveness based on a sample of 600 Polish firms. The fourth chapter prepared by Krisztina András and Zsolt Havran entitled *"Examination of Central and Eastern European Professional Football Clubs' Sport Success, Financial Position and Business Strategy in International Environment"* examines the competitiveness of professional football clubs in the Central and Eastern European region. The authors compare the sport-related and financial competitiveness of the clubs from nine countries of the CEE region (Bulgaria, Croatia, Czech Republic, Hungary, Poland, Romania, Serbia, Slovakia and Slovenia) to those of German and Russian professional leagues. The last chapter of the book authored by Miklós Stocker titled *"Local Heroes in Hungary"* draws on the notion of "Local Heroes" and identifies this category of firms in Hungary, while exploring their characteristics, business performance and export intensity.

We believe that the structure and content of this book will provide the readers with an insight into the developments in the CEE and let them discover a sample of the research carried out in the region.

Warsaw, Poland	Mirosław Jarosiński
Poznań, Poland	Łukasz Puślecki
Poznań, Poland	Piotr Trąpczyński

Part I
Country-Level Developments

The Competitiveness of EU Member States from Central and Eastern Europe in 2007–2014

Marzenna Anna Weresa

Abstract This chapter aims to examine changes in the competitiveness of 11 European Union member states in Central and Eastern Europe (CEE11) from 2007 to 2014. The empirical research builds on a synthesis of key theories that explain the concept of competitiveness and expand it to include sustainable competitiveness, a new notion that takes into account social and environmental factors determining the quality of life.

The research shows that Estonia maintained its competitive lead in the CEE region from 2007 to 2014. Five of the 11 analysed CEE countries, namely the Czech Republic, Poland, Romania, Bulgaria, and Latvia, improved their competitive positions and continued the process of catching up with Estonia. The competitiveness of Croatia, Hungary, Slovakia, and Slovenia deteriorated, pushing their rankings to the bottom of the league table of the 11 analysed CEE countries. However, if competitiveness is measured by including its sustainable components (i.e. social and environmental sustainability), the competitive positions of all of the analysed CEE countries except Croatia, Romania, and Slovakia are higher than those exclusively based on traditional competitiveness factors.

Keywords Competitiveness • Sustainability • Innovation • Central and Eastern Europe • European Union

Introduction

The main objective of this chapter is to determine the current competitive position of 11 European Union countries from Central and Eastern Europe (CEE) and to find out how it changed over the 2007–2014 period. For this purpose, competitiveness is defined as a broad category embedded in a nation's prosperity, and the following assessment criteria are applied: (1) the current condition of the economy measured by GDP; (2) living standards reflected by GDP per capita (in purchasing power standard terms), as well as by key indicators of social sustainability, such as life

M.A. Weresa
SGH Warsaw School of Economics, Warsaw, Poland
e-mail: marzenna.weresa@sgh.waw.pl

© Springer International Publishing Switzerland 2016
P. Trąpczyński et al. (eds.), *Competitiveness of CEE Economies and Businesses*, DOI 10.1007/978-3-319-39654-5_1

expectancy, school enrolment, the Human Development Index, income inequalities, and the incidence of poverty; (4) environmental sustainability measured by resource productivity; (3) position in external economic relations, determined by the capability to sell goods and services on the global market and the ability to attract FDI and to invest abroad.

What Is Competitiveness?

Although it has been 25 years since Michael E. Porter published his book *Competitive Advantage of Nations* (Porter 1990), explaining how nations compete internationally, the term "competitiveness" is still not clearly defined at the macroeconomic level. This multidimensional economic category is understood and interpreted in many different ways. There are many facets of competitiveness, each with a different focus; the focus can be on price, productivity, technology or structure (Aiginger et al. 2013:11). However, there is a consensus among scholars that the competitiveness of a country is linked with its economic system, which shapes the business environment and is location-specific (Bieńkowski et al. 2010; Misala 2014). In the broad sense, competitiveness can be defined as a country's ability to increase the standard of living, along with improving its role in the global marketplace and its investment attractiveness (Weresa 2015a:7).

There are, however, attempts to develop a new definition of competitiveness that captures a new growth path and includes new goals beyond GDP growth, such as social inclusion and environmental protection. In this case, competitiveness means "the ability of a country (region, location) to deliver beyond-GDP goals for its citizens today and tomorrow" (Aiginger et al. 2013:13). This extended definition corresponds to the concept of sustainable competitiveness defined as "the set of institutions, policies, and factors that make a nation productive over the longer term while ensuring social and environmental sustainability" (Corrigan et al. 2014:55). Social sustainability is understood in terms of reducing inequality, ensuring security, and providing broad access to the healthcare system. Environmental sustainability means the efficient management of resources in order to secure prosperity for present and future generations. It includes low CO_2 emissions, proper wastewater treatment and all other factors that help to improve the quality of the natural environment (Corrigan et al. 2014:55).

Such a re-definition of competitiveness and inclusion of social and environmental sustainability into this concept implies shifts in the relative importance of factors shaping the competitive advantages of different locations. For instance, social innovations, inclusive and frugal innovations, and eco-innovations can gain importance as competitiveness determinants (Weresa 2015b:350). Furthermore, the new concept of sustainable competitiveness calls for a new approach in assessing and comparing the competitive positions of countries and regions, which includes a broader spectrum of economic, social, and environmental indicators. Such a broader approach is applied in this chapter.

Competitiveness of CEE Countries in 2007–2014: Macroeconomic Perspective

Using this new framework of sustainable competitiveness, the competitive positions of EU countries from Central and Eastern Europe will be analysed for 2007–2014. This group consists of the 11 countries that joined the European Union in 2004 (Poland, the Czech Republic, Hungary, Slovakia, Slovenia, Latvia, Lithuania, and Estonia), in 2007 (Romania and Bulgaria), and in 2013 (Croatia). In order to determine the competitiveness of these countries and identify the changes in 2007–2014, a set of economic, social, and environmental indicators will be analysed and compared with their average values for the EU as a whole. The starting point for this assessment is the potential resulting from the size of national income (Table 1).

In 2014, the GDP of the 11 EU member states from the CEE region measured in current prices constituted 7.9 % of the total EU28 GDP, and the region's share increased by only 0.8 percentage points from 2007. Poland was the largest country among the EU member states from the CEE region in terms of GDP, its share growing from 2.5 % in 2007 to 2.9 % in 2014. The Czech Republic and Romania shared second place in 2014. Romania has had mild gains since 2007. Slovakia ranked third among the CEE11 countries in terms of GDP; its share in the EU28 grew only slightly, from 0.4 % in 2007 to 0.5 % in 2014.

Table 1 GDP of EU member countries from CEE in current prices: 2007, 2010 and 2014 compared (million euros and percentage)

Country	Gross domestic product at market prices (million euros)					
	Current prices (million euros)			% of EU28 total		
	2007	2010	2014	2007	2010	2014
European Union (28 countries)	12,915,385.9	12,794,719.3	13,958,351.8	100.0	100.0	100.0
Bulgaria	32,708.0	37,723.8	42,750.9	0.3	0.3	0.3
Czech Republic	138,004.0	156,369.7	154,738.7	1.1	1.2	1.1
Estonia	16,246.4	14,718.5	19,962.7	0.1	0.1	0.1
Croatia	43,925.8	45,004.3	43,019.8	0.3	0.4	0.3
Latvia	22,639.5	17,772.4	23,580.9	0.2	0.1	0.2
Lithuania	29,040.7	28,027.7	36,444.4	0.2	0.2	0.3
Hungary	101,605.9	98,198.4	104,239.1	0.8	0.8	0.7
Poland	313,654.1	361,744.3	410,844.6	2.4	2.8	2.9
Romania	125,403.4	126,746.4	150,230.1	1.0	1.0	1.1
Slovenia	35,152.6	36,252.4	37,303.2	0.3	0.3	0.3
Slovakia	56,090.6	67,387.1	75,560.5	0.4	0.5	0.5
CEE (11 countries)	914,471.0	989,945.0	1,098,674.9	7.1	7.7	7.9

Source: Author's elaboration based on Eurostat data, http://ec.europa.eu/eurostat/data/database, accessed 25 January 2016

Table 2 GDP per capita in CEE in PPS (euros and percentage)

Country/year	Current prices in euros (PPS)		% of EU28 average	
	2007	2014	2007	2014
European Union (28 countries)	25,800	27,400	–	–
Czech Republic	21,600	23,200	83.7	84.7
Slovenia	22,500	22,600	87.2	82.5
Slovakia	17,300	21,100	67.1	77.0
Estonia	17,700	20,900	68.6	76.3
Lithuania	15,600	20,600	60.5	75.2
Hungary	15,700	18,600	60.9	67.9
Poland	13,700	18,600	53.1	67.9
Latvia	15,400	17,500	59.7	63.9
Croatia	15,800	16,100	61.2	58.8
Romania	10,700	15,200	41.5	55.5
Bulgaria	10,600	12,800	41.1	46.7

Source: Author's elaboration based on Eurostat data, http://ec.europa.eu/eurostat/data/database, accessed 25 January 2016

A more detailed picture of the competitiveness of CEE countries and how it changed during the 2007–2014 period can be obtained by comparing GDP per capita measured in purchasing power standards (PPS[1]) (Table 2).

With the exception of Slovenia and Croatia, the competitive position of CEE countries measured by GDP per capita (in PPS terms) has improved since 2007 (Table 2). There are, however, huge differences among CEE countries in this ranking. In 2014, the highest level of GDP per capita measured in PPS terms among CEE countries was noted in the Czech Republic, followed by Slovenia and Slovakia. In the Czech Republic, GDP per capita accounted for 84.7 % of the EU28 average in 2014, while in Bulgaria the figure was only 46.7 %. The greatest improvements in GDP per capita in PPS terms from 2007 to 2014 took place in Poland (by 14.8 p.p.), Lithuania (by 14.7 p.p.), and Romania (by 14.0 p.p.). This means that, for instance, Poland's development gap towards the EU28 average has narrowed by nearly 15 percentage points. On the other hand, there were also processes of divergence from the EU28 average in some CEE countries, namely in Slovenia and Croatia (Table 2).

Looking at the competitiveness of CEE countries from the GDP growth perspective related to the GDP per capita level, some differences should be pointed

---

[1] According to the Eurostat definition, Purchasing Power Standards (PPS) are obtained as a weighted average of relative price ratios in respect to a homogeneous basket of goods and services, both comparable and representative for each country. They are fixed in a way that makes the average purchasing power of 1 euro in the European Union equal to one PPS.

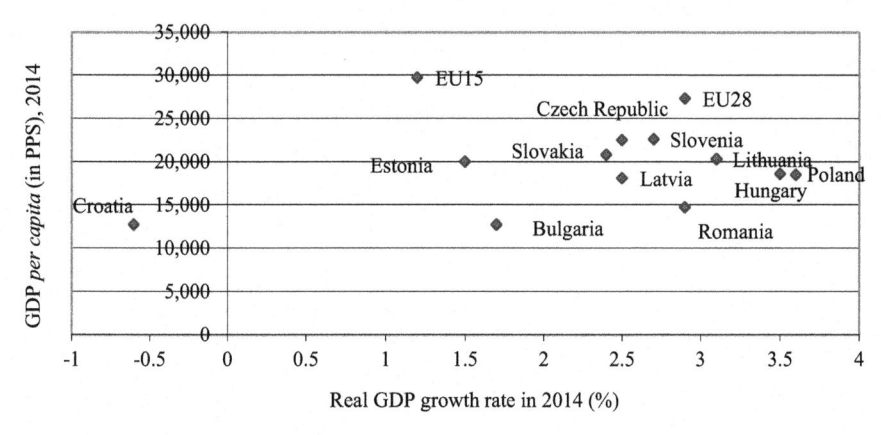

Fig. 1 Competitiveness of the EU member states from CEE measured by GDP growth rate and GDP per capita, 2014. *Source*: Weresa (2015b:352)

out. Poland, Hungary and Lithuania led the way in terms of real GDP growth in 2014, albeit with relatively low GDP per capita levels (in PPS terms). The Czech Republic, Slovenia, and Slovakia grew at a relatively slower rate, but had the highest competitive positions measured by GDP per capita (Fig. 1).

When assessing prosperity, apart from the current income levels and their growth rates, it is necessary to take income disparities into account. A conventional indicator that measures inequalities in household income is the Gini coefficient. It is defined by Eurostat as "the relationship of cumulative shares of the population arranged according to the level of equivalised disposable income, to the cumulative share of the equivalised total disposable income received by them" (Eurostat 2015).

The 2007–2014 period produced a slight increase in income disparities in the European Union measured by the average values of the Gini index (Table 3). Only 4 of the 11 EU member states from the CEE region have seen a decrease in income disparities since 2007. These countries are Romania, Poland, Croatia, and the Czech Republic. In the same period the greatest increases were recorded in Hungary, Estonia, and Slovenia. However, when it comes to the level of income disparities in 2014, 5 of the 11 analysed CEE countries, namely Estonia, Latvia, Bulgaria, Lithuania, and Romania, showed disparities higher than the EU28 average. The lowest income disparities were seen in Slovenia and the Czech Republic (Table 3).

The European Union's Europe 2020 strategy promotes social inclusion, and this goal corresponds with the concept of sustainable competitiveness. In particular, the aim of the Europe 2020 strategy is to reduce poverty by lifting at least 20 million people out of the risk of poverty and social exclusion. Looking at the CEE economies from this angle, in 2014 only 3 of the 11 countries, namely the Czech Republic, Slovakia, and Slovenia, had risk-of-poverty rates lower that the EU28. In Slovenia, this rate has been growing since 2007. In Estonia and

Table 3 Income inequalities in CEE countries measured by the Gini coefficient, 2007–2014

	2007	2008	2009	2010	2011	2012	2013	2014
EU (28 countries)	n.a.	n.a.	n.a.	30.4	30.8	30.4	30.5	30.9
EU (27 countries)	30.6	31.0	30.6	30.4	30.7	30.4	30.5	30.9
Bulgaria	35.3	35.9	33.4	33.2	35.0	33.6	35.4	35.4
Czech Republic	25.3	24.7	25.1	24.9	25.2	24.9	24.6	25.1
Estonia	33.4	30.9	31.4	31.3	31.9	32.5	32.9	35.6
Croatia	n.a.	n.a.	n.a.	31.6	31.2	30.9	30.9	30.2
Latvia	35.4	37.5	37.5	35.9	35.1	35.7	35.2	35.5
Lithuania	33.8	34.5	35.9	37.0	33.0	32.0	34.6	35.0
Hungary	25.6	25.2	24.7	24.1	26.8	26.9	28.0	27.9
Poland	32.2	32.0	31.4	31.1	31.1	30.9	30.7	30.8
Romania	37.8	36.0	34.9	33.3	33.2	33.2	34.0	34.7
Slovenia	23.2	23.4	22.7	23.8	23.8	23.7	24.4	25.0
Slovakia	24.5	23.7	24.8	25.9	25.7	25.3	24.2	26.1

Source: Author's elaboration based on Eurostat data, http://ec.europa.eu/eurostat/data/database, accessed 25 January 2016
n.a. data not available

Hungary, this indicator also increased from 2007 to 2014 despite the fact that it was already higher than the EU average in 2007. The highest percentage of the population at risk of poverty or social exclusion in CEE countries was recorded in Romania and Bulgaria, although the rate decreased from 2007 to 2014. Declines were also noted in Poland, Lithuania, Croatia, and Latvia (Fig. 2), which shows that the social pillar of competitiveness has improved in some CEE countries.

The quality of life in the 11 CEE countries, measured by yardsticks such as life expectancy, the school enrolment ratio, and tertiary educational attainment, differs significantly. In most of the analysed CEE countries, educational indicators (e.g. the percentage of population with a tertiary education, early school leavers) are better that the EU average, while health indicators (e.g. life expectancy) are worse. However, in 2014 the competitive position of CEE countries assessed by means of the Human Development Index (HDI), was somewhat better than when expressed in GDP per capita terms alone. The biggest differences were observed in Bulgaria, Slovenia, and Estonia, and the smallest changes were noted in Hungary, Latvia, and Slovakia (Table 4). Although with regard to the HDI values, the analysed CEE countries continued to lag behind most other EU countries, the gap decreased steadily. In the latest HDI league table in 2015, only two EU members from CEE, namely Romania and Bulgaria, were classified as countries with a high human development index, while the remaining nine analysed countries were classed into a group with a very high HDI.

When it comes to the environmental pillar of sustainable competitiveness, resource productivity can be used as a possible indicator that captures this

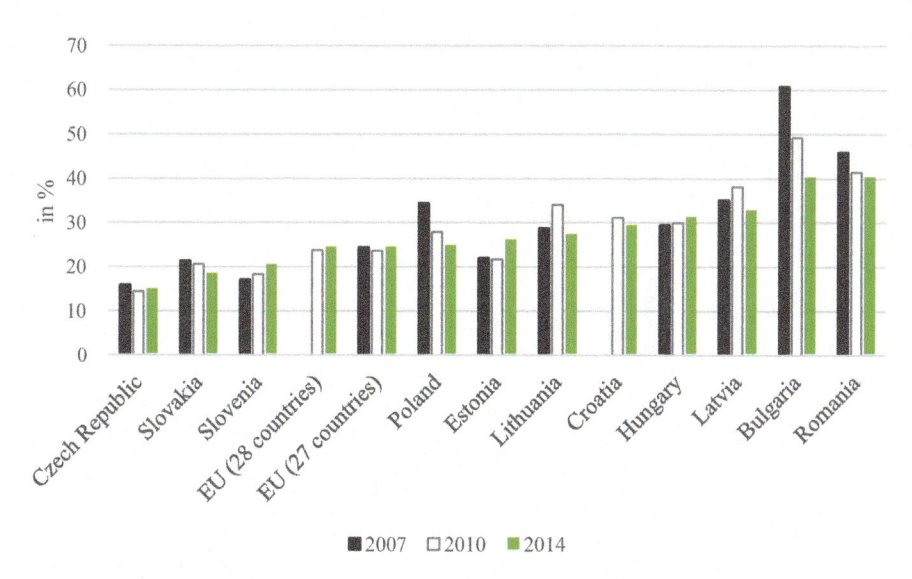

Fig. 2 People at risk of poverty or social exclusion in CEE countries as a percentage of total population: 2007, 2010 and 2014 compared. *Source*: Author's elaboration based on Eurostat data, http://ec.europa.eu/eurostat/data/database, accessed 26 January 2016

competitiveness component. It is calculated as the ratio of a country's GDP to its domestic material consumption, understood as the annual quantity of raw materials extracted from the domestic territory plus all physical imports and minus all physical exports (definition by Eurostat 2015). This indicator can be expressed in Euros per kilogramme (which makes it possible to compare the same country in different periods), in PPS per kilogramme (for comparing different countries in the same year), or in terms of an index as of 2010, which makes it possible to compare countries in different years.

Figure 3 presents resource productivity in terms of the 2010 indices for the analysed CEE countries in 2007 and 2014, and compares them with the EU average.

Hungary and Slovakia were the leading CEE countries in terms of resource productivity increases in both 2007 and 2014; their indices grew much faster than EU averages. In 2014, apart from these two leaders, significant improvements in resource productivity were observed in Slovenia, Croatia, and the Czech Republic. This indicates that these five countries made significant progress from 2007 to 2014 in terms of the environmental pillar of competitiveness.

Table 4 Human Development Index (HDI) and its components in CEE countries, 2014

HDI rank	Country	Human Development Index (HDI) (index value)	Life expectancy at birth (years)	Expected years of schooling (years)	Mean years of schooling (years)	Gross national income (GNI) per capita (2011 PPP USD)	GNI per capita rank minus HDI rank
25	Slovenia	0.880	80.4	16.8	11.9	27,852	12
28	Czech Republic	0.870	78.6	16.4	12.3	26,660	10
30	Estonia	0.861	76.8	16.5	12.5	25,214	12
35	Slovakia	0.844	76.3	15.1	12.2	25,845	5
36	Poland	0.843	77.4	15.5	11.8	23,177	10
37	Lithuania	0.839	73.3	16.4	12.4	24,500	7
44	Hungary	0.828	75.2	15.4	11.6	22,916	3
46	Latvia	0.819	74.2	15.2	11.5	22,281	4
47	Croatia	0.818	77.3	14.8	11.0	19,409	11
52	Romania	0.793	74.7	14.2	10.8	18,108	10
59	Bulgaria	0.782	74.2	14.4	10.6	15,596	13
	World	0.711	71.5	12.2	7.9	14,301	–

Source: UNDP (2015:208)

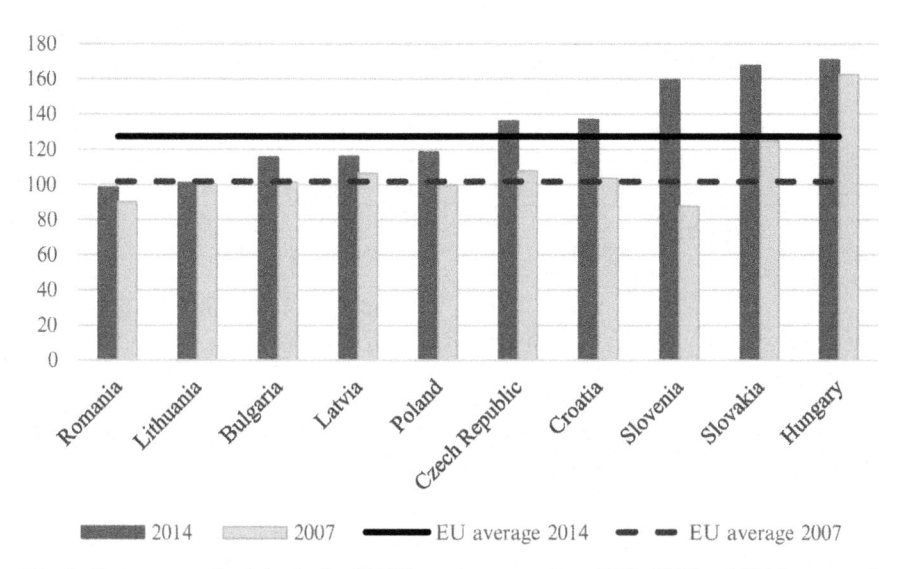

Fig. 3 Resource productivity in the 11 EU member states from CEE: 2007 and 2014 compared. *Source*: Author's elaboration based on Eurostat data, http://ec.europa.eu/eurostat/data/database, accessed 26 January 2016

Competitive Positions in International Relations: Leaders and Laggards in CEE

A crucial element of a country's international competitiveness is its ability to compete in an international environment, in particular its ability to export and to attract foreign factors of production.

While assessing the international dimension of the competitive position of the 11 EU countries from CEE, it should be noted that in 3 countries (Bulgaria, Estonia, and Lithuania) exports declined in absolute terms in 2014, while in others they continued to increase. A similar trend was recorded for imports. Estonia, Latvia, and Lithuania decreased their imports in 2014, while other CEE countries experienced increases. Despite these shifts, the shares of individual countries in the foreign trade of the CEE region as a whole were rather stable. Poland led the way with a 27.5 % share in the total exports of these 11 CEE countries and accounting for 28.3 % of their imports in 2014. Both figures grew compared with those recorded in 2007 (Tables 5 and 6).

The Czech Republic and Hungary were the other regional leaders in foreign trade values, though the role of Hungary in CEE foreign trade decreased (Tables 5 and 6).

When it comes to the balance of trade, the Czech Republic enjoyed the largest surplus among the analysed countries. All these countries improved their trade balances from 2007 to 2014. Some of them, including Poland, Romania, Lithuania, Estonia, and Bulgaria, reduced their trade deficits. Others, including Hungary,

Table 5 CEE11 exports, 2007–2014

Country	Exports in millions of euros						Share in total exports of the 11 CEE countries (%)	
	2007	2010	2011	2012	2013	2014	2007	2014
Bulgaria	13,512	15,561	20,265	20,770	22,271	22,054	3.3	3.7
Czech Republic	89,382	100,311	117,054	122,230	122,184	131,797	22.1	22.3
Estonia	8034	8743	12,003	12,518	12,294	12,090	2.0	2.0
Croatia	9004	8905	9582	9629	9531	n.a.	2.2	n.a.
Latvia	6062	7191	9433	10,983	10,893	10,960	1.5	1.9
Lithuania	12,509	15,651	20,151	23,048	24,545	24,361	3.1	4.1
Hungary	69,610	72,024	80,684	80,612	80,941	83,236	17.2	14.1
Poland	102,259	120,483	135,558	144,282	154,342	163,067	25.3	27.5
Romania	29,543	37,398	45,284	45,020	49,570	52,494	7.3	8.9
Slovenia	21,964	22,026	24,968	25,033	25,614	27,074	5.4	4.6
Slovakia	42,696	48,777	57,349	62,742	64,565	65,153	10.6	11.0
Total 11 CEE countries	404,575	457,070	532,331	556,867	576,750	592,286	100.0	100.0

Source: Author's elaboration based on Eurostat data, http://ec.europa.eu/eurostat/data/database, accessed 26 January 2016

Table 6 CEE11 imports, 2007–2014

Country	Imports in millions of euros						Share in total imports of the 11 CEE countries (%)	
	2007	2010	2011	2012	2013	2014	2007	2014
Bulgaria	21,862	19,245	23,407	25,460	25,829	26,182	4.6	4.5
Czech Republic	86,224	95,536	109,285	110,066	108,621	116,203	18.1	19.8
Estonia	11,439	9268	12,543	13,848	13,889	13,745	2.4	2.3
Croatia	18,833	15,137	16,281	16,214	16,581	n.a.	4.0	n.a.
Latvia	11,180	8819	11,703	13,409	13,451	13,303	2.3	2.3
Lithuania	17,813	17,653	22,826	24,882	26,208	25,889	3.7	4.4
Hungary	69,730	66,514	73,592	74,078	75,379	78,745	14.6	13.4
Poland	120,912	134,306	151,291	154,934	156,319	165,508	25.4	28.3
Romania	51,305	46,850	54,943	54,645	55,280	58,542	10.8	10.0
Slovenia	23,027	22,700	25,522	24,934	25,129	25,551	4.8	4.4
Slovakia	44,229	49,050	57,358	60,241	61,543	61,848	9.3	10.6
CEE (11 countries)	476,554	485,078	558,751	572,711	578,229	585,516	100.0	100.0

Source: Author's elaboration based on Eurostat data, http://ec.europa.eu/eurostat/data/database, accessed 26 January 2016

Slovakia, and Slovenia, turned deficits into surpluses. The EU remained their most important trading partner, though the geographical structure of their foreign trade changed gradually, with a steadily decreasing role for EU markets, especially in the case of imports.

Most of the new EU member states compete on international markets chiefly in the segment of labour-intensive goods. Some of these countries (Poland, for instance) have developed comparative advantages in marketing-based industries since their EU entry. However, only a few countries (for example Hungary and Slovakia) enjoy comparative advantages in the trade of technology-intensive goods (Weresa 2013).

In order to capture trends in comparative advantages in foreign trade, further detailed analysis will cover a longer period, specifically the 2000–2012 time frame. The following evaluation of changes in the comparative advantages of selected EU member states from Central and Eastern Europe will be made using the Revealed Comparative Advantage (RCA) index (Balassa 1965, 1979, 1989). The original Balassa index has been modified to the following formula:

$$RCA = \ln\left(\frac{x_{ij}^K}{m_{ij}^K} \div \frac{X_j^K}{M_j^K}\right),$$

where: x_{ij}^K—exports of commodity group "i" from country "K" to country/group of countries "j";

m_{ij}^K—imports of commodity group "i" to country "K" from country/group of countries "j";

X_j^K—total exports from country "K" to country/group of countries "j";

M_j^K—total imports to country "K" from country/group of countries "j";

i—sector according to the above mentioned classification;

K—studied country;

j—rest of the world.

An RCA_i greater than 0 indicates the existence of a revealed comparative advantage, while an RCA_i lower than zero means a revealed comparative disadvantage. Due to the logarithmic form of the equation, the positive and negative RCA_i indices are symmetrically distributed around zero.

RCA indices showing either the existence, or a lack of a revealed comparative advantage in the trade of the analysed CEE countries were calculated for groups of industries singled out in the classification based on the use of tangible and intangible inputs in the manufacturing process. Industries have been classified with the use of tangible and intangible factor inputs in the production process (Peneder 1999). The classification originates from the Schumpeterian notion of competition, in which an important part of the competitive advantage is an ability to create new products and processes in order to meet changing consumer tastes and needs. This classification makes it possible to distinguish exogenous competitive advantages (resulting from being endowed with tangible factors of production such as physical capital and labour) from endogenous factors (resulting from investment in intangible resources, including investment in innovation and marketing). Manufacturing industries have been divided into five groups based on how different types of inputs contribute to production costs:

- mainstream manufacturing industries, in which tangible factors (labour and capital) are as important in the manufacturing process as intangible factors (research and marketing), with labour prevailing over capital among the tangible factors;
- labour-intensive industries, in which labour plays a predominant role in the production of goods, while marketing inputs tend to be more intensive than other intangible factors;
- capital-intensive industries, in which investment in physical capital plays a dominant role;
- marketing-driven industries, with relatively high spending on advertising and brand building accompanied by a relatively low intensity of investment in capital;
- technology-driven industries, with high expenditure on research and development (R&D).

Goods produced by technology-driven industries have the most enduring competitive advantages that are at the same time less sensitive to price changes. This is because these advantages are based on innovation. Competitive advantages in marketing-driven industries are also relatively stable because they are based on consumer brand loyalty.

In order to achieve a comparable picture, the analysis below focuses exclusively on the six largest CEE11 countries. It excludes the three Baltic states, as well as Slovenia and Croatia because the role and structure of trade in these small economies differ considerably from those in their larger CEE peers. The analysis shows that only two of the studied countries (the Czech Republic and Slovakia) had comparative advantages in the trade of goods produced by mainstream manufacturing industries throughout the studied period and these advantages were relatively stable over time. The remaining CEE countries did not have advantages in the trade of goods produced by mainstream manufacturing industries. Poland showed the smallest comparative disadvantage for this group of goods, while the strongest disadvantage was revealed in Hungary (Fig. 4).

A different trend was at work in the trade of labour-intensive products. All the studied CEE countries had comparative advantages in the trade of products from labour-intensive industries, but these advantages tended to decrease over time. Hungary, the Czech Republic, and Slovakia had the smallest advantages in this segment of goods, while Bulgaria and Romania had the strongest, though diminishing, advantages (Fig. 5).

The structure of comparative advantages in the trade of capital-intensive goods was far more diverse. Romania, Bulgaria, and Slovakia had comparative advantages in the trade of such products, but these advantages decreased steadily. Meanwhile, the EU as a whole gradually increased its advantages in the trade of capital-intensive goods. Poland, the Czech Republic, and Hungary steadily

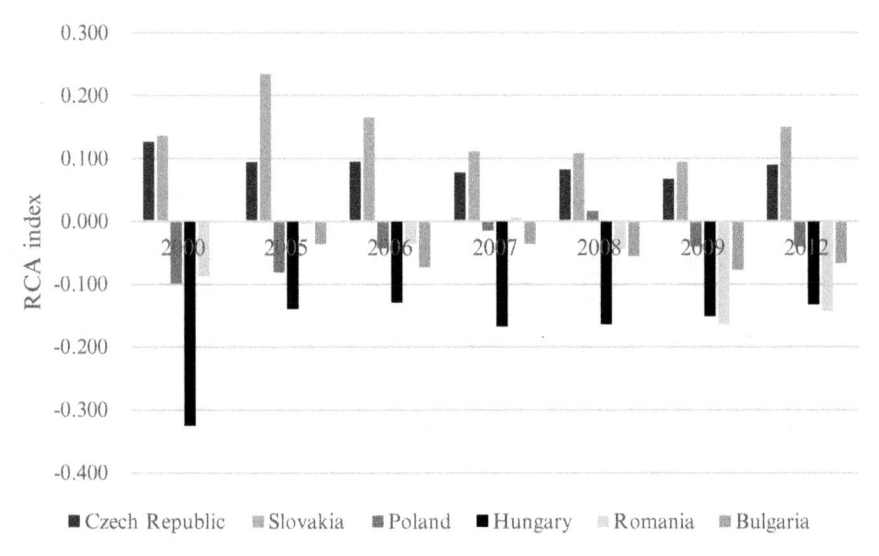

Fig. 4 The comparative advantages of selected CEE11 countries in the trade of goods produced by mainstream manufacturing industries, 2000–2012. *Source*: Author's calculations based on data from the United Nations Commodity Trade Statistics Database

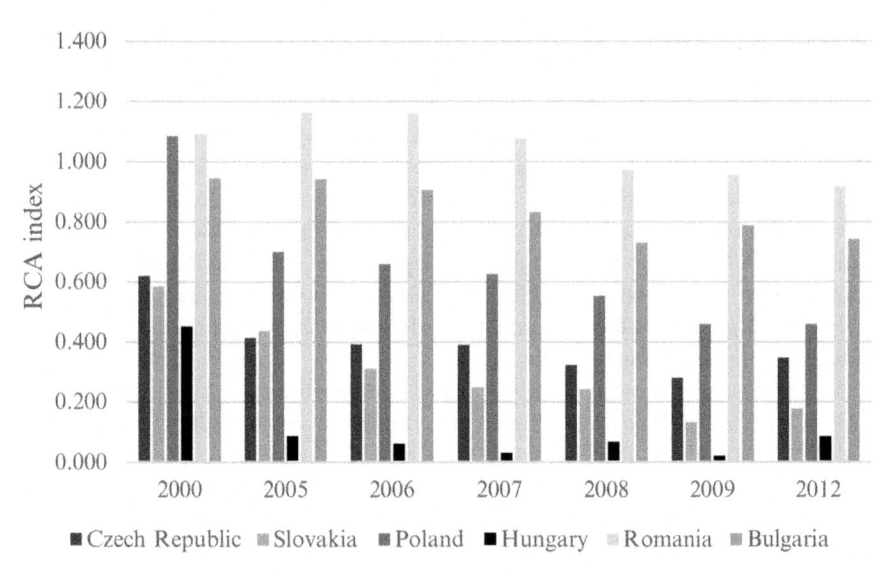

Fig. 5 The comparative advantages of selected CEE11 countries in the trade of goods produced by labour-intensive industries. *Source*: Author's calculations based on data from the United Nations Commodity Trade Statistics Database

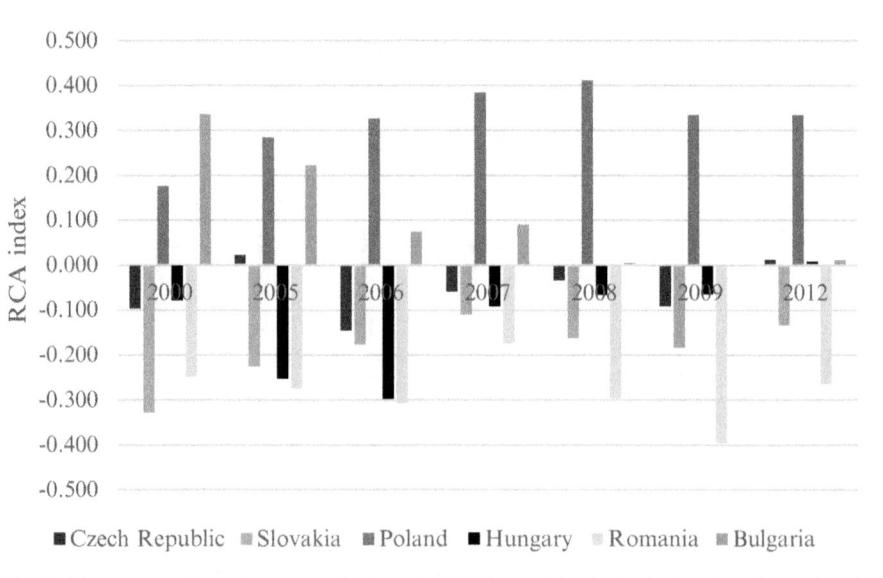

Fig. 6 The comparative advantages of selected CEE11 countries in the trade of goods produced by marketing-driven industries. *Source*: Author's calculations based on data from the United Nations Commodity Trade Statistics Database

improved their positions, but failed to achieve competitiveness in this area; their RCA indices rose but stayed below zero throughout the studied period. Poland stands out positively in the trade of goods produced by marketing-driven industries. Poland had stable and relatively strong comparative advantages, while Bulgaria produced only slight advantages in the trade of this group of products (Fig. 6).

In the case of products from technology-driven industries, the structure of comparative advantages in the studied countries changed the most substantially. Hungary and Slovakia had a relatively strong position in the trade of this group of goods, while the remaining studied CEE countries were not competitive. Nevertheless, their competitiveness increased gradually, as evidenced by the rising RCA indices in all these countries (Fig. 7).

Summing up the above analyses, it can be concluded that the convergence of the CEE countries' GDP per capita levels with the EU average leads to a situation in which the existing sources of competitiveness, including low labour costs and cheap raw materials, are declining. Consequently, these countries are being forced to look for new sources of competitive advantage that will enable them to sustain their growth through efforts such as increased involvement in international trade and a shift in the structure of trade toward high-value-added goods (Weresa 2014). This conclusion raises the question of the role of innovation in shaping competitiveness, in particular its sustainable (social and ecological) pillars. A concise answer can be given by plotting a summary innovation index (SII) that captures different dimensions of the innovation performance of CEE countries with a social progress index reflecting competitiveness in the broad sense, including its social and ecological components (Porter et al. 2015). The results of such an exercise for

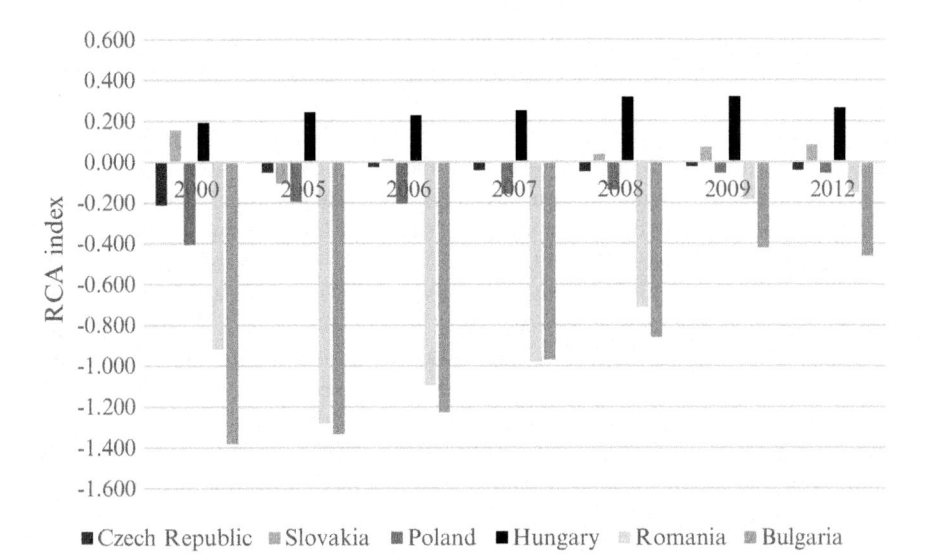

Fig. 7 The comparative advantages of selected CEE11 countries in the trade of goods produced by technology-driven industries. *Source*: Author's calculations based on data from the United Nations Commodity Trade Statistics Database

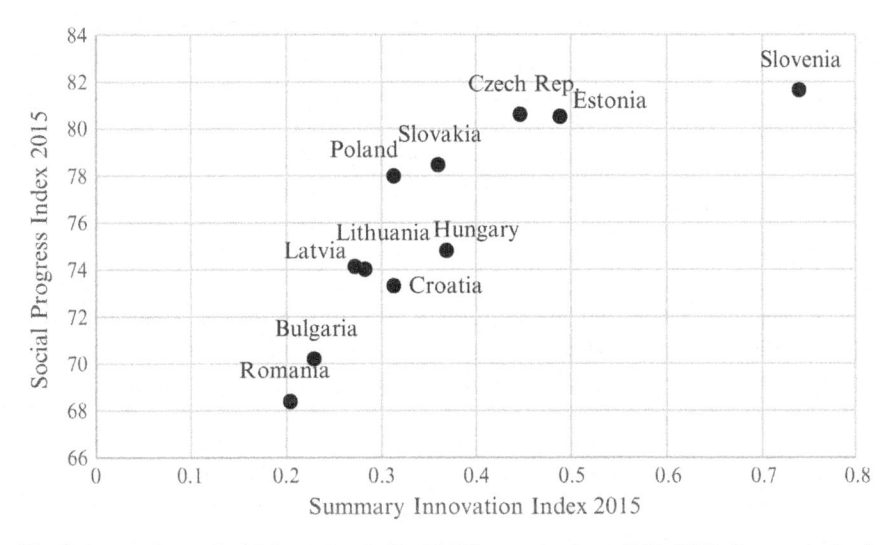

Fig. 8 Innovation and social progress in the 11 EU countries from CEE, 2015. *Source*: Author's elaboration based on EC (2015:92) and Porter et al. (2015:148–149)

the 11 EU member states from CEE are presented in Fig. 8. It reveals that social progress in the studied CEE countries is highly correlated with innovation performance (correlation coefficient = 0.82). A higher innovation index corresponds with higher values of the social progress index.

Another component of the CEE countries' external competitiveness is measured by the ability to attract foreign factors of production, in particular foreign direct investment.

Most of the analysed CEE countries experienced a sharp decline in FDI inflows as a result of the global crisis. However, some countries from this group were less severely affected. Hungary and the Czech Republic, for example, experienced only mild fluctuations in FDI inflows and their shares of total inflows to the analysed region increased sharply from 2007 to 2012. Poland has been gradually losing its leadership in the region in terms of investment attractiveness (Table 7). New investment opportunities, combined with lower labour costs offered by other countries in the region, make the competition for FDI much fiercer than in the past.

For several years, most of the CEE countries that joined the European Union in 2004 and later were primarily seen as attractive FDI destinations. In recent years, however, these countries have started to invest abroad, as well. This new trend reflects the desire of many companies from the CEE region to strengthen their position on both regional and more distant markets and to search for resources that are not available or are too expensive in their domestic economies. Since traditional FDI theories do not sufficiently explain outward FDI from CEE, the issue can be analysed from a broader perspective of FDI from emerging economies (Goldstein 2009; Demirbag and Yaprak 2015). According to Narula and Verbeke, outward FDI depends on "the capacity of the firm to 'extract' value from country-specific advantages by making them firm-specific" (Narula and Verbeke 2015:619). Therefore, investment abroad can be regarded as an indicator of the extent to which the ownership advantages of domestic firms, as well as the advantages of their countries of origin are transferrable to foreign countries in order to generate profits higher than those at home. Thus, outward investment could be treated as a test demonstrating just how successful local businesses are in coping with global competition.

The 2007–2012 period saw strong fluctuations in outward FDI from Central and Eastern European EU member states. This was due to the global crisis, along with reasons related to the internal situation in these countries. Poland, Hungary, and the Czech Republic were the largest foreign investors from the CEE region in 2007–2012, but their ranking according to capital outflows underwent some changes. In 2007, Poland topped the list among the analysed countries; in 2012 Hungary took the lead (Table 7).

Competitiveness measured by the ability to attract FDI and to invest abroad can be summarised using an FDI flow intensity indicator. The index measures the intensity of investment integration within the international economy. It is calculated as an average of inward and outward FDI flows as a percentage of GDP. Relating FDI flows to GDP makes it possible to compare different economies as it removes the effect of differences in their size.

The indices varied significantly in individual CEE countries from 2007 to 2012 (Fig. 9). The average index in the EU decreased from 4.0 in 2007 to 2.4 in 2012. Indices close to the EU average in 2012 were noted in the Czech Republic and Latvia, which might indicate moderate levels of internationalisation for these economies. The highest fluctuations in the indices from 2007 to 2012 were observed

Table 7 Foreign direct investment (FDI) flows in CEE, 2007–2012

Country	FDI inflows in millions of euros			FDI outflows in millions of euros			Share in total FDI inflows from 11 CEE countries in %		Share in total FDI outflows from 11 CEE countries in %	
	2007	2010	2012	2007	2010	2012	2007	2012	2007	2012
Bulgaria	9052	1151	1142	206	174	270	15.9	3.7	1.7	2.3
Czech Republic	7633	4638	6215	1184	881	1394	13.4	20.2	9.7	11.8
Estonia	1985	1208	1051	1276	107	813	3.5	3.4	10.4	6.9
Croatia	3637	286	1057	181	−121	−73	6.4	3.4	1.5	−0.6
Latvia	1704	284	871	271	14	151	3.0	2.8	2.2	1.3
Lithuania	1473	604	545	437	−4	305	2.6	1.8	3.6	2.6
Hungary	2886	1662	10,716	2646	866	8668	5.1	34.9	21.6	73.6
Poland	17,221	10,473	4716	3927	5455	557	30.3	15.4	32.1	4.7
Romania	7254	2219	2137	204	−16	−89	12.8	7.0	1.7	−0.8
Slovenia	1309	272	−58	1465	−156	−226	2.3	−0.2	12.0	−1.9
Slovakia	2618	1336	2321	438	714	7	4.6	7.6	3.6	0.1
Total FDI flows to 11 CEE countries	56,772	24,133	30,713	12,235	7914	11,777	100	100	100	100

Source: Author's elaboration based on Eurostat data, http://ec.europa.eu/eurostat/data/database, accessed 28 January 2016

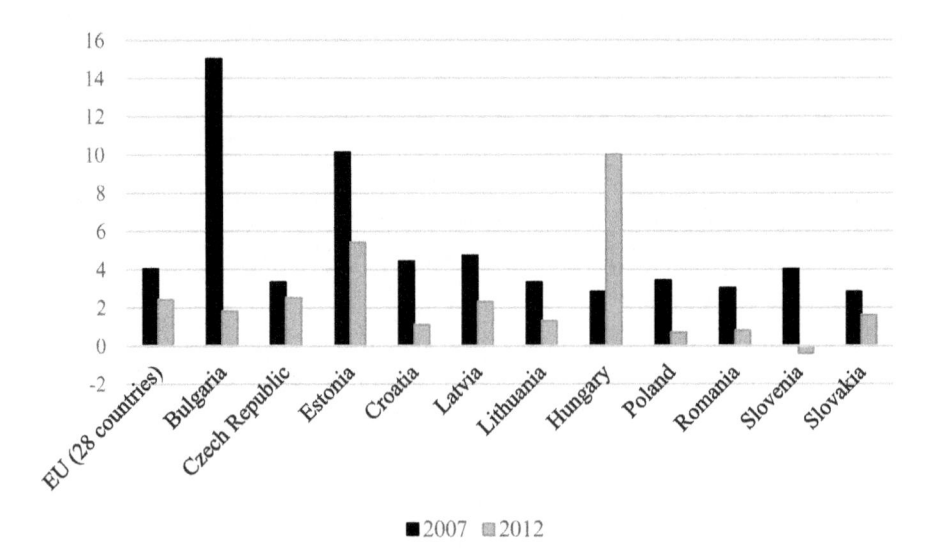

Fig. 9 FDI flow intensity in the EU member states from CEE: 2007 and 2012 compared. *Source*: Author's elaboration based on Eurostat data, http://ec.europa.eu/eurostat/data/database, accessed 28 January 2016

in Bulgaria, Estonia and Hungary, which may be a sign of uneven growth paths in these countries.

Summary and Conclusions

Summarising the results of the analyses made in this chapter, it can be concluded that the competitive positions of most of the analysed CEE countries improved from 2007 to 2014 even though some of these countries suffered from the global crisis. Estonia maintained its competitive lead in the region, while five other countries from this group, the Czech Republic, Poland, Lithuania, Romania, and Bulgaria, improved their standings in international competitiveness league tables published by the World Economic Forum, and continued to catch up with Estonia. However, the remaining countries, among them Slovakia, Slovenia, Hungary, and Croatia, saw their competitive positions deteriorate from 2007 to 2014 (Schwab 2015; see also Fig. 10).

However, if competitiveness is measured by including its sustainable components (i.e. social and environmental sustainability), 8 of the 11 analysed countries had higher competitive positions than when exclusively based on traditional competitiveness factors (Fig. 11).

Three countries from the analysed region, Croatia, Romania, and Slovakia, did not have strong sustainability pillars. However, Slovenia has improved in both

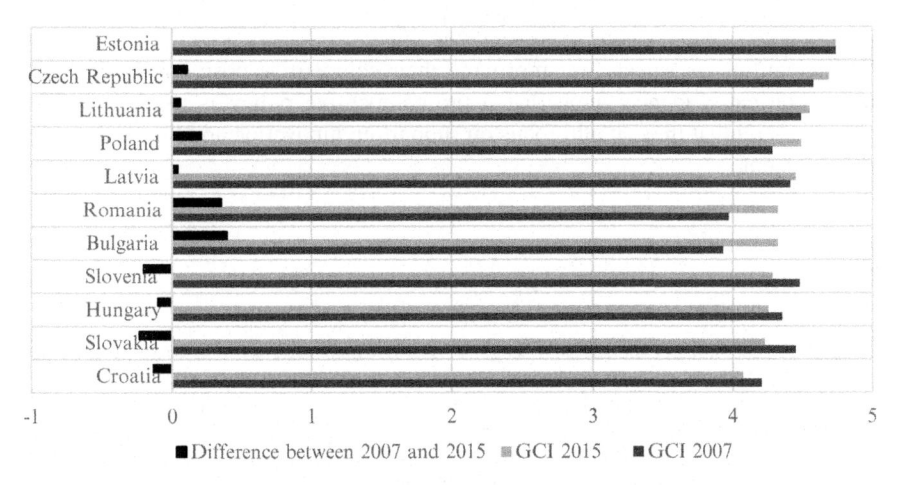

Fig. 10 The competitiveness of the 11 EU member states from CEE and how it changed in 2007–2015 (as measured by the WEF's Global Competitiveness Index). *Source*: Author's elaboration based on Schwab (2007:10, 2015:7)

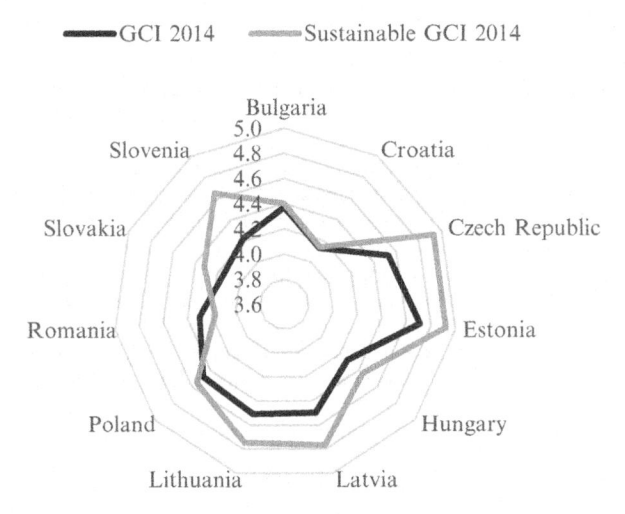

Fig. 11 The Global Competitiveness Index (GCI) and a sustainability-adjusted Global Competitiveness Index compared, 2014. *Source*: Author's elaboration based on Schwab (2014:68–69)

components of sustainable competitiveness—social and environmental sustainability—while Slovakia has made some progress in environmental sustainability. In Croatia, there has been no change in either pillar.

Looking at long-term trends in a set of competitiveness measures, it can be concluded that the CEE countries that managed to improve their competitive positions from 2007 to 2014 did it mainly through better use of internal resources. In some countries, among them Poland, another success factor was relative resilience to external shocks compared with other economies. When it comes to the CEE countries' prospects for improving their competitive positions, both theory and empirical evidence show that a pro-competitive policy is needed in these countries and that they should focus on supporting innovation and human resource development.

References

Aiginger, K., Bärenthaler-Sieber, S., & Vogel, J. (2013). *Competitiveness under new perspectives.* Working Paper 44. www.foreurope.eu.
Balassa, B. (1965). Trade liberalization and 'revealed' comparative advantage. *The Manchester School, 33*, 99–123.
Balassa, B. (1979). The changing pattern of comparative advantage in manufactured goods. *Review of Economics and Statistics, 61*(2), 259–266.
Balassa, B. (1989). *Comparative advantage, trade policy and economic development.* New York: Harvester Wheatsheaf.
Bieńkowski, W., Weresa, M. A., & Radło, M.-J. (Eds.). (2010). *Konkurencyjność Polski na tle zmian gospodarczych w krajach OECD.* Warszawa: Oficyna Wydawnicza SGH.
Corrigan, G., Crotti, R., Drzeniek Hanouz, M., & Serin, C. (2014). Assessing progress toward sustainable competitiveness. In K. Schwab (Ed.), *Global competitiveness report 2014–15* (pp. 53–83). Geneva: World Economic Forum.
Demirbag, M., & Yaprak, A. (Eds.). (2015). *Handbook of emerging market multinational corporations.* Cheltenham: Edward Elgar.
EC. (2015). *Innovation union scoreboard.* Brussels: European Union. http://ec.europa.eu/growth/industry/innovation/facts-figures/scoreboards/index_en.htm.
Eurostat. (2015). http://ec.europa.eu/eurostat/data/database.
Goldstein, A. (2009). *Multinational companies from emerging economies: Composition, conceptualization and direction in the global economy.* New York: Palgrave Macmillan.
Misala, J. (2014). Theoretical grounds of the development of long-term competitive advantages in international trade. In M. A. Weresa (Ed.), *Innovation, human capital and trade competitiveness. How are they connected and why do they matter?* (pp. 3–51). Cham: Springer.
Narula, R., & Verbeke, A. (2015). Making internalization theory good for practice: The essence of Alan Rugman's contributions to international business. *Journal of World Business, 50*, 612–622.
Peneder, M. (1999). *The new WIFO taxonomy of manufacturing industries.* WIFO Working Papers 114, Vienna.
Porter, M. E. (1990). *The competitive advantage of nations.* New York: The Free Press.
Porter, M. E., Stern, S., & Green, M. (2015). *Social Progress Index 2015.* Washington, DC: Social Progress Imperative. www.socialprogressimperative.org.
Schwab, K. (Ed.). (2007). *Global competitiveness report 2007–2008.* Geneva: World Economic Forum.
Schwab, K. (Ed.). (2014). *Global competitiveness report 2014–2015.* Geneva: World Economic Forum.
Schwab, K. (Ed.). (2015). *Global competitiveness report 2015–2016.* Geneva: World Economic Forum.
UNDP. (2015). *Human development report 2015.* New York: United Nations Development Programme.
Weresa, M. A. (2013). *Innovation system restructuring in new EU member states in competition with Asia.* Innovation for Growth – i4g Policy Brief 19, High Level Expert Group 'Innovation for Growth' – i4g, Collection of i4g Policy Briefs, European Commission Brussels. https://ec.

europa.eu/research/innovation-union/pdf/expert-groups/i4g-reports/i4g_policy_brief__19_-_innovation_system_restructuring_new_member_states.pdf.

Weresa, M. A. (Ed.). (2014). *Poland: Competitiveness report 2014. A decade in the European Union*. Warsaw: Warsaw School of Economics Publishing.

Weresa, M. A. (2015a). Preface. In M. A. Weresa (Ed.), *Poland: Competitiveness report 2015. Innovation and Poland's performance in 2007–2014* (pp. 7–8). Warsaw: Warsaw School of Economics Publishing.

Weresa, M. A. (2015b). Toward sustainable competitiveness: An overall assessment of changes in the innovative position and competitiveness of the Polish economy in 2007–2014. In M. A. Weresa (Ed.), *Poland: Competitiveness report 2015. Innovation and Poland's performance in 2007–2014* (pp. 345–355). Warsaw: Warsaw School of Economics Publishing.

Competitiveness, Entrepreneurship and Economic Growth

Romana Korez-Vide and Polona Tominc

Abstract In this chapter we explored country competitiveness and entrepreneurship as drivers of economic growth. The research was carried out on a sample of Central and Eastern European (CEE) member states of the European Union (EU). The analysis shows that economic growth as measured by GDP per capita growth rates, and global competitiveness of a country as measured by the World Economic Forum's (WEF) Global Competitiveness Index scores' growth rates, are positively related to each other. The comparative analysis also reveals that efficiency-driven and certain transition CEE EU Member States have made the highest progress at various competitiveness pillars, which is reflected in their economic growth. The opposite has been found for two innovation-driven CEE EU Member States. When testing the hypothesis on the relationship between the average growth of quality of early-stage entrepreneurship indices and average growth of GDP per capita, no significant relationship was found. This finding is in accordance with the general thesis that entrepreneurial activity supports economic growth only as part of a favourable broader business environment. The research results constitute a preliminary analytical framework for policymakers and managers in the analysed countries.

Keywords Competitiveness • Entrepreneurship • Economic growth • Central and Eastern Europe

Introduction

There is a broad ongoing debate among politicians and scholars alike about the meaning and components of the concept of competitiveness. Boltho (1996) explains it as an ability of an economy to secure a higher standard of living than comparable economies, whilst Porter (1998) argues that the only meaningful concept of competitiveness is national productivity. The World Economic Forum's (WEF) Global Competitiveness Index (GCI), which has been extensively referenced as a credible

R. Korez-Vide (✉) • P. Tominc
University of Maribor, Maribor, Slovenia
e-mail: romana.korez@um.si; polona.tominc@um.si

metric instrument of national competitiveness, is based on Porter's (1998) definition. According to this definition, a country's competitiveness is a set of macroeconomic and microeconomic factors that determine its productivity and economic growth, respectively (WEF 2014).

There is no doubt that the developed entrepreneurial sector has a critical effect on economic growth and the success of national economies (Acs and Szerb 2009; Baumol 1990; Bosma and Levie 2010; Leibenstein 1968; Rebernik et al. 2015; Schumpeter 1934; Von Mises 1949; etc.). Two basic drivers of economic growth through entrepreneurship can be distinguished: the existence of major established firms and the entrepreneurial process taking place in new and growing enterprises—the early-stage entrepreneurship (Reynolds et al. 2002). Early-stage entrepreneurs are identified as those individuals who are personally involved in the creation of a new venture and are at the same time employed as owners/managers of a new firm that is less than 3½ years old (Reynolds et al. 2005). The dynamic entrepreneurship sector is crucial for economic growth, regardless of the stage of economic development—although entrepreneurial characteristics, as well as characteristics of the impact of entrepreneurship sector on economic growth, vary. In this chapter we explore the relationship between national competitiveness, as defined by WEF (2014), and entrepreneurship and economic growth, as measured by gross domestic product (GDP) per capita growth rates. The existing studies on the relationship between competitiveness and economic growth have predominantly focused on one dimension of competitiveness (e.g. Harrison 1996), or on a specific region (e.g. Gardiner et al. 2004). Our empirical analysis is conducted on a sample of Central and Eastern European (CEE) European Union (EU) member states that had a similar political heritage and hence also comparable opportunities of socio-economic development. The latter have been increased by the transformation of political systems in the beginning of the 1990s and by the stepwise accession of these countries to the EU in the past two decades. Authors variously define Central and Eastern European region. According to OECD's (2014) definition, this region comprises Albania, Bulgaria, Croatia, Czech Republic, Estonia, Hungary, Latvia, Lithuania, Poland, Romania, Slovak Republic and Slovenia. The empirical analysis of our chapter is conducted on the sample of 11 CEE EU member states. The existent analyses of CEE countries' competitiveness focus on one or two competitiveness dimensions (e.g. Petrariu et al. 2013; Wilinski 2012), discuss competitiveness in one particular year (e.g. European Commission 2014), or evaluate competitiveness for selected CEE countries (e.g. Niessner 2013). There is no comprehensive insight into the progress and regression of all competitiveness dimensions in a longer period and their possible impacts on CEE EU member states' economic growth rates.

Since the entrepreneurial activity is not directly included in the WEF's Global Competitiveness Index, and due to its confirmed impact on economic growth by several empirical studies, we tested this relationship on a sample of CEE EU member states. There are several studies analysing the impact of the quantity of entrepreneurial activity on economic growth (usually measured by GDP per capita) (Wennekers et al. 2010), which show that the level of entrepreneurial activity and

GDP per capita have a U-shaped relationship. Since the characteristics of entrepreneurial activity on average differ depending on the stage of economic development, the quality of entrepreneurial activity may play a potentially crucial role. This is the reason why, instead of focusing on volume or quantity of entrepreneurship in the economy, we focused on the quality of entrepreneurial activity.

This chapter is structured as follows: in section "Theoretical Background and Hypotheses" we conceptualise a country's competitiveness and describe the impacts of competitiveness pillars on economic growth; we then formulate hypotheses for our research. Section "Methodology and Data" provides a detailed explanation of the methodology and data gathering. In section "Empirical Analysis", the empirical analysis is conducted and the hypotheses are tested. In section "Conclusion", we discuss the empirical findings and state the limitations of our research.

Theoretical Background and Hypotheses

According to WEF (2014), a country's competitiveness is a set of 12 pillars, structured into three groups. The first group is related to the basic requirements of institutions, infrastructure, macroeconomic stability, health and primary education. The second group represents the sources of efficiency—higher education, goods market efficiency, labour market efficiency, financial market development, technological readiness, market size and business sophistication. The third group includes innovation and business sophistication factors. All 12 pillars tend to reinforce each other, and a weakness in one area often has a negative impact in others (WEF 2014). All of the pillars matter to a certain extent for all economies; however, due to different stages of countries' development, they affect them in different ways. The basic requirements are critical for countries still in the factor-driven stage, and the efficiency enhancers are important for countries that had progressed towards the efficiency-driven stage. The innovation and sophistication factors affect the countries in the innovation-driven stage. All countries falling in between two of the three stages can be considered to be in transition. For each of the 12 pillars of a country's competitiveness, there exists empirical evidence about their impact on economic growth.

The quality of a country's *institutions*, which can be determined by the legal and administrative framework within which individuals, firms, and governments interact to generate wealth, has been proven as a factor of economic growth by several studies (e.g. Acemoglu et al. 2002; North 1989; Rodrik et al. 2002). According to Miller et al. (2014), public institutions can impose significant economic costs on businesses and slow the process of economic development (e.g. excessive bureaucracy and red tape, overregulation, corruption, dishonesty in dealing with public contracts, lack of transparency, inability to provide appropriate services for the business sector, improper management of public finances and political dependence of the judicial system). Besides public institutions, good governance of private institutions and maintenance of investor and consumer confidence is also an important element of the process of wealth generation (see Zingales 1998).

The quality and extensiveness of *infrastructure* networks integrate the national market and connect it at low cost to markets in other countries, enable businesses to get their goods and services to market in a secure and timely manner, allow for a rapid and cheap flow of information, determine the location of economic activities, facilitate the movement of workers, prevent interruptions and shortages of energy supplies, etc. Their impact on economic growth has been identified, for example, by Canning and Pedroni (1999) and Calderon and Serven (2004).

Although extant research (e.g. Fischer 1993) finds only weak effects of *macroeconomic stability* on productivity and growth, there exists clear evidence about its impact on short-term economic activity. For example, the impacts of low and moderate levels of inflation are studied by Goodfriend (2007) and Temple (2000), the impacts of public debt levels are examined by Reinhart and Rogoff (2010), and the impacts of the level of taxes, structure of taxation and the way government spends money are studied by Johansson et al. (2008), among others.

Healthy employees are vital to a country's productivity. Thus, investment in the provision of *health services* is a critical factor of economic development and growth, respectively (see Sachs 2001). The quantity and quality of the *basic education* received by the population increases the workers' efficiency and contributes more to devising or executing innovations, which eventually helps businesses to move up the value chain by producing more sophisticated or value-intensive products (see WEF 2014).

Secondary and tertiary enrolment rates, as well as the quality of *higher education*, are also key factors for economies that want to move up the value chain (see Krueger and Lindahl 2001).

Goods market efficiency is related to the production of the right mix of products and services, given a country's particular supply-and-demand conditions, as well as to the effectiveness of trading with these goods (WEF 2014). The best possible environment for the exchange of goods requires a high level of market competition and a minimum of government intervention that impedes business activity (see Branstetter et al. 2010). Openness to international competition via trade and investment enables a country to improve productivity, expand the most productive local industries and access more advanced knowledge and technology from abroad (Delgado et al. 2012). A positive relationship between openness and prosperity has been found by several researchers (e.g. Alesina et al. 2005; Baldwin 2003; Dollar and Kraay 2003), as well as the positive influence of trade on the transfer of knowledge and firm innovation in a country (e.g. Branstetter 2006). Market efficiency also depends on demand conditions, such as customer orientation and buyer sophistication (see Porter 1998). More demanding customers force companies to be more innovative and customer-oriented and thus impose the discipline necessary for market efficiency.

To achieve *labour market efficiency*, the workers have to be allocated to their most effective use in the economy and provided with incentives to invest their best effort in their jobs. Thus, the labour market supports economic growth if it is flexible enough to shift workers from one economic activity to another one rapidly and at a low cost, and allows for wage fluctuations without much social disruption (see Kaplan 2009).

Efficient access to capital is important for companies to make long-term investments needed to raise productivity levels (see Levine 2005). Thus, *financial market development* is reflected in the allocation of financial resources to those entrepreneurial or investment projects with the highest expected rates of return, rather than to the politically connected ones. Furthermore, it is reflected in its sophistication, which enables the provision of capital from various sources (WEF 2014). In order to fulfil all those functions, financial markets need appropriate regulation to protect investors and other actors in the economy.

For an economy to prosper, it is important to be agile in adopting existing technologies to enhance the productivity of its industries (see Barro and Sala-i-Martin 2003). Thus, contemporary *technological readiness* is reflected in the information-communication technology (ICT) access and usage.

Market size, as one of a country's endowments, affects productivity through the opportunities for achieving economies of scale. In the era of globalisation, international markets have become a substitute for domestic markets, especially for small countries. Thus, exports and the membership in the regional integration (which allows cheaper and simpler access to other markets) can be thought of as a substitute for domestic demand in determining the size of the market for the firms of a country. The effects of a country's international markets are shown in studies such as that of Parteka and Wolszczak-Derlacz (2013).

Business sophistication is concerned with the quantity and the quality of local suppliers, service providers and associated institutions in a particular field and the extent of their interactions. It raises productivity due to higher efficiency, creates greater opportunities for innovation in processes and products and reduces entry barriers for new firms (see Delgado et al. 2010). Furthermore, the firms' advanced operations and strategies (branding, marketing, distribution, advanced production processes, and the production of unique and sophisticated products) spill over into the economy and lead to sophisticated and modern business processes across the country's business sectors, which contributes to higher productivity (see WEF 2013). Several empirical studies confirm the importance of companies operations and strategies for productivity (e.g. Bloom and Van Reenen 2007).

The positive impact of *technological innovation* (including institutions and policies supporting innovation) on productivity has been empirically proven by studies such as those of Grossman and Helpman (1991) and Furman et al. (2002). According to Romer (1990), technological innovation is particularly important for economies that can no longer improve their productivity only by integrating and adapting exogenous technologies.

Based on the theoretical background and evidence from the literature, where we have explained the concept of a country's competitiveness and the impact of each competitiveness pillar on economic growth, we formulated the following hypothesis:

> Hypothesis H1. The growth of a national economy's GDP per capita and the growth of a national economy's competitiveness are positively related to each other.

Our chapter focuses also on the analysis between the quality of entrepreneurial activity and economic growth. The existing research results support the idea that the relationship between the level of entrepreneurial activity in the economy and economic growth follows the U-shape (Wennekers et al. 2010). The upward trend of the U-shaped relationship is due to the quality of entrepreneurial activity. In fact, the solo self-employed at the lower end of the entrepreneurial spectrum and ambitious innovative entrepreneurs at the upper end should be distinguished. In innovation-driven economies, a positive correlation between the prevalence rates of business start-ups and average per capita income may be predominant; on the other hand, in factor- and efficiency-driven economies the correlation may even be negative, with the regime switch somehow depending on the qualitative characteristics of entrepreneurship. A similar situation is found regarding the relationship between the entrepreneurship levels and the competitiveness of economies. Recent publications (see WEF 2015) revealed that as the competitiveness of an economy increases, lower proportions of the working-age population start with entrepreneurial activity. As the authors explain, several hypotheses exist to explain this situation: "In highly competitive economies, there are a larger number of attractive existing employment opportunities than in less competitive economies, which raises the opportunity costs of starting a business in these highly competitive economies. Also the higher skill level required to start a business that can compete in a highly competitive market environment raises the barrier to entry for new entrepreneurs in highly competitive economies" (WEF 2015:10).

However, scant research exists about the impact of quality of entrepreneurial activity, which is in the focus of our research. Therefore, our hypothesis H2 posits that the quality of early-stage entrepreneurial activity in the economy and the growth of national economy's GDP per capita are related, but the sign of their relationship is not hypothesised.

> Hypothesis H2. The growth of a national economy's GDP per capita and the growth of quality of early-stage entrepreneurial activity are related to each other.

Methodology and Data

This chapter is a macroeconomic dynamic research, based on secondary data. The calculations of average growth rates of competitiveness indices and GDP per capita for each of the CEE EU member states are followed by comparative analyses of these variables for the discussed countries and by the exploration of relations between variables. The data for the period 2008–2014 we collected from the World Economic Forum's Global Competitiveness Reports and Eurostat Database. The research on the impact of quality of early-stage entrepreneurial activity on economic growth is based on the Global Entrepreneurship Monitor (GEM) indicators.

GEM is a project carried out since 1999 by a research consortium dedicated to understanding the relationship between entrepreneurship and national economic development. GEM enables research and analyses of characteristics, relationships and interdependencies at the level of individuals, as well as at the aggregated country level. It also explores the characteristics of early-stage entrepreneurs and their start-ups, which was utilised in the present study. The data collected and assembled as part of the GEM research programme are consistent with the current technical standards in social science research. The GEM research provides cross-national harmonised datasets on several components and aspects of entrepreneurship. The methodology of GEM research and survey are described in more detail in Reynolds et al. (2005).

CEE EU member states did not all participate in Global Entrepreneurship Monitor (GEM) in the same years: Romania, Croatia, Hungary, Latvia and Slovenia participated in GEM every year from 2008 to 2015; Czech Republic, Lithuania, Poland and Slovak Republic participated 2011–2013; Estonia participated in 2012 and 2013 and Bulgaria first participated in 2015. With the purpose of making the analysis comparable, a time period of 3 successive years was taken into account: ten countries analysed participated in years 2011–2013 (Czech Republic, Croatia, Hungary, Latvia, Lithuania, Poland, Romania, Slovak Republic, and Slovenia). Estonia, however, participated only in 2012 and 2013.

Empirical Analysis

In the first part of the empirical analysis, we compared the average Global Competitiveness Index (GCI) scores of 11 CEE EU member states and the average growth of these scores in the period of 2008–2014. The goal of this comparative analysis was to reveal the state of competitiveness of these countries after the beginning of the financial and economic crisis, and establish each country's record of improvement or deterioration regarding the pillars of competitiveness in the observed period of time. To achieve detailed insight into each country's competitiveness, we have analysed each group of pillars—basic requirements, efficiency enhancers and innovation and sophistication factors.

Figure 1 shows that the highest average levels of competitiveness in the period from 2008 to 2014 were achieved by Estonia and Czech Republic. It is also evident that some transition countries (Lithuania and Poland) achieved higher average levels of competitiveness than some countries at the innovation-driven stage of development (Slovenia and Slovak Republic). According to WEF (2014), Bulgaria and Romania are classified as countries at the efficiency-driven stage of development; Croatia, Hungary, Latvia, Lithuania and Poland as countries in the transition stage of development; and Czech Republic, Estonia, Slovak Republic and Slovenia as countries at the innovation-driven stage of development.

Figure 2 reveals the average growth levels of total competitiveness and the average growth levels of three groups of competitiveness pillars for CEE EU

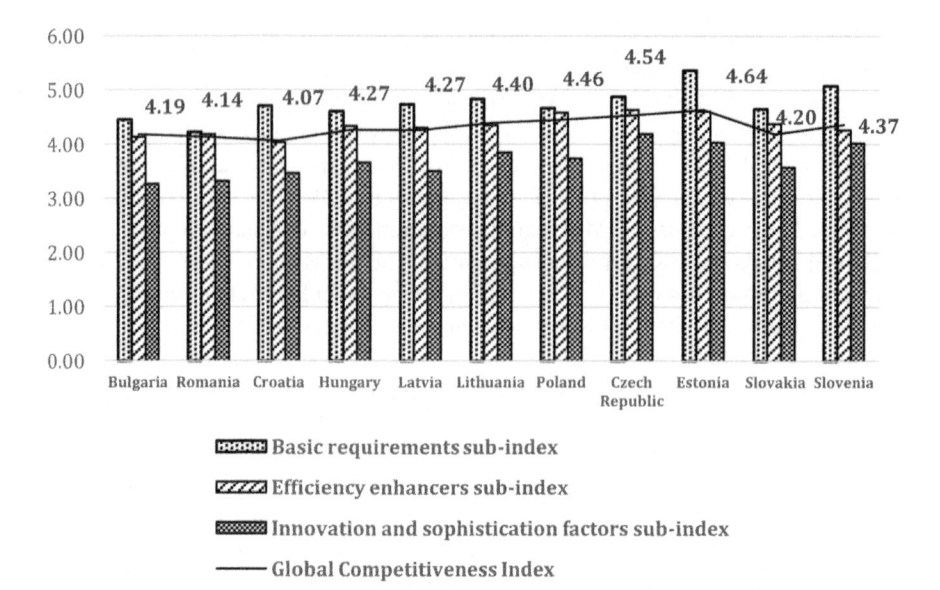

Fig. 1 Average global competitiveness of CEE EU member states (scores, 2008–2014). *Sources of data*: WEF (2008, 2009, 2010, 2011, 2012, 2013, 2014) and authors' calculations. *Notes*: see WEF (2013:10) for the explanation of countries' classification according to their level of development and for the sub-indices weights in the GCI according to the stage of development

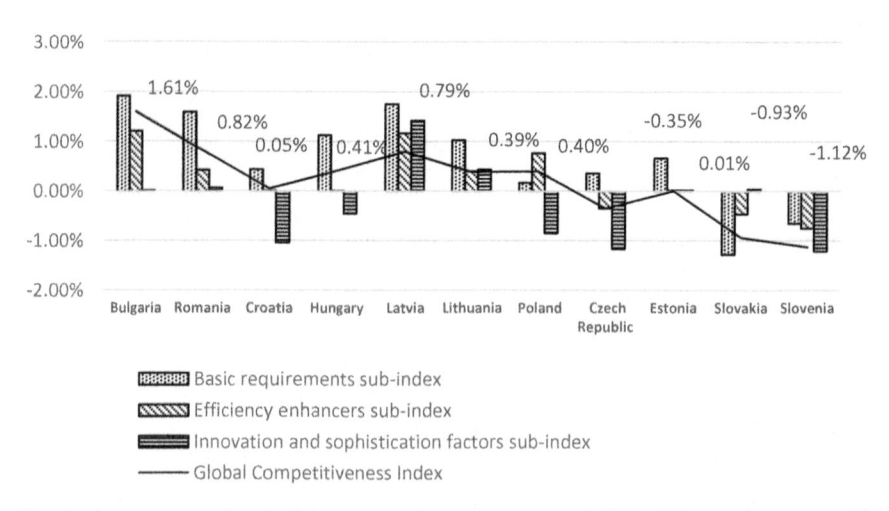

Fig. 2 Average growth of global competitiveness scores of CEE EU member states (%, 2008–2014). *Sources of data*: WEF (2008, 2009, 2010, 2011, 2012, 2013, 2014) and authors' calculations

member states. Herewith we gain an insight into the main fields of progress and regression in competitiveness of CEE EU member countries in the observed period of time. Slovenia's position worsened in all three groups of competitiveness factors;

the highest decrease was seen within the group of innovation and sophistication factors, which endangers Slovenia's future growth prospects with regard to its achieved stage of development. Similar observations are valid for Czech Republic, which recorded high deterioration in the most important group of competitiveness pillars according to its level of development. Slovakia, classified among innovation-driven countries as well, recorded the highest deterioration of basic requirements, even though they represent the foundations for ending a country's transition period.

Among the transition countries, the data show that the worst position was held by Croatia. The other transition countries achieved better positions regarding their average growth of global competitiveness, although Poland and Hungary deteriorated competitiveness in the field of innovation and sophistication factors. According to the data, Bulgaria—one of the two CEE EU member countries at the efficiency-driven stage of development—outperformed all other countries in the field of average competitiveness growth in the observed period of time.

A more detailed picture of a country's position regarding basic factors of competitiveness is shown by Fig. 3. All CEE EU member states managed to improve their total competitiveness in this field, with the exception of Slovakia and Slovenia. These two countries recorded the highest rates of regression in the field of institutions and macroeconomic environment. The deterioration of institutional environment has been observed also for Croatia, Hungary, Lithuania, Poland and Czech Republic. The highest levels of competitiveness in the field of basic requirements were recorded by Bulgaria, Latvia and Romania. Bulgaria, Romania, Latvia and Croatia made the highest progress in the field of infrastructure. Estonia, however, is the leading country in terms of progress in the field of institutional environment.

Figure 4 shows that the lowest positions with regard to efficiency enhancers were achieved by some countries at the innovation-driven stage of development—Slovenia, Slovakia and Czech Republic. The other countries managed to improve their competitiveness in this group of factors. Most of the countries under study had witnessed a deterioration of competitiveness levels in the field of financial development, with Slovenia faring the worst in this pillar. The deterioration of labour market efficiency was the second-most important reason for the decline of overall competitiveness in this group of pillars. However, most of the CEE EU member states recorded progress in the field of technological readiness development; the best results in this field were achieved by Croatia, Bulgaria, Latvia and Lithuania.

The group of business sophistication and technological innovation factors (including institutions and policies supporting innovation) substantially worsened in two countries that compete on this basis—Slovenia and Czech Republic—and in Croatia, as well as in Poland and Hungary, where this factor could contribute to the faster progress of the innovation-driven stage of development (see Fig. 5).

Table 1 is the synthesis of the state of competitiveness of CEE EU member states in the period from 2008 to 2014. The findings are the following: Bulgaria and Latvia have recorded improvement at the highest number of competitiveness pillars

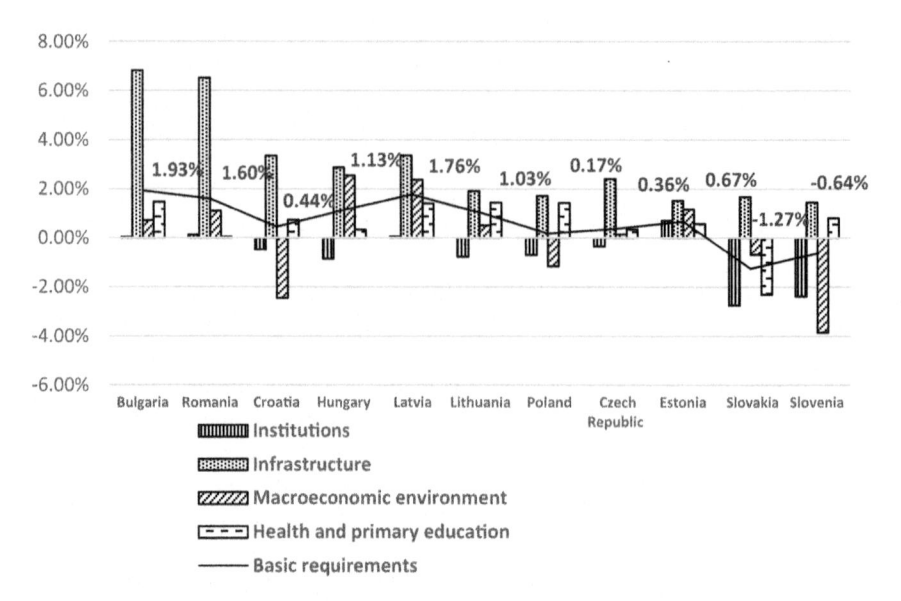

Fig. 3 Average growth of global competitiveness of CEE EU member states in the field of basic requirements (%, 2008–2014). *Sources of data*: WEF (2008, 2009, 2010, 2011, 2012, 2013, 2014) and authors' calculations

(11), Estonia and Romania have each improved at 9 pillars, Poland and Lithuania improved at 8 pillars, Hungary has improved at 7 pillars, Slovakia and Czech Republic improved at 6 pillars and Croatia and Slovenia have each improved at 5 pillars.

In the second part of the empirical analysis, we calculated average GDP per capita and average growth of GDP per capita of CEE EU countries in the period from 2004 to 2013 (see Fig. 6). We found that the highest growth of GDP per capita were recorded in two efficiency-driven countries (Romania and Bulgaria) and two transition countries (Latvia and Lithuania), which also displayed the lowest average levels of GDP per capita. Two innovation-driven countries—Slovenia and Czech Republic—achieved the lowest average growth of GDP per capita. This was not the case for the other two innovation-driven countries with the highest average level of GDP per capita—Slovakia and Estonia.

With the intention to test the Hypothesis 1 of our research, we have ranked the observed countries according to average GDP per capita, average growth of GDP per capita, average GCI scores and average growth of GCI scores (Table 2).

The relationship between the growth of a national economy's GDP per capita and the growth of a national economy's competitiveness was tested using the Spearman non-parametric correlation coefficients, since we wanted to establish the relationship between rankings rather than between values themselves. While the correlation between average GDP per capita ranks and average GCI ranks is not significant, the important result supporting our Hypothesis 1 is that growth of GDP

Competitiveness, Entrepreneurship and Economic Growth 35

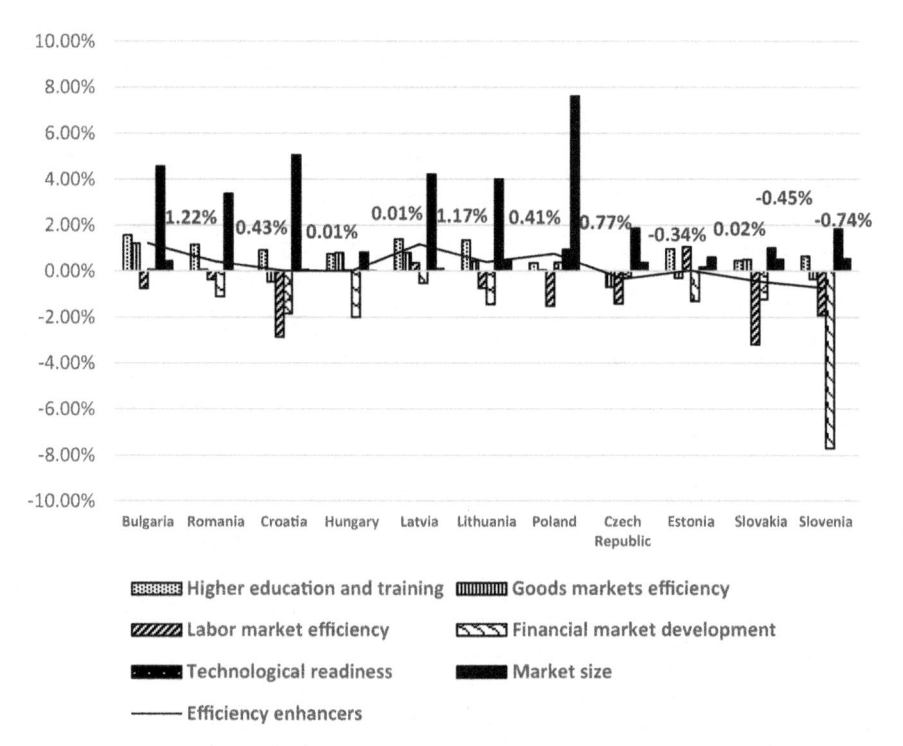

Fig. 4 Average growth of global competitiveness of CEE EU member states in the field of efficiency enhancers (%, 2008–2014). *Sources of data*: WEF (2008, 2009, 2010, 2011, 2012, 2013, 2014) and authors' calculations

per capita ranks and growth of GCI ranks are statistically significantly positively related (Correlation coefficient = 0.649; $p < 0.05$), thus supporting Hypothesis 1.

Country differences in the quality of early-stage entrepreneurial activity were measured by five indicators:

- Percentage within the early-stage entrepreneurs in a country that believe that their products/services are new to all or at least some of the potential customers;
- Percentage within the early-stage entrepreneurs in a country that believe that regarding their products/services, there are only a few or even zero competitors in a country's market;
- Percentage within the early-stage entrepreneurs in a country that use the latest technologies for producing their products/services (technologies not older than a year);
- Percentage within the early-stage entrepreneurs in a country that believe that they will employ at least 10 employees in the next 5 years (at least 50 % growth);
- Percentage within the early-stage entrepreneurs in a country that intend to export their products/services (at least 1 % of their potential customers come from abroad).

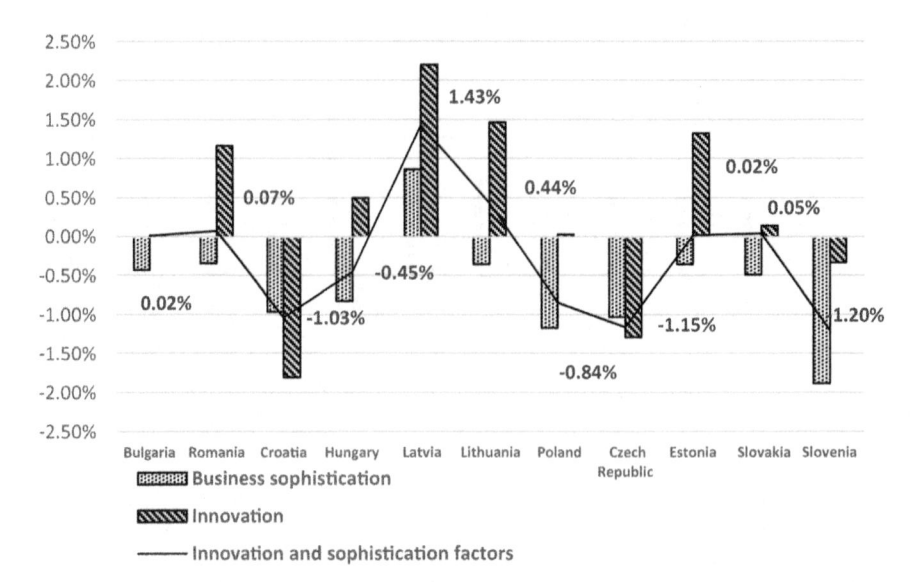

Fig. 5 Average growth of global competitiveness of CEE EU member states in the field of innovation and sophistication factors (%, 2008–2014). *Sources of data*: WEF (2008, 2009, 2010, 2011, 2012, 2013, 2014) and authors' calculations

Figure 7 shows that in all ten countries, the growth of all entrepreneurial indices is very modest, except regarding the percentage within the early-stage entrepreneurs in a country that use the latest technologies for producing their products/services. In that category, all countries except Czech Republic and Slovakia recorded positive average rates. Results have to be interpreted with caution, since the assessment of period of availability of technologies depends on the level of technological development (for example, something assessed as a new technology in an efficiency economy is probably not assessed as new in an innovation-driven economy). Similar caution in interpretation is necessary regarding the assessment of novelty of product/services produced, where efficiency-driven Romania recorded the highest average growth rate.

In almost all countries, the average rate of growth of start-ups that would operate in an identified market niche with few or none competitors is negative—only in Estonia and Slovenia positive values were recorded (in both cases 1.12 %). Similarly, the average growth rates of expected new employment were mainly negative.

Three countries recorded the positive growth rates regarding the export. In Estonia, Slovenia and Slovak Republic, the growth of percentage of early-stage entrepreneurs who expected that at least 1 % of their (potential) customers came from abroad was positive.

Altogether, the Czech Republic reported zero non-negative growth rates of entrepreneurial indices. Croatia, Hungary and Latvia each reported one out of five growth rates as non-negative. Romania recorded three and Slovenia recorded five.

Table 1 The synthesis of the state of competitiveness of CEE EU member states (2008–2014)

Country	Basic requirements					Efficiency enhancers							Innovation and sophistication factors		
	Tc	Ins	Inf	Me	Hpe	Tc	Het	Gme	Lme	Fmd	Tr	Ms	Tc	Bs	In
Bulgaria	Im	+	+	+	+	Im	+	+	+	+	+	+	Im	−	+
Romania	Im	+	+	+	+	De	+	+	−	−	+	+	Im	−	+
Croatia	Im	−	+	−	+	De	+	−	−	−	+	+	De	−	−
Hungary	Im	−	+	+	+	Un	+	+	Un	−	+	Un	De	−	+
Latvia	Im	+	+	+	+	Im	+	+	+	−	+	+	Im	+	+
Lithuania	Im	−	+	+	+	De	+	+	−	−	+	+	Im	−	+
Poland	Im	−	+	−	+	Im	+	+	−	+	+	+	De	−	+
Slovakia	De	−	+	−	−	De	+	−	−	−	+	+	Im	−	+
Estonia	Im	+	+	+	+	De	+	−	+	−	+	+	Im	−	+
Czech Republic	De	−	+	+	+	De	+	−	−	−	+	+	De	−	−
Slovenia	De	−	+	+	+	De	+	−	−	−	+	+	De	−	−

Sources of data: WEF (2008, 2009, 2010, 2011, 2012, 2013, 2014) and authors' calculations

Tc total competitiveness, *Ins* institutions, *Inf* infrastructure, *Me* macroeconomic environment, *Hpe* health and primary education, *Het* higher education and training, *Gme* goods market efficiency, *Lme* labour market efficiency, *Fmd* financial market development, *Tr* technology readiness, *Ms* market size, *Bs* business sophistication, *In* innovation, *Im* improvement, *Un* unchanged, *De* deterioration

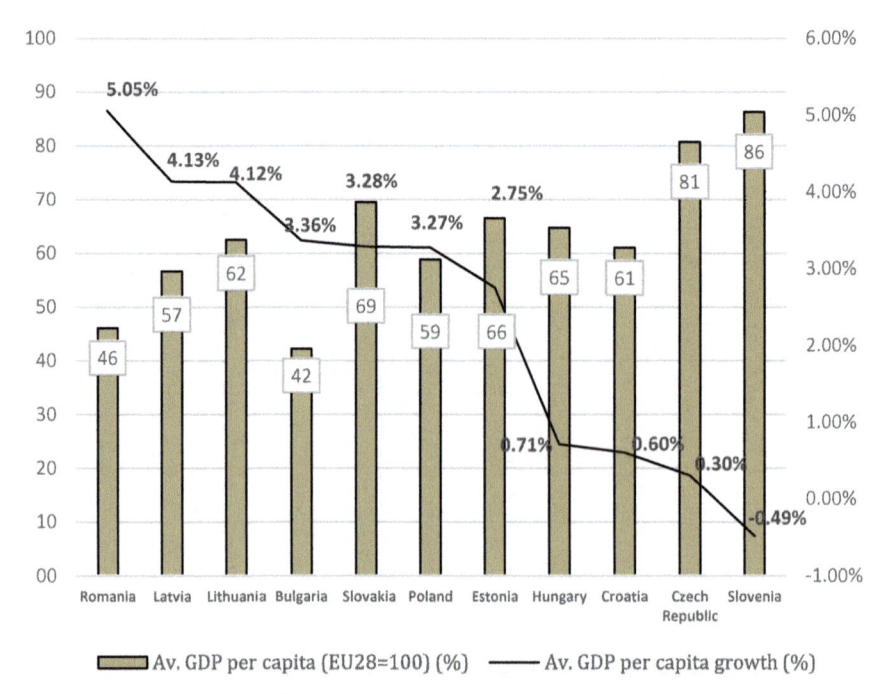

Fig. 6 Average GDP per capita EU28 = 100 and average growth of GDP per capita EU28 = 100 (%, 2004–2013). *Sources of data*: Eurostat (2015) and authors' calculations

When testing the significance of relationship between average growth of quality of the early-stage entrepreneurship indices and average growth of GDP per capita, no significant relationship was found. Moreover, some correlation coefficients indicated positive and some indicated negative signs of a relationship, thus providing no support for Hypothesis 2. These results were generally consistent with some previous findings of studies, which investigated the commonly assumed relationship that innovation and entrepreneurship were positively related to each other, and that both of them drove economic growth. However in their study, Anokhin and Wincent (2012) found that this was not always true. They explored the joint effect of country-level start-up entrepreneurship rates, relative wealth (GDP per capita) and R&D per capita on country-level patents and total factor productivity (TFP). Their results suggested that the quality and impact of entrepreneurial activity could vary significantly across countries. High start-up rates and high-aspiration-entrepreneurs contributed positively to country-level innovation and Total Factor Productivity only when the right framework conditions were in place. The important point was that policy investments in new firm creation alone would not advance economic growth; they would have to be accompanied by investments in education and innovation in general. The main conclusion was that entrepreneurship could support economic growth, but only as part of a broader policy toolset.

Table 2 Countries' ranks according to GDP per capita and GCI scores

Country	Av. GDP per capita EU28 = 100 (%)	Av. GDP per capita EU28 = 100 (ranks)	Av. GDP per capita EU28 = 100 growth (%)	Av. GDP per capita EU28 = 100 growth (ranks)	Av. GCI (scores)	Av. GCI (ranks)	Av. GCI growth (%)	Av. GCI growth (ranks)
Bulgaria	42.1	11	3.36	5	4.19	10	1.61	2
Croatia	60.9	7	0.60	12	4.07	12	0.05	9
Czech Republic	80.6	2	0.30	13	4.54	2	−0.35	12
Estonia	66.4	4	2.75	9	4.64	1	0.01	11
Hungary	64.6	5	0.71	11	4.27	7	0.41	6
Latvia	56.5	9	4.12	3	4.27	6	0.79	4
Lithuania	62.4	6	4.13	2	4.40	4	0.39	8
Poland	58.7	8	3.27	8	4.46	3	0.40	7
Romania	46.0	10	5.05	1	4.14	11	0.82	3
Slovakia	69.4	3	3.28	7	4.20	9	−0.93	13
Slovenia	86.2	1	−0.49	14	4.20	5	−1.12	14

Sources of data: WEF (2008, 2009, 2010, 2011, 2012, 2013, 2014); Eurostat (2015) and authors' calculations

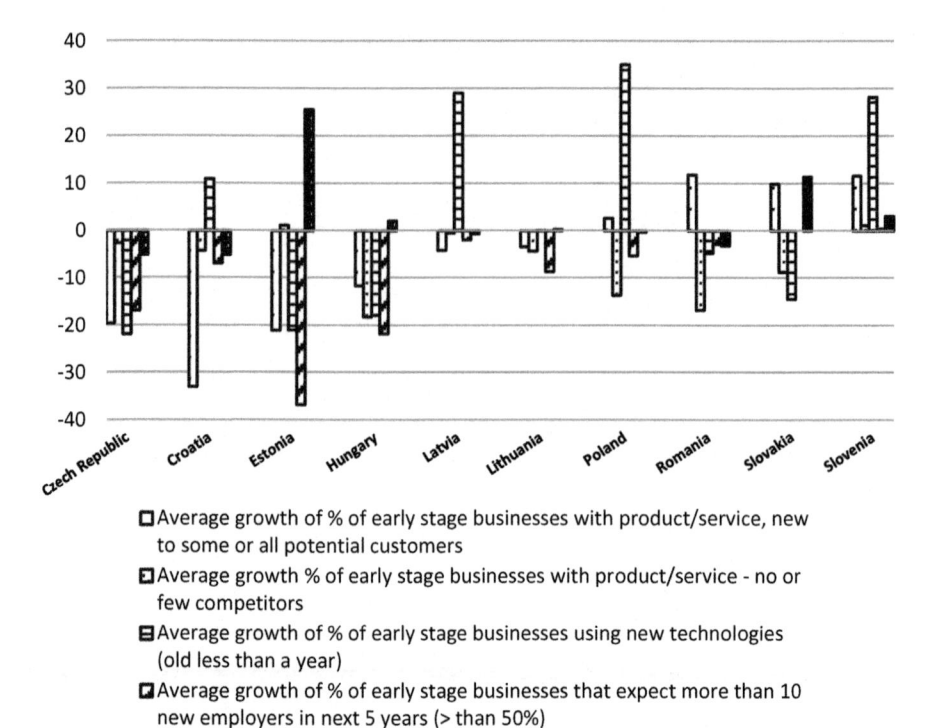

Fig. 7 Average growth of quality of early-stage entrepreneurship indicators (%, 2011–2013; for Estonia only 2012–2013). *Sources of data*: Amoros and Bosma (2014), Kelley et al. (2012), Xavier et al. (2013) and authors' calculations

Conclusion

A country's economic growth and consequently the standard of living of its population are related to many factors that are inside or outside the control of policymakers, institutions, companies and individuals. Although variously conceptualised and measured, a country's competitiveness comprises endogenous and exogenous variables of economic growth. The key goal of this chapter was to find out if a country's competitiveness and its economic growth are related. As a measure of competitiveness, we used the World Economic Forum's Global Competitiveness Index, as a measure of economic growth, however, GDP per capita was used. The research was conducted on a sample of Central and Eastern European EU Member States due to their similar political past and similar opportunities after their political transformations in the beginning of the 1990s. The observed period was partly the period from 2004 to 2013, when all of these countries became members of the EU, and partly the period from 2008, when the financial and economic crisis began.

Based on the calculations of average growth rates, determination of countries' ranks and calculations of their correlations, we supported Hypothesis 1 that the growth of a national economy's GDP per capita and the growth of a national economy's competitiveness are positively related. Similar observations were found in previous studies such as that of Dobrinsky and Havlik (2014). The findings show that particularly efficiency-driven and some transition CEE EU Member States recorded high growth of GDP per capita in the observed periods, which is accompanied by their higher competitiveness; on the other hand, some innovation-driven CEE EU Member States deteriorated in this regard. In general, each country has to emphasise the development of those competitiveness pillars that are the most important for that country's level of development. However, as all competitiveness pillars are mutually dependent, a country should not neglect the development of the others. Our research has shown main gaps in the competitiveness of each observed country and thus it can be used as an initial analytical foundation for the development of policies and managerial measures in the areas where significant changes are necessary. Some possible implications for policymakers and managers are evident from the theoretical background of our research, where each competitiveness pillar is described in detail. It is obvious that while the observed countries have established a record of growth and economic progress in the years before the global economic crisis (see Labaye et al. 2013:3), most of them need a new growth model that would enable them to finish the transition period and to fully modernise their economies. Other studies (see Gorzelak 2015:9) stress the importance of further institutional and industrial restructuring that leads to higher productivity and higher value-added segments in international markets, which would help to improve the self-funding capabilities of these economies and stimulate an endogenous growth pattern. Regarding foreign direct investment (FDI), economic policies should not only consider the quantity but also the structure of incoming FDI (ibid.:53).

We had to reject Hypothesis 2 (the growth of a national economy's GDP per capita and the growth of quality of early-stage entrepreneurial activity are related). This confirmed the findings of some previous studies, namely that entrepreneurial activity supports economic growth only as a part of a favourable broader business environment.

The key limitation of our research is that the Global Competitiveness Index is a composite indicator, composed also from proxy indicators, and according to a set methodology. Possible limitations can also be related to the short periods of observations and the small sample of observed countries.

Several extensions of our research are possible. When analysing the relationship between the growth of a national economy's GDP per capita and the growth of a national economy's competitiveness, we analysed only the composite index GCI. Future studies might go deeper into analysis of factors within each group of pillars that affect the country's competitiveness. Such analysis would be especially interesting for countries that have dramatically weakened or improved their competitiveness. Also, selection of other measures of competitiveness should be considered in subsequent studies.

References

Acemoglu, D., Johnson, S., & Robinson, J. (2002). Reversal of fortune: Geography and institutions in the making of the modern world distribution of income. *Quarterly Journal of Economics, 117*(4), 1231–1294.

Acs, Z., & Szerb, L. (2009). *The Global Entrepreneurship Index* (Jena Research papers). Jena: Max Planck Institute of Economics.

Alesina, A., Spolaore, E., & Enrico, R. (2005). Trade, growth and the size of countries. In P. Aghion & S. Durlauf (Eds.), *Handbook of economic growth* (1st ed., pp. 1499–1542). Amsterdam: Elsevier.

Amoros, J. E., & Bosma, N. (2014). *The global entrepreneurship monitor, 2013 executive report.* Babson Park, MA, London: Babson College, London Business School, GERA.

Anokhin, S., & Wincent, J. (2012). Start-up rates and innovation: A cross-country examination. *Journal of International Business Studies, 43*(1), 41–60.

Baldwin, R. (2003). *Openness and growth: What's the empirical relationship* (NBER Working Paper No. 9578). Cambridge, NY: National Bureau of Economic Research.

Barro, R. J., & Sala-i-Martin, X. (2003). *Economic growth* (2nd ed.). Cambridge, MA: MIT Press.

Baumol, W. (1990). Entrepreneurship: Productive, unproductive, and destructive. *Journal of Political Economy, 98*(5), 893–921.

Bloom, N., & Van Reenen, J. (2007). Measuring and explaining management practices across firms and countries. *Quarterly Journal of Economics, 122*(4), 1351–1408.

Boltho, A. (1996). The assessment: International competitiveness. *Oxford Review of Economic Policy, 12*(3), 1–16.

Bosma, N., & Levie, J. (2010). *Global entrepreneurship monitor, 2009 executive report.* Babson Park, MA, London: Babson College, London Business School, GERA.

Branstetter, L. (2006). Is foreign direct investment a channel of knowledge spillovers? Evidence from Japan's FDI in the United States. *Journal of International Economics, 68*(2), 325–344.

Branstetter, L., Lima, M., Lowell, J. T., & Venancio, A. (2010). *Do entry regulations deter entrepreneurship and job creation? Evidence from recent reforms in Portugal* (NBER Working Paper No. 16473). Cambridge, NY: National Bureau of Economic Research.

Calderon, C., & Serven, L. (2004). *The effects of infrastructure development on growth and income distribution* (World Bank Policy Research Working Paper No. 3400). Washington, DC: World Bank.

Canning, D., & Pedroni, P. (1999). *Infrastructure and long run economic growth.* Accessed April 5, 2015, from http://citeseerx.ist.psu.edu/viewdoc/download?doi=10.1.1.489.6497&rep=rep1&type=pdf

Delgado, M., Ketels, C., Porter, E. M., & Stern, S. (2012). *The determinants of national competitiveness* (NBER Working Paper No. 18249). Cambridge, NY: National Bureau of Economic Research.

Delgado, M., Porter, M. E., & Stern, S. (2010). Clusters and entrepreneurship. *Journal of Economic Geography, 10*(4), 495–518.

Dobrinsky, R., & Havlik, P. (2014). *Economic convergence and structural change: The role of transition and EU accession.* Vienna: The Vienna Institute for International Economic Studies.

Dollar, D., & Kraay, A. (2003). Institutions, trade and growth. *Journal of Monetary Economics, 50*(1), 133–158.

European Commission. (2014). *Reindustrializing Europe. Member states competitiveness report.* SWD (2014) 278. Brussels: European Commission.

Eurostat. (2015). *Statistics A–Z.* Accessed April 3, 2015, from http://ec.europa.eu/eurostat/data/database

Fischer, S. (1993). The role of macroeconomic factors in growth. *Journal of Monetary Economics, 32*(3), 485–512.

Furman, J., Porter, M., & Stern, S. (2002). The x. *Research Policy, 31*(6), 899–933.

Gardiner, B., Ron, M., & Tyler, P. (2004). *Competitiveness, productivity and economic growth across the European Regions.* Accessed March 27, 2015, from http://www-sre.wu-wien.ac.at/ersa/ersaconfs/ersa04/PDF/333.pdf.

Goodfriend, M. (2007). How the world achieved consensus on monetary policy. *Journal of Economic Perspectives, 21*(4), 47–68.

Gorzelak, G. (Ed.). (2015). *Growth-innovation-competitiveness: Fostering cohesion in Central and Eastern Europe.* GRINCOH Project Final Report, Contr. Nr. 290657. Accessed August 10, 2015, from http://www.grincoh.eu/reports

Grossman, G. M., & Helpman, E. (1991). Quality ladders in the theory of growth. *The Review of Economic Studies, 58*(1), 43–61.

Harrison, A. (1996). Openness and growth: A time-series, cross-country analysis for developing countries. *Journal of Development Economics, 48*, 419–447.

Johansson, A., Heady, C., Arnold, J., Brys, B., & Vartia, L. (2008). *Tax and economic growth* (Economics Department Working Paper No. 620). Paris: OECD.

Kaplan, D. (2009). Job creation and labor reform in Latin America. *Journal of Comparative Economics, 37*(1), 91–105.

Kelley, D. J., Singer, S., & Herrington, M. (2012). *The global entrepreneurship monitor, 2011 executive report.* Babson Park, MA, London: Babson College, London Business School, GERA.

Krueger, A., & Lindahl, M. (2001). Education for growth: Why and for whom? *Journal of Economic Literature, 39*(4), 1101–1136.

Labaye, E., Sjåtil, E. P., Bogdan, W., Novak, J., Mischke, J., Fruk, M., & Ionuţiu, O. (2013). *A new dawn: Reigniting growth in Central and Eastern Europe.* Accessed August 10, 2015, from http://www.mckinsey.com/insights/economic_studies/a_new_dawn_reigniting_growth_in_central_and_eastern_europe

Leibenstein, H. (1968). Entrepreneurship and development. *American Economic Review, Papers and Proceedings, 58*(2), 72–83.

Levine, R. (2005). Finance and growth: Theory and evidence. In P. Aghion & S. Durlauf (Eds.), *Handbook of economic growth.* Amsterdam: Elsevier.

Miller, T., Kim, A., & Holmes, K. R. (2014). *2014 Index of economic freedom.* Washington, DC: The Heritage Foundation.

Niessner, B. (2013). *Convergence 2.0.* Vienna: Erste Group.

North, D. C. (1989). Institutions and economic growth: An historical introduction. *World Development, 17*(9), 1319–1332.

OECD. (2014). *Glossary of statistical terms.* Accessed March 23, 2015, from http://stats.oecd.org/glossary/detail.asp?ID=303.

Parteka, A., & Wolszczak-Derlacz, J. W. (2013). The impact of trade integration with the EU on productivity in a posttransition economy: The case of Polish manufacturing sectors. *Emerging Markets Finance and Trade, 49*(2), 84–104.

Petrariu, I. R., Bumbac, R., & Ciobanu, R. (2013). Innovation: A path to competitiveness and economic growth. The case of CEE countries. *Theoretical and Applied Economics, 20*(5), 15–26.

Porter, M. E. (1998). *The competitive advantage of nations* (2nd ed.). New York: Free Press.

Rebernik, M., Tominc, P., Crnogaj, K., Širec, K., Bradač Hojnik, B., & Rus, M. (2015). *Pomanjkanje vitalnosti slovenskega podjetništva – GEM Slovenija 2014.* Maribor: Ekonomsko-poslovna fakulteta.

Reinhart, C. M., & Rogoff, K. S. (2010). Growth in a time of debt. *American Economic Review: Paper and Proceedings, 100*, 573–578.

Reynolds, P., Bosma, N., Autio, E., Hunt, S., De Bono, N., Servais, I., Lopez-Garcia, P., & Chin, N. (2005). Global entrepreneurship monitor: Data collection design and implementation 19982003. *Small Business Economics, 24*(3), 205–231.

Reynolds, P., Bygrave, W. D., Erkoo, A., & Hay, M. (2002). *GEM 2002 executive report.* Babson College, London Business School, E.M. Kauffman Foundation.

Rodrik, D., Subramanian, A., & Trebbi, F. (2002). *Institutions rule: The primacy of institutions over geography and integration in economic development*. Mimeo: Harvard University.

Romer, P. (1990). Endogenous technological change. *Journal of Political Economy, 98*, S71–S102.

Sachs, J. (2001). *Macroeconomics and health: Investing in health for economic development: Report of the commission on macroeconomics and health*. Geneva: World Health Organization.

Schumpeter, J. A. (1934). *The theory of economic development*. Cambridge, MA: Harvard University Press.

Temple, J. (2000). Inflation and growth: Stories short and tall. *Journal of Economic Surveys, 14*(4), 395–426.

Von Mises, L. (1949). *Human action: A treatise of economics*. Edition 1998. Ludwig von Mises Institute, Auburne, AL.

Wennekers, S., Van Stel, A., Caree, M., & Thurik, A. R. (2010). The relationship between entrepreneurship and economic development: Is it U-shaped? *Foundations and Trends in Entrepreneurship, 6*(3), 167–237.

Wilinski, W. (2012). Beginning of the end of cost competitiveness in CEE countries – Analysis of dependence between Labour Costs and internationalization of the region. *Comparative Economic Research, 15*(1), 43–59.

World Economic Forum. (2008). *The global competitiveness report 2008–2009*. Geneva: World Economic Forum.

World Economic Forum. (2009). *The global competitiveness report 2009–2010*. Geneva: World Economic Forum.

World Economic Forum. (2010). *The global competitiveness report 2010–2011*. Geneva: World Economic Forum.

World Economic Forum. (2011). *The global competitiveness report 2011–2012*. Geneva: World Economic Forum.

World Economic Forum. (2012). *The global competitiveness report t 2012–2013*. Geneva: World Economic Forum.

World Economic Forum. (2013). *The global competitiveness report 2013–2014*. Geneva: World Economic Forum.

World Economic Forum. (2014). *The global competitiveness report 2014–2015*. Geneva: World Economic Forum.

World Economic Forum. (2015). *Leveraging entrepreneurial ambition and innovation: A global perspective on entrepreneurship, competitiveness and development*. Geneva: World Economic Forum.

Xavier, S. R., Kelley, D., Kew, J., Herrington, M., & Vorderwuelbecke, A. (2013). *The global entrepreneurship monitor, 2012 executive report*. Babson Park, MA, London: Babson College, London Business School, GERA.

Zingales, L. (1998). Corporate governance. In P. Newman (Ed.), *The new Palgrave dictionary of economics and the law*. New York: MacMillan.

Facilitating Outward Foreign Direct Investment (OFDI): The Perspective of Support Providers in Poland in the Aftermath of 2008+ Economic Crisis

Marta Götz and Barbara Jankowska

Abstract In this chapter we focus on the role of formal institutions and in particular the home country government and its policy in pursuing the most advanced form of foreign expansion, which is foreign direct investment (FDI).

Specifically, by discussing and evaluating the policy towards outward FDI in Poland, we seek to assess the significance of state support in the (post)crisis realm. The crisis years in the world economy (2008–2009) have had an impact on Polish OFDI flows. However, in the case of Poland, the decrease of outflows was not very significant. Having this fact in mind, we formulate the following research questions: what are the measures used by the Polish government to support OFDI? Has the policy toward Polish indigenous firms investing abroad changed since the outbreak of the global economic crisis?

In an attempt at answering the questions and presenting the challenges involved in designing and implementing policies oriented at facilitating investment outflows, we first provide a literature overview on OFDI in general, and the role of the government in supporting OFDI, in specific. Secondly, we indicate the measures used by the Polish government and other public institutions to encourage Polish firms to invest abroad. Thirdly, based on a case study and expert survey, we present the results of our primary study on the measures fostering OFDI used by the national government, regional authorities and business support institutions in Poland.

Keywords Policy towards OFDI • Economic crisis • Poland • Internationalisation

M. Götz (✉)
Vistula University, Warsaw, Poland
e-mail: m.gotz@vistula.edu.pl

B. Jankowska
Poznan University of Economics and Business, Poznan, Poland
e-mail: barbara.jankowska@ue.poznan.pl

Introduction

In this chapter we focus on the role of formal institutions, particularly the home country government and its policy in pursuing outward foreign direct investment (OFDI) during and after the global economic crisis which started in 2008. We embedded our study in the Polish context. OFDI policy as such has been studied in terms of the support measures available for Polish firms' international expansion (see e.g. Gorynia et al. 2015). However, we aim to contribute to that discussion investigating the effect of the economic crisis 2008+ on the possible post-crisis change of the perception of OFDI and subsequently of the respective policy towards a more beneficial one in Poland. The choice of the country under the study was intentional. The Investment Development Path theory suggests that along with the process of economic development, countries turn from being FDI receptors to FDI providers (Gorynia et al. 2010). This concept is reflected in the Polish economic reality. Along with the process of economic transformation and development, indigenous firms emerged and soon started establishing their affiliates in foreign markets. According to the National Bank of Poland, the Polish OFDI stock has been systematically increasing since 1996. In the period from 1996 till 2013 it has grown from 365 million euros to 20,650 million euros.

Having in mind the regular growth of Polish OFDI stock in the world and being aware of the relatively successful operations of Polish investors in foreign markets, we formulate the following research questions: what are the institutional measures used by the Polish government to foster OFDI? Has the policy toward Polish indigenous firms investing abroad changed since the outbreak of the world economic crisis? Which of the measures, if any, were used by Polish firms investing abroad?

This chapter was divided into two parts: the conceptual and empirical one. Within the conceptual section, we have briefly presented the role of institutions, particularly the role of the home country government in supporting the OFDI. The empirical part starts with the methodological remarks. Next, we indicate some facts about Polish OFDI and briefly characterise the measures currently used by the Polish government and other public institutions to encourage Polish firms to invest abroad. Data pertaining to Polish OFDI and supportive measures for OFDI in Poland provide the context for the results of the empirical investigation. Our primary study based on in-depth interviews with representatives of national government, regional authorities and business support institutions, depicts the measures used to foster OFDI, particularly with regard to the economic crisis 2008+. We close the chapter with conclusions and recommendations.

Literature Review: OFDI Policy as a Topic Within the Institutional Approach

The role of the government and FDI policy is an issue discussed within the institutional perspective, which has become one of the leading approaches in the international business studies focused particularly on the phenomenon of FDI (Peng et al. 2008; Xu and Meyer 2012). Institutions can be defined as the rules of the game in a society (North 1990; Williamson 1998). They are constraints that structure political, economic and social interactions (North 1991). According to Scott (1995), institutions impose restrictions by defining legal, moral and cultural boundaries, separating legitimate activities from illegitimate ones. Institutions characteristic of home countries of foreign investors are significant as they create external conditions in which MNE headquarters operate and develop their international strategies (e.g. Andersson and Holm 2010).

Governments are institutions *per se* and are responsible for establishing institutions recognised as the "rules of the game" that is why they affect the firms' FDI operations. Since FDI operations create links between host and home countries, respective governments can impact foreign investors. In other words, the role of government for FDI operations can be presented from the perspective of the host country or home country government and in the context of inward or outward FDI.

The literature studies led us to the conclusion that research on the involvement of government and on FDI policy has predominantly focused on FDI undertaken by MNEs from developed economies, or exposed issues related to inflows of FDI to emerging, transition or developing markets (Bellak et al. 2008; Demekas et al. 2007; Huidumac-Petrescu and Joia 2013; Krifa-Schneider and Matei 2010; Oman 2000; Rajan 2004; Te Velde 2007). Accordingly, it is the significant host country government which was predominantly raised in the aforesaid studies. There is still a research gap to be addressed with regard to the involvement of the home country government in facilitating the OFDI, especially from emerging markets.

The significance of the home government's actions aimed at fostering OFDI can be explained in the context of the liability of foreignness (e.g. Hymer 1976; Zaheer 1995; for a review, see Eden and Miller 2004) and an organisational legitimacy perspective (Dowling and Pfeffer 1975; Scott 1995). It has been confirmed that MNEs prefer entering institutionally similar countries (Boisot and Meyer 2008; Xu and Shenkar 2002; Yeung 2006). Institutional similarity is crucial for achieving organisational legitimacy. An organisation to be "accepted by its environment" (Kostova and Zaheer 1999: 64) has to respond positively to external settings. However, being a foreign subsidiary means functioning in accordance with the rules of the parent company that are defined and developed within the institutional context of the home country. The potential conflict between the internal responsiveness (following the strategy imposed by the parent firm) and external responsiveness related to host country institutional context generates pressures and costs for MNEs. To ease the pressures and lower the costs of unfamiliarity with host markets (Gaur and Lu 2007; Phillips et al. 2009; Xu et al. 2004), home country governments can use different measures. The measures can reduce institutional differences between the home and host country or make MNEs familiar with those differences which may result in incorporation of particular alterations in the strategies of MNEs.

The aforementioned institution-based view highlights the relationships between the firms and the context of their operations, and home country conditions, among others. The impact of home country settings on the international expansion of domestic firms can be indirect or direct. As Cuervo-Cazurra and Genc (2011) noted, the direct influence is related to the perception of the home country. In fact, the image of a country may be an asset or a liability. The indirect impact means that home-based firms are induced to develop particular adaptive resources and capabilities which constitute the firm-specific advantage and determine firm strategy. The government and FDI policy are institutional factors that may be regarded as factors transmitting the direct and indirect influences of the home country on the international strategy of firms, including, *inter alia*, their OFDI operations. The distinction between direct and indirect influence refers not only to the home country factors, in general terms, but to the measures of the home country government policy focused on FDI and in particular on OFDI, likewise (Brewer 1993). The discrimination between direct and indirect measures corresponds to the classification of OFDI support instruments proposed by some Polish researchers (Gorynia et al. 2013, 2015). The classification was developed with the use of two criteria—the financial and non-financial character of the measures and their dedication or not to OFDI operations. The indirect impact related to non-dedicated measures that can affect OFDI pertains to broad internationalisation efforts and competitiveness of firms. These efforts can result in OFDI in the long run (Gorynia et al. 2013). Thus, among home country measures (HCMs) which can affect the readiness to OFDI indirectly, we can mention the monetary policy, capital controls and other restrictions on international funds' transfers, wage policies and/or price controls in home countries (Brewer 1993).

In our empirical study, we focused on the impact of the home country measures (HCMs) on OFDI, while not distinguishing between direct and indirect impacts. According to Kline (2003) who based his studies on UNCTAD (1995: 309–351), there are six main types of HCMs that promote FDI outflows: policy, information provision and technical assistance, technology transfer, financial and fiscal incentives, investment insurance, market access regulations. The six types of measures were indicated as the appropriate HCMs in case of investors from developed countries investing in developing countries. However, four of them can support OFDI undertaken by firms from emerging and transition markets since they are not specific to the situation in which the investor comes from a developed country and the host location is the developing country. The specific types of HCMs mentioned above refer to technology transfer and market access regulations. The latter is rather a measure used by host countries in order to attract inward FDI.

Policies aimed at fostering OFDI can, in general, take the form of bilateral investment treaties (BITs) that declare the home country's intention to encourage

FDI flows. The BITs can be regarded as triggers of OFDI as they motivate the home country to develop other, more specific HCMs.

Information provision and technical assistance depend on the collection and dissemination of information on the investment climate, external environment and opportunities for FDI in the host country. The provision of data on the conditions of doing business in a particular host country to a potential investor supports the latter's efforts to identify a particular host market. Moreover, dedicated information is needed to contact potential investors with potential host country partners. An attractive group of HCMs are financial and fiscal incentives. Financial incentives can take different forms, including grants, loans, loan guarantees and equity participation in the project. Fiscal incentives are support measures relating to taxation—e.g. tax exemptions, deferrals or credits for taxation of foreign source income and general tax sparing provisions. OFDI can be affected by transfer pricing standards, monitoring, enforcement and information sharing arrangements. The eagerness of firms to undertake OFDI is sometimes diminished by various types of risks, including the political one. HCMs that cover different types of risks usually not included in traditional private insurance policies can also promote OFDI. Investment insurance is of greater importance particularly to FDI located in countries with a less stable macroeconomic environment.

Peng et al. (2008) noted that the OFDI supporting policy in Western economies tends to be taken for granted. However, the significance of the home country government for OFDI particularly in emerging economies has been largely neglected. The explanation for that may be the dominance of FDI inflows from developed countries. In 2000s FDI outflows from developing countries accounted just for 12 % of global FDI outflows (UNCTAD 2014: ix). In 2013, FDI outflows from developing and transition economies reached the level of 39 % of global FDI outflows, which is 553 billion USD, and MNEs from these countries have been increasingly acquiring foreign affiliates of multinationals from developed countries located in their regions (UNCTAD 2014: ix). Poland has been trying to keep pace with other emerging markets.

Methodology of the Study

The system of international promotion of Poland abroad and the measures dedicated to Polish outward investors seem to be comprehensive. However, the occurrence of the economic turmoil raises the question about the alterations that could have been introduced with regard to support measures. Representatives of Polish Ministry of Economy assess the (post)crisis modification in FDI policy as negligible.[1] To deepen investigate that issue, we conducted interviews with representatives

---

[1] An official from the Department of Support Instruments, Ministry of Economy mail response 21.11.2014.

of assistance providers for Polish outward investors. We used the non-probabilistic sampling technique—the purposive sampling. As our goal was to obtain a relatively broad picture of policy facilitating OFDI in Poland shortly after the economic crisis, we have used the expert survey in order to glean the knowledge from individuals that have particular expertise in this area. We conducted interviews with representatives of the national government, regional authorities and business support institutions. We decided to survey experts since their views as stakeholders involved in both designing and pursuing policy decisions seem critical for thorough and evidence-based research in this area. The expert pool included representatives of the Ministry of Foreign Affairs, the Marshal Office of Wielkopolska (a region in the Western part of Poland), ARAW (Wroclaw Agglomeration and Development Agency), PAIIZ (Polish Agency for Information and Foreign Investment), and the think tank "Poland, Go global!".

We took an open approach to conducting interviews with the representatives of the supportive institutions, whereby experts were asked to express their opinions and comment on the possible post-crisis changes of OFDI policy.

Results of the Empirical Study

Facts About Polish OFDI

The economic crisis that took place in the global economy during the years 2008–2009 turned firms' external settings into hypercompetitive and made them face substantial challenges (Schmitt et al. 2010). Along with subsequent declines in output, employment, and trade, global FDI flows also began to fall—by 16 % in 2008. In 2009 FDI decreased by a further 40 % for the first time in 60 years and in 2010 the FDI levels stagnated just above 1 trillion USD (Poulsen and Hufbauer 2011). The FDI outflows in the world in 2008 declined by 9.4 % in relation to 2007 (UNCTAD 2009:13). The decline was visible especially in the developed economies—the growth rate of the OFDI flows in 2008 was −11.9 %. However, the transition economies experienced the growth rate at the level of 13.9 % (UNCTAD 2009: 12).

The Polish OFDI stock in the period 2008–2013 increased from 17,030 million euros to 20,650 million euros and the leading position of Europe as the main location of Polish OFDI was visible (see Table 1). The share of Polish FDI hosted in Europe in total stock oscillated around 93 % in the studied period. It is evident that the Polish OFDI stock in 2013 was lower than in 2012. The biggest decline refers to the Polish OFDI stock located in Belgium, Bulgaria, Luxembourg, Germany, Greece, Spain, France, Ireland, Italy, Netherlands, Portugal, United Kingdom, Austria, Finland and Sweden (NBP 2013). However, this slump has to be interpreted carefully as in 2013 the National Bank of Poland introduced a new methodology and any comparisons are difficult.

Table 1 Basic information on Polish OFDI stock (million euros)

	2008	2009	2010	2011	2012	2013
Europe	15,738	19,026	30,565	37,969	40,596	19,278
Rest of the World	1293	1481	2699	2919	2896	1372
Total World	17,030	20,507	33,264	40,888	43,492	20,650

Source: NBP (2010, 2013)

The main destinations of Polish investment in Europe in terms of the total value of the outward stock in 2013 were Luxembourg, the Netherlands, Cyprus, the Czech Republic, Lithuania and Switzerland. However, in the cases of Luxembourg and Cyprus we can talk only about the capital-in-transit rather than genuine investment related to production or other economic activity and hiring new staff.

Polish investors have preferred Europe as the host region for their facilities, but there are companies investing in North America and Asia. The most attractive market in the North America were the United States in 2013 with the Polish OFDI stock of 397 million euros. Polish firms have systematically increased their presence in the United States since 2008. The growth in the value of the stock has been very strong since 2010. It is the time when the North American economy, especially that of the United States was recovering from the financial crisis. It could mean that Polish companies exploited the gaps in the market that appeared after the economic downturn. The share of North America in the total value of Polish OFDI was at the level of 2 % in 2013. Asia accounted for 3 % of total Polish outward stock in 2013. The most attractive Asian markets for Polish investors were India, China and Japan. China was the number one till 2010.

Other regions in the world worth mentioning are South America and Africa. However, the share of Polish OFDI stock in total stock located in the South American markets was lower than 1 % in 2013. The highest value of the stock was characteristic for the crisis period—the years 2008–2009. This region is still to be explored by Polish investors. However, there is one country in the South America luring Polish firms—namely Brazil where the Polish OFDI stock recorded 17 million euros in 2013 in comparison to 2.5 million euros in 2008. Next to South America, Africa can be mentioned as an underexplored region by Polish investors. The share of Polish OFDI stock in Africa in total Polish outward stock fluctuated in the analysed period around 1 %. The most popular African markets among Polish investors were Liberia (113 million euros in 2013), Senegal (41 million euros in 2013) and Morocco (32 million euros in 2013). Polish firms intensified their operations in Africa since 2009 when the developed countries experienced the economic turmoil.

The Polish OFDI flows were relatively volatile in the period 2008–2013 (Table 2). The crisis period—the years 2008–2009—brought less optimistic results in terms of the OFDI flows. The Polish outflows amounted to 3011 million euros and 3745 million euros in 2008 and 2009, respectively.

In 2013 Polish entities withdrew from abroad 1063 million euros. The outflows directed towards Europe were decreased and recorded −1310 million euros. The

Table 2 Basic information on flows of Polish OFDI in million euros

	2008	2009	2010	2011	2012	2013
Europe	2521	3541	5105	5796	395	−1310
Rest of the World	491	203	350	71	162	247
Total World	3011	3745	5455	5867	557	−1063

Source: NBP (2010, 2013)

Table 3 The sectoral structure of Polish OFDI stock in million euros

	2008	2009	2010	2011	2012	2013
Services	10,437	12,116	16,531	25,839	28,060	15,830
Manufacturing	1662	2952	12,795	11,914	12,529	4271
Construction	320	293	1077	1555	1526	−188
Mining	30	88	480	744	793	894
Other	4582	5059	2381	835	583	−157
Total	17,030	20,507	33,264	40,888	43,492	20,650

Source: NBP (2010, 2013)

reduction of Polish outflows was the biggest in the case of Luxembourg (to −2139 million euros), Sweden (−299 million euros) and Ukraine (−244 million euros). In 2012 we could observe the reduced FDI activity especially with Luxembourg (−716 million euros), Switzerland (−647 million euros) and Sweden (−489 million euros). Cyprus (444 million euros), Great Britain (325 million euros), Denmark (267 million euros) and Germany (187 million euros) were the key destinations of Polish outgoing FDI flows in 2013.

As far as the sectoral structure of Polish OFDI is concerned, there is a visible predominance of services (Table 3). The period from 2008 till 2013 brought a strong rise in the share of services in total outward stock from 61 % in 2008 to 77 % in 2013. The services include wholesale and retail trade, repairs, transportation and storage, accommodation and food services, information and communication, as well as financial and insurance activities. The financial and insurance services contributed to the largest extent to the outward stock in 2013 with 43 % share in total outward stock in 2013. High growth was recorded by the financial intermediation, too. This subsector increased its share in total outward stock from 25 % in 2008 to 42 % in 2013. Amongst industry sectors, manufacturing prevailed clearly with a strong position of food products, beverages and tobacco products since 2008 till 2010. In 2011 this subsector recorded a decline, but in 2013 the stock grew again. Manufacturing was followed by construction and mining. Mining and quarrying contributed to the positive development in the value of Polish outward stocks, too. This subsector recorded a substantial increase since 2010.

The sectoral structure of Polish OFDI flows was changing in the analysed period (Table 4). In 2008 there was a visible predominance of services with 2286 million euros. Five years later this sector experienced a decline as the flows amounted to −2296 million euros and the highest value of flows was characteristic for

Table 4 The sectoral structure of Polish OFDI flows in million euros

	2008	2009	2010	2011	2012	2013
Services	2286	1886	2766	4503	1096	−2296
Manufacturing	443	1495	1145	932	84	155
Construction	−136	8	152	703	−318	1108
Mining	38	90	110	78	116	236
Other	380	266	1283	−349	−422	−267
Total flows	3011	3745	5455	5867	557	−1063

Source: NBP (2010, 2013)

construction (1108 million euros). The second position belonged to financial and insurance activities (248 million euros).

In general, despite the recent trend of an increasing role of services and a relatively significant share of transit flows counted as OFDI, neighbouring European countries and manufacturing sector prevails at least in terms of measures, such as the number of affiliates, staff employed overseas or the share of foreign sales (GUS 2012).

To sum up, based on our examination of OFDI statistics we can conclude that basic information on Polish OFDI stocks does not reveal any radical modification related to the period of the economic crisis and shortly after the economic downturn. TA relatively strong decline in the value of total outflows in 2012 can be discerned. In order to obtain a more reliable picture of Polish OFDI, we can compare the data from NBP with the data from UNCTAD. According to UNCTAD, the Polish outflows in 2008 amounted to 4414 million USD, in 2009 to 4699 million USD and in 2013 to −4652 million USD. These data reflect similar trends as the statistics provided by NBP. Neither the year 2008, nor the year 2009 when the economic turmoil broke out, brought any radical changes to Polish FDI outflows.

In this context the need to develop a consistent policy fostering Polish OFDI and promote pro-expansionary attitudes among Polish investors should not be traced back to the recent crisis only, as the motives and rationale of internationalisation go much deeper. However, the justification for the development of OFDI policy in Poland can relate to the still relatively low involvement of this economy in global FDI outflows. According to UNCTAD, the share of Polish FDI outflows in global FDI outflows was at the level of 0.2 % in 2008, 0.4 % in 2009 and dropped to −0.3 % in 2013 (UNCTAD statistics 2015). The share of Polish OFDI stock in the global stock of OFDI recorded in 2008 and in 2009 0.15 % and in 2013 increased to 0.24 % (UNCTAD statistics 2015). The impact of the economic crisis has not been reflected in the decline of outflows and outward stock of Polish OFDI in the crisis years 2008 and 2009 and shortly after the crisis period embracing the years 2010 and 2011.

However, taking the micro-economic perspective into consideration, we can conclude that the economic turmoil has certainly affected Polish firms involved in foreign expansion. Studies conducted by some researchers highlight the ambiguous nature of this phenomenon (Caruana et al. 2000; Welch and Welch 2009; Wennberg and Holmquist 2008). Being aware of that it is useful to investigate the policy towards OFDI in Poland, since the measures and actions undertaken by the Polish government and other public institutions can help to better exploit the potentially positive impact of the crisis on internationalisation efforts. They may help to increase the share of Poland in the global outflows of FDI and global stock of OFDI, or to encourage Polish investors to reformulate their foreign expansion strategies in order to increase the sustainability of their businesses.

Policy Facilitating OFDI in Poland

Poland as one of CEE countries has started its economic transformation in 1990. The development of market economy in Poland and hence the liberalisation of the economy has been related *inter alia* to the growing openness of Poland towards foreign investors. Poland as an advanced emerging market is characterised by an intense development of market-supporting institutions (Arnold and Quelch 1998; Hoskisson et al. 2000). That assertion is reflected in the trends related to OFDI policy and Polish government's activity in the field of OFDI.

The system of Poland's promotion abroad encompasses five areas (Promocja Polskiej gospodarki za granicą 2014). We can distinguish between:

- measures aiming at advertising Poland as a brand and improving the image of Polish firms (addressing Polishness as a liability);
- during state visits Polish officials are frequently accompanied by representatives of Polish business (economic missions);
- departments of Polish Embassies (Trade and Investment Promotion Sections) offer assistance to Polish firms setting up business there;
- special system of information provision has been set up which provides insight into conditions for business activities on foreign markets;
- financial support for export is made available.

The systemic help offers the network of exporters and investors support centres dedicated to particular administrative regions in Poland. This programme embraces 16 branches located in each region. The aim of the programme is to support exporters and potential investors and complement prior direct assistance offered in the form of grants and loans. The programme endorses expansion in 15 strategic sectors. To strengthen the image of Poland as a reliable strategic partner among business and public opinion in Germany, Czech Republic, Ukraine, China, or Russia, an informational campaign—"Made in Poland" was launched in 2013 (Bonikowska et al. 2013).

Polish firms' efforts to expand abroad are supported by some unconventional measures. Innovative companies that commercialise research findings and outcomes globally are invited to participate in a contest organised by the National Centre for Research and Development. Within that contest, a broad set of measures and actions can be financed. Such firms are offered support to develop their international strategy, formulate their business plans and analyse foreign markets.

The purchase of specialised market research reports, participation in training and coaching in how to adjust to the legislative and cultural demands of a given market, intellectual property management, preparation of bids for negotiation, identification of key customers and business partners, cooperation with foreign business advisors in developing innovative markets to establish business relations, fine-tuning of market strategies and preparation of market entry tactics, workshops for prospective financial investors, professional valuation of offerings by venture capital, and launches of cooperation in R&D or production are among the areas of potential assistance.

Polish smaller and innovative companies are supported in the process of networking, developing partnerships with entities operating in the Silicon Valley or establishing their businesses in the Valley. They can be assisted by the US-Poland innovation hub of Palo Alto.

There is a series of contests for firms successfully investing in foreign markets. Such entities can participate in a prestigious contest "Polish Firm—International Champion" organised by PricewaterhouseCoopers under the auspices of the *Rzeczpospolita* daily. The basic criterion to enter the competition is to have established a foreign business facility in the preceding 5 years (e.g. service point or another business location, or foreign company acquisition), or to successfully develop international sales. Another viable option is the think tank Poland Go Global, which is an initiative of the ICAN Institute (the publisher of *Harvard Business Review Polska*) and KGHM which commenced its activities with a conference in 2012. Its main purpose was to support the internationalisation of Polish businesses by exchanging good practices and carrying out joint commercial projects. In a more remote future, the think tank is to examine the international activities of Polish businesses, establish collaboration with organisations dealing with economic issues in Europe (associated in the Stockholm Network), hold regular conferences and maintain joint scholarly-business fora. Support for the international expansion of Polish enterprises is also offered by Citi Bank Handlowy in cooperation with the *Puls Biznesu* daily within the programme "Time for Economic Patriots".

The policy towards OFDI by Polish firms seems to have gradually evolved. After years of a certain *laissez faire* approach, when companies had been on their own and could not have expected any particular help from the state, a more friendly attitude assuming tangible support has been initiated.

In this chapter we go beyond simply describing available instruments covered already by various reports and papers (see Éltető et al. (2015) for a detailed review of existing measures). But before turning to our field study and experts' survey, we would like to embed the results of our primary research in a broader context. We present the opinions of representatives of firms that can be found in secondary sources. In one of interviews, the CEO of Selena, a leading chemical Polish company claims that more protection and support for national firms is needed in order to redress the unfair conditions enabling foreign companies to obtain access to Polish market, whereas Polish firms cannot count on any privileges (Stodolak 2014). The competitive conditions of doing business vary considerably, so we witness an unfavourably asymmetrical opening of our market without due reciprocity. Well-meant economic patriotism, unfortunately feared by administration due to the allegation of siding with business, abuses, etc. discourage politicians to undertake the needed measures. However, even simple steps matter such as less red tape, simpler and more transparent rules, a streamlined taxation system, a more business friendly environment enabling domestic firms to thrive and facilitating their start abroad. Another important issue is the removal of artificial barriers disabling growth of local firms, encouraging local administration and private households and other customers to source at Polish firms—issue of public procurement. Firms expanding abroad are necessary for the whole economy, their prosperity translates and defines the economic performance of the whole country, their HQ hire best employees, conduct R+D activities, represent upper value chain tasks. However, the number of such firms in Poland is still limited. This problem is additionally aggravated by mass emigration. Hence new initiatives are established to bring emigrants back and, as a result, some Polish MNE are setting such platforms facilitating their return. These appeals and manifestos can be regarded as a first necessary step to raise awareness of current problems and to draw decision makers' attention to neglected issues.

Worth mentioning is the initiative by the Selena CEO to set up foundation "Inteligentny Start" (Panek 2014). It is tasked with arranging and facilitating the recruitment processes for Polish firms venturing abroad. Its aim is thus to harness the skills, contacts and know-how of Polish migrants living abroad and prevent any future waist of their brain power.

If the internationalising companies shared their experience and expressed their opinions more openly, then the right design of OFDI policy could be facilitated. Such feedback information would help better formulate and organise the whole support system. Difficulties to obtain information from firms undergoing internationalisation and active abroad, which seem to be a commonplace unfortunately, may suggest the urgent need to consider launching some sort of reporting system (Éltető et al. 2015). Obligatory reporting, which is a duty to provide official statistical offices with some basic information on a regular basis, which will then be publicly available, should not be underestimated particularly from a research perspective, but not exclusively. It is even more important from the perspective of promotion of Polish firms in the international market. Their successful expansion changes the perception of the attractiveness of Poland as a host country for investors, as well. Strong Polish players are a kind of confirmation that even in a transition economy there are emerging firms able to face the hypercompetitive conditions in the international market.

Polish investors mention their expansion ambitions and plans often just by the way, while informing about other facts related to their operations. An example can be the announcement made once by the Polish capital group Gerda that they bought the famous international brand of heating systems Ulrich. It was mentioned while presenting the plans to invest in the SEZ Starachowice (Grzegorczyk 2013). Publicly listed companies and more experienced investors are more eager to share the information about foreign expansion. Among the publicly listed firms one can mention the CCC Group that declared its plans for speeding up its investment in new shops to become the biggest shoe seller in Hungary, Czech Republic and Slovakia. The set of new markets encompasses more locations—Austria (four new shops to be opened), Slovenia (three shops to be opened), Croatia (seven shops to be opened) and Turkey (one shop to be opened). Among more experienced investors one can mention the packaging producer Can-Pack that attempts to achieve the position of a global company being yet a regional player. In January 2013 the firm bought 35 % of shares in Can Asia, Inc. from San Miguel Yamamura Packaging Corporation (http://www.canpack.eu/?p=614). Can-Pack operates an aluminium can production facility at Aurangabad, in the state of Maharashtra, India (Can-Pack... 2016). The facility has been working since 2008 and was the largest Polish investment made in India in recent years. The company plans to make further investments depending on market trends. An interesting example is the Group Azoty. The company's plans related to the foreign expansion confirm that Polish firms have ambitions to go into more remote locations than Europe. In fact, the announced strategy for years 2013–2020 targets operations not only in Europe, but in Africa, as well. The firm invested in a phosphate mine in Senegal (Fertile prospects... 2015: 30–33).

Supporting OFDI in Poland: Results of Experts' Survey

In this section of our chapter we present the opinions and comments of the selected experts on the potential change of perception of OFDI in Poland and any alterations within the outward FDI policy in Poland in the aftermath of 2008+ crisis. As each of the experts represents a particular organisation of public administration or a business support institution, their opinions were not combined, but intentionally presented separately. Their comments cannot be generalised as they represent distinct cases. We attempted to report the views of the experts precisely, possibly avoiding our own interpretations.

In the opinion of the representative of the Marshal Office in Wielkopolska, the crisis acted rather as a catalyst. It accelerated the internationalisation process and made it clear that the EU can be vulnerable, weak and preoccupied with solving own problems. Polish firms need to reorient, to seek other markets to invest and simply to diversify in order to be more secure. The events of 2008 and later acted as a filter illuminating the risk associated with excessively relying on one market—the EU. However, it seems that a defensive strategy prevails over an offensive one. Stimulating expansion results from the fear of losing market and the need to compensate losses, rather than from proactive long term strategy of conquering new markets.

Interviews with representatives of the ARAW—The Wroclaw Agglomeration and Development Agency led to the conclusion that since the outset of the crisis in 2008, we have not observed a clear change of perception of OFDI policy towards a more beneficial one. No visible shift either in Poland or elsewhere in Europe can be discerned, apart from perhaps some more occasions for favourably priced acquisitions. Polish firms seem to have weathered the crisis well and continue to expand abroad regardless of the global turbulences. Political voices advocating some economic patriotism or nationalism even is one thing, but actual economic calculations, profits and losses analysis are another one. Shrewd business evaluation is crucial for any firm's decision to invest or to relocate. As long as Poland is still a relatively cheap location and offers good quality for low prices, its attractiveness is not endangered. Koelner's acquisition of the UK-based Rawplug, Selena's investment in Brazil, Toya's purchase of the Chinese Jato or KGHM's expansion to Chile are among the most prominent examples that the internationalisation of Polish firms did not cease due to the economic crisis. It should be stressed, however, that the specificity of the current foreign expansion as the traditional division "pure export vs. FDI" does not hold anymore. Hybrid forms such as participation in joint large scale projects (subway in Dubai), setting up subsidiaries or starting distribution make simple division trade vs. investment blurred.

Concerning the issue of a potential impact of the economic crisis on OFDI policy in Poland, in the opinion of PAIIZ crisis changes attitude in a sense it makes decision-makers and investors realise how fragile relying only on Europe might be. It might have raised interest in distant third markets. There paradoxically Poland has got both advantages and disadvantages. On the one hand, in Africa, for instance, competition is already high, where besides European countries China is establishing its foothold dynamically. On the other hand, Polish investors there do not suffer from the colonial stigma and may be more welcome. The topical change following the crisis is, however, the tightening of fiscal policies. Apart from austerity measures, steps have been taken to make the tax system more watertight, to prevent abuses, erase tax loopholes etc. Available incentives in SEZ are granted only to new investments and only those, which under no condition would be linked to some relocation, or factory or subsidiary closure somewhere else. In other words, investment cannot be carried out at the expense of another location. Supported are mainly greenfield projects, as there is currently no climate for M&A or brownfield, although these types do not involve restrictions as no particular type of help is usually offered to them. Economic support comes mainly from public budget and it is its size that in fact determines the value of assistance offered. The stark difference between the German budget and funds earmarked on help, and the Polish budget is illustrative.

In the opinions of the representative of the think tank "Poland, Go Global!", as far as expansion of Polish firms is concerned it seems that rather long-term tendencies dominate. The crisis highlighted the advantages of Polish companies, such as extremely high and appreciated worldwide flexibility and ability to react swiftly to scale up or down if necessary and to adjust to clients' needs. This unique combination of low costs with high efficiency offers competitive advantage and makes Polish firms' expansion particularly successful in mid-income countries which are not that attractive for the slightly "spoiled" Western European firms expecting higher and faster returns. In this sense, Polish firms and their investments act as bridges. The brand "Made in Poland" is becoming more and more popular.

Survey results point to some decline in export dynamics over last year but those who decided to venture abroad are more successful. Still, many companies are risk averse and shy expansion to foreign markets. It is not the lack of funding which deter them from internationalisation, but rather uncertainty. Many still claim that the Polish market remains priority and still offers much growth possibility. In a discrete manner, Chinese companies are purchasing many well-established European firms. Some cases got more media attention, but this process is happening relatively fast and on a massive scale, but since many acquired firms do not change their brand, they escape public opinion. The Polish firm Morliny or Swedish Volvo are cases in the point. Apparently there are no defense mechanisms or selection procedures which may better regulate these processes. This, however, may in the end lead to massive expansion by Chinese capital and emergence of Chinese companies which, being themselves in possession of Western technologies, can refrain from importing them from Europe. This monopolisation might endanger the future economic position of European firms. The crisis underlines the need among Polish firms to diversify markets yet the high level of uncertainty discourages them from venturing abroad. It also stresses the relative benefits of M&A over Greenfield projects clearly requiring more funding. The recent Ukrainian crisis and collapse of the Russian market become a next challenge for Polish firms, on the one hand. But on the other hand, this acceleration of diversification processes also gave rise to more flexibility.

The opinions of representatives of local authorities and business support institutions can be complemented by the reflections of the representative of the Polish Ministry of Foreign Affairs that were expressed during a conference on the 15th of December 2014. The speech and presentation in the conference delivered some comments and answers to the research issues highlighted in our research questions. In the year 2014 there has been a visible intensification of the promotional activities of the Ministry of Foreign Affairs, particularly in the area of economic diplomacy. It is tough to assess whether it results from crisis developments in the EU. New initiatives have been launched, such as the award for the most effective embassy in supporting Polish firms' expansions on foreign markets. Currently, an inherent component of all state visits are economic issues. In 2014, globally 20 visits have been accompanied by 1000 Polish companies interested in a given market, in Europe in 10 visits participated 50 firms, in Africa in 30 visits—450 companies. The African market attracts new potential Polish investors being aware of successful operations of such Polish firms. Some examples include Kulczyk Investments that obtained production licenses in Nigeria and is going to develop its operations in this continent within the oil and gas sector, Polskie LNG involved in building regasification plants, the company H. Cegielski-Poznań that builds turnkey power plants, Grupa Azoty, Consus Carbon Engineering—a firm that owns facilities in Togo and Ghana and intends to build a power station, Exallo Drilling operating in Mozambique and Uganda with future expansion plans and Krezus SA in Guinea (Rostowska 2013). The most popular sectors for Polish OFDI in Africa are oil and gas, energy, and mining sectors. However, there are even Polish IT companies, such as Asecco, that are winning the African market.

Conclusions

This study provides a contribution to research on the role of formal institutions and in particular the home government in supporting the outward foreign direct investment. We investigated the issue in the context of the last global economic crisis 2008 and embedded the empirical part of the chapter in the Polish context. The topic has become significant especially for advanced emerging economies, such as Poland, where the trend towards internationalisation, even via FDI, is relatively strong. The significance of the primary findings on the role of the Polish government in supporting OFDI can be explained in the context of the liability of foreignness. Polish firms still have to face the challenge of Polish liability, including negative stereotypes and prejudice limiting the success in a given foreign market. That issue has been visible even before the economic crisis and, unfortunately, seems to remain a valid concern today.

The statistics and the behaviour of some Polish firms indicated in the chapter may suggest that they exploited the crisis phenomena as an opportunity to win new foreign markets. Polish OFDI flows during the crisis period did not decline substantially, which may confirm the relatively strong resilience of Polish investors to the crisis. A positive aspect is that Polish firms are still eager to consequently increase their international experiences and do not diminish their pre-crisis internationalisation ambitions. The already mentioned growing internationalisation aspirations, particularly in the most advanced form of FDI on the side of Polish firms, even shortly after the economic crisis can be confirmed by the mentioned rising popularity of state arranged foreign economic missions (Firmy... 2014). While in 2012–2013 460 companies took part, only in the first half of 2014 there were already 350 of them. There have been more missions and they gathered more members.

Simultaneously we have to admit, that it could be a little surprising that the support measures used by the Polish government and other public bodies were not significantly reformulated during the crisis and shortly afterwards. At first glance, we could take the more proactive fostering of Polish OFDI in the aftermath of the economic crisis for granted. Nonetheless, a careful analysis of opinions and comments of the experts led us to different conclusions. Experts draw attention rather to other issues like the general problem with the unawareness among companies of the availability of any internationalisation support, and the resulting low interest among firms to apply for such help. Initiatives like the contest among Embassies rewarding the most effective ones suggest that this approach is changing and attention is being paid not just to provision of assistance, but also to monitoring it, evaluating its effectiveness and utility and, in consequence, upgrading it. Experts also stress the opposite role played by information flowing from investors to decision makers, which relates to feedback, an input that is necessary for a right formulation of policy.

The expected more friendly and active approach towards internationalisation of Polish firms, which is still not a rule, seems just to coincide with the crisis, but it has not been triggered by it. It is true that the foreign venturing by Polish entities in the form of FDI is a new phenomenon as compared to exporting, which started in fact only after joining the EU in 2004. However, the crisis may just have facilitated this tendency by providing more opportunities for cheaper acquisitions. Additionally, the economic downturn exposed the fragility of the strategy of excessive reliance on one market, or Western markets in general, as it clearly illuminated the need to diversify and rebalance geographic destinations while venturing abroad.

Our findings based on in-depth interviews revealed that the crisis has certainly reinforced the necessity of broader internationalisation. The attention by designing and providing assistance is indeed paid by policy makers to fostering expansion to the distant, more promising "perspective markets". From this perspective, the EU internal market seems accessible, it is characterised by cultural proximity and offers only negligible margins and fierce competition, all of which explain the relatively low interest in this area with regard to OFDI support policy. Distant markets, which are usually much riskier, remote yet rewarding, require more information for seizing opportunities there that may justify the offered help. In some experts' view, it is also worth underlining that there are advanced hybrid forms of presence in foreign markets which in fact combine some augmented export servicing with investing in specific modules of the value chain, or explicitly extending the production network.

This recently witnessed intensification of pro-expansionary actions could therefore be described as path-dependent. Internationalisation is not a reaction to crisis, but rather subsequent step in the comprehensive processes of strengthening the economy by building up larger multinational companies capable of weathering global competition. A further exploration of this area is of relevance not just for involved practitioners, but also scholars and decision makers designing the support system. The growing volumes of Polish export and investment abroad are the consequence of developments which started 25 years ago.

The presentation of HCMs' terms that we have outlined and the opinions of firms on the HCMs highlighted in the secondary sources are a first step in the process of evaluation of such HCMs. To continue and develop the discussion on the role of home government in fostering OFDI, the evaluation of particular HCMs on the side of investors should be conducted. The evaluation could be complemented by the identification of strengths and weaknesses of these measures.

We are aware that our research suffers from some limitations. One of the most important is limited sample size. We have conducted the in-depth interviews with meaningful, albeit few entities representing the government, regional authorities and business support institutions. In the future, their perspective should be accompanied by a broader view of beneficiaries of the support.

Acknowledgement This chapter draws on the findings of the research project No. 11430010 of the Small Grants Programme of the International Visegrad Fund "Outward FDI policies in Visegrad Countries". We would like to thank anonymous reviewers for their valuable comments.

References

Andersson, U., & Holm, U. (2010). *Managing the contemporary multinational: The role of headquarters*. Cheltenham: Edward Elgar.
Arnold, D. J., & Quelch, J. A. (1998). New strategies in emerging markets. *Sloan Management Review, 40*(1), 7–20.
Bellak, C., Leibrecht, M., & Stehrer, R. (2008). *Policies to attract foreign direct investment: An industry-level analysis*. Paris: OECD.
Boisot, M., & Meyer, M. W. (2008). Which way through the open door? Reflections on the internationalization of Chinese firms. *Management and Organization Review, 4*(3), 349–365.
Bonikowska, M., Rabiej, P., Turkowski, A., & Żurek, K. (2013). Obudzić uśpionego olbrzyma. *ThinkTank magazyn, 19*, 50–59.
Brewer, T. L. (1993). Government policies, market imperfections, and foreign direct investment. *Journal of International Business Studies, 24*(1), 101–120.
Can-Pack aluminium can manufacturing plant, India. Accessed January 5, 2016, from http://www.packaging-gateway.com/projects/can-pack/
Caruana, A., Ewing, M. T., & Ramaseshan, B. (2000). Effects of economic recession on export activity. *Journal of Global Marketing, 13*(2), 93–106.
Cuervo-Cazurra, A., & Genc, M. (2011). Transforming disadvantages into advantages: Developing-country MNEs in the least developed countries. *Journal of International Business Studies, 39*(6), 957–979.
Demekas, D. G., Balász, H., Ribakova, E., & Wu, Y. (2007). Foreign direct investment in European transition economies – The role of policies. *Journal of Comparative Economics, 35*(2), 369–386.
Dowling, J., & Pfeffer, J. (1975). Organizational legitimacy: Social values and organizational behavior. *The Pacific Sociological Review, 18*(1), 122–136.
Eden, L., & Miller, S. R. (2004). Distance matters: Liability of foreignness, institutional distance and ownership strategy. *Advances in International Management, 16*, 187–221.
Éltető, A., Ferenčíková, S., Götz, M., Hlušková, T., Jankowska, B., Kříž, E., & Sass, M. (2015). *Outward FDI policies in Visegrad countries*. Final Report, IZ Policy Papers, No. 16.
Fertile prospects. *World Business Journal*, January–February 2015, 30–33.
Firmy coraz chętniej zwracają się o wsparcie do dyplomacji, Rzeczpospolita 21.07.2014.
Gaur, A. S., & Lu, J. W. (2007). Ownership strategies and survival of foreign subsidiaries: Institutional distance and experience. *Journal of Management, 33*(1), 84–110.
Gorynia, M., Nowak, J., Trąpczyński, P., & Wolniak, R. (2013, June 25–29). Overview and evaluation of policy measures supporting outward FDI: The case of Poland. In E. Kaynak & T. D. Harcar (Eds.), *Flexibility, innovation and adding value as drivers of global competitiveness: Private and public sector challenges* (pp. 108–115). Proceedings of the Twenty Second World Business Congress, Taipei, Republic of China (Taiwan). National Taipei University.
Gorynia, M., Nowak, J., Trąpczyński, P., & Wolniak, R. (2015). Government support measures for outward FDI: An emerging economy's perspective. *Argumenta Oeconomica, 1*(34), 229–258.
Gorynia, M., Nowak, J., & Wolniak, R. (2010). Foreign direct investment of Central and Eastern European countries, and the investment development path revisited. *Eastern Journal of European Studies, 1*(2), 21–36.
Grzegorczyk, M. (2013). Polskie firmy obiecują inwestycje zagraniczne. Accessed January 5, 2016, from http://www.obserwatorfinansowy.pl/forma/rotator/polskie-firmy-obiecuja-inwestycje-zagraniczne/
GUS. (2012). Działalność podmiotów posiadających udziały w podmiotach z siedzibą za granicą w 2012 roku, Warszawa, 30.04.2014 r. Accessed May 10, 2015, from http://stat.gov.pl/download/gfx/portalinformacyjny/pl/defaultaktualnosci/5502/5/5/7/informacja_biezaca_wyniki_wstepne_dzialalnosc_podmiotow_posiadajacych_udzialy_w_podmiotach_za_granica_w_2012.pdf

Hoskisson, R. E., Eden, L., Lau, C. M., & Wright, M. (2000). Strategy in emerging economies. *Academy of Management Journal, 43*(3), 249–267.

Huidumac-Petrescu, C. E., & Joia, R. M. (2013). National policy measures. Right approach to foreign direct investment flows. *Theoretical and Applied Economics, 2*(579), 103–112.

Hymer, S. (1976). *The international operations of national firms, a study of direct foreign investment.* Cambridge, MA: MIT Press.

Kline, J. M. (2003). Enhancing the development dimension of home country measures. In *The development dimension of FDI: Policy and rule-making perspectives* (pp. 101–113). Proceedings of the Expert Meeting, Geneva, 6–8 November 2002. UNCTAD.

Kostova, T., & Zaheer, S. (1999). Organizational legitimacy under conditions of complexity: The case of the multinational enterprise. *Academy of Management Review, 24*(1), 64–81.

Krifa-Schneider, H., & Matei, I. (2010). Business climate, political risk and FDI in developing countries: Evidence from panel data. *International Journal of Economics and Finance, 2*(5), 54–65.

NBP. (2010). *Polskie inwestycje bezpośrednie za granicą w 2009 roku.* Accessed May 15, 2015, from http://www.nbp.pl/publikacje/pib/pib_2009_n.pdf

NBP. (2013). *Polskie inwestycje bezpośrednie za granicą w 2013 roku.* Accessed May 15, 2015, from http://www.nbp.pl/publikacje/pib/pib_2013_n.pdf

North, D. C. (1990). *Institutions, institutional change, and economic performance.* Cambridge, MA: Harvard University Press.

North, D. C. (1991). Institutions. *The Journal of Economic Perspectives, 5*(1), 97–112.

Oman, C. (2000). *A study of competition among governments to attract FDI.* Paris: Development Centre of OECD. Policy Competition for Foreign Direct Investment.

Panek, W. (2014). Ważny jest udany początek. *Poland go global Magazine, 2*(4), 8–9.

Peng, M. W., Wang, D. Y. L., & Jiang, Y. (2008). An institution-based view of international business strategy: A focus on emerging economies. *Journal of International Business Studies, 39*(5), 920–936.

Phillips, N., Tracey, P., & Karra, N. (2009). Rethinking institutional distance: Strengthening the tie between new institutional theory and international management. *Strategic Organization, 7*(3), 339–348.

Poulsen, L. S., & Hufbauer, G. C. (2011, January 3). *Foreign direct investment in times of crisis.* (Working Paper Series). Peterson Institute for International Economics.

Promocja Polskiej gospodarki za granicą. (2014). Raport PISM, Warszawa, styczeń 2014.

Rajan, R. S. (2004). Measures to attract FDI: Investment promotion, incentives and policy intervention. *Economic and Political Weekly, 39*(1), 12–16.

Rostowska, M. (2013). Investment in sub-Saharan Africa: Opportunities for Polish companies. *PISM Strategic File, 4*(31), 1–6.

Schmitt, A., Probst, G., & Thusman, M. (2010). Management in times of economic crisis: Insights into organizational ambidexterity. *Management, 13*(3), 128–150.

Scott, W. R. (1995). *Institutions and organizations.* Thousand Oaks, CA: Sage Publications.

Stodolak, S. (2014). Naiwny liberalizm gospodarczy szkodzi. Obserwator Finansowy, 24.09.2014.

Te Velde, D. W. (2007). Understanding developed country efforts to promote foreign direct investment to developing countries: The example of the United Kingdom. *Transnational Corporations, 16*(3), 83–104.

UNCTAD. (1995). *World investment report 1995.* New York/Geneva: Transnational Corporations and Competitiveness/UNCTAD.

UNCTAD. (2009). *Assessing the impact of the current financial and economic crisis on global FDI flows.* Geneva: UNCTAD.

UNCTAD. (2014). *World investment report. Investing in the SDGs: An action plan.* Geneva: UNCTAD.

UNCTAD Statistics. (2015). http://unctadstat.unctad.org/wds/ReportFolders/reportFolders.aspx?IF_ActivePath=P,5

Welch, C. L., & Welch, L. S. (2009). Re-internationalisation: Exploration and conceptualization. *International Business Review, 18*(6), 567–577.
Wennberg, K., & Holmquist, C. (2008). Problemistic search and international entrepreneurship. *European Management Journal, 26*(6), 441–454.
Williamson, O. (1998). The institutions of governance. *The American Economic Review, 88*(2), 75–79.
Xu, D., & Meyer, K. E. (2012, February). *Linking theory and context: "Strategic research in emerging economies" after Wright et al. (2005)* (CEIBS working paper). Shanghai, China.
Xu, D., Pan, Y., & Beamish, P. W. (2004). The effect of regulative and normative distances on MNE ownership and expatriate strategies. *Management International Review, 44*(3), 285–307.
Xu, D., & Shenkar, O. (2002). Institutional distance and the multinational enterprise. *Academy of Management Review, 27*(4), 608–618.
Yeung, H. W. (2006). Change and continuity in Southeast Asian ethnic Chinese business. *Asia Pacific Journal of Management, 23*(3), 229–254.
Zaheer, S. (1995). Overcoming the liability of foreignness. *Academy of Management Journal, 38*(2), 341–363.

Attracting FDI to the New EU Member States

Tomasz Dorożyński and Anetta Kuna-Marszałek

Abstract In the present chapter we have made an attempt to identify factors determining the investment attractiveness of the new EU Member States, which may have an impact upon the scale of foreign direct investment (FDI) in these countries. This chapter is structured as follows. First, it explores the existing literature on FDI definition and main effects of its inflow into the host country. Subsequently, we discuss the investment attractiveness and its determinants in theory and based on empirical studies. Further, we review investment attractiveness assessment of the new EU Member States based on selected international rankings. The final part examines relationships between selected determinants of investment attractiveness and FDI inflows to new EU Member States. The presented study is particularly focused on the correlation between selected variables pertaining to investment incentives and the inflow of FDI. The study is based on appropriate statistical methods, such as Spearman's rank correlation and Pearson correlation. Finally, we present the key conclusions of the chapter.

Keywords FDI • EU Member States • Incentives

Introduction

Economic growth and development of countries are determined by a number of factors, among which foreign direct investment (FDI) plays a vital role. Although theoreticians agreed a long time ago that the effects of FDI inflows are rather ambiguous and empirical analyses conducted in all continents suggest that its impact upon the welfare of countries may be heterogeneous, although in most cases they turn out to be positive.

Thus, FDI is considered to be the safest and the most beneficial form of capital flows. FDI supplements capital shortages, contributes to technological modernisation of economies, creates new jobs, improves export capacity of countries and increases the welfare of societies. It is often perceived as a way to intensify

---

T. Dorożyński (✉) • A. Kuna-Marszałek
University of Lodz, Lodz, Poland
e-mail: tdorozynski@uni.lodz.pl; akuna@uni.lodz.pl

economic mobilisation of less developed regions. This is the reason why both developed and developing countries compete to offer the best conditions so as to attract FDI. In practice, it requires the knowledge about the motivation behind the FDI and, first of all, about location-related decision determinants crucial for the investment. In other words, the awareness of mechanisms and interdependences linked to decisions made by foreign investors facilitates a more intentional development of conditions to attract FDI and may also help to focus on investment projects which are the most beneficial from the point of view of the host economy.

The policy can be observed also in the group of the EU Member States, which have been attracting FDI for more than two decades, now. Integration with the European Union accelerated the dynamic process of development of the region and facilitated the mobilisation of investment resources for economic and social projects, which additionally enhanced its attractiveness. Most of these countries offer relatively good location and human resources at a relatively low operational cost to investors, and by investing in infrastructure have become attractive investment locations. Overall security situation, related to their membership in international organisations and being a part of the European single market, is their additional asset. Investors can meet their specific expectations there and may benefit from all sorts of allowances and preferences, and hence boost business development.

The main goal of this chapter is to identify factors decisive for investment attractiveness of the new EU Member States, which may affect the scale of foreign direct investment in these countries. It is another contribution within the series of publications of the authors devoted to FDI location determinants. Previous ones discussed predominantly the cases of Visegrad Group countries (Dorożyński and Kuna-Marszałek 2014, 2016a) and investment incentives as valid FDI motives (Dorożyński and Kuna-Marszałek 2016b).

FDI Definition

The widely accepted definition of FDI[1] is known as the IMF/OECD benchmark definition. It was provided by a joint workforce of these two international organisations with the objective of providing standards to national statistical offices for compiling FDI statistics (Contessi and Weinberger 2009). According to this definition, *foreign direct investment* "reflects the objective of establishing a lasting interest by a resident enterprise in one economy (*direct investor*) in a firm (*direct investment enterprise*) that is resident in an economy other than that of the direct investor" (OECD 2008:48). The usual threshold that allows a particular investment to be classified as FDI is ownership by the foreign investor of at least 10 % of the stock or shares of the direct investment enterprise.

---

[1]The benchmark definition was first published in 1983 based on a report by the OECD Group of Financial Statisticians, subsequent revisions were published in 1990, 1992, and 2008.

In contemporary economy, FDI represents a specific type of international capital flows. As a result, it leads to the transferring of not only capital, but also investment goods. FDI may be undertaken not only as greenfield or brownfield investment outside of the borders of the investor's home country, but also includes the transfer of licences, patents, know-how or copyright in return for shares in a business. FDI may also cover capital flows in the form of borrowings, loans, donations, and reinvested earnings. FDI is usually a long-term undertaking. In practice it means that capital involvement is connected with a long-term perspective of an investor's presence in a given foreign market.

As we have already mentioned, FDI is also connected with the notion of direct investment enterprises. The term covers those entities that are (IMF 2015):

1) subsidiaries (enterprises in which a non-resident investor owns more than 50 %);
2) associates (enterprises in which a non-resident investor owns between 10 and 50 %);
3) branches (unincorporated enterprises, wholly or jointly owned by a non-resident investor);

and are either directly or indirectly owned by the direct investor.

FDI flows can be observed from the perspective of the host economy, which records them as *inward* FDI, or from the perspective of the home economy, which records them as *outward* FDI, a category of assets. International statistics often provide aggregate FDI flows, which are the sum of equity capital, reinvested earnings, and other direct investment capital. Then, aggregate FDI flows and stocks include all financial transfers aimed at the financing of new investments, plus retained earnings of affiliates, internal loans, and financing of cross-border mergers and acquisitions (Contessi and Weinberger 2009).

Largely simplifying, direct investment capital transactions are made up of three basic components (BIS 2015):

1) equity capital—comprising equity in branches, subsidiaries and associates (except non-participating, preferred shares that are treated as debt securities and are included under other direct investment capital) and other capital contributions (e.g. provisions of machinery),
2) reinvested earnings—consisting of the direct investor's share of earnings not distributed (e.g. dividends by subsidiaries or associates and earnings of branches not remitted to the direct investor),
3) other capital, including intercompany transactions such as borrowing and lending of funds.

A voluminous literature explores the impact of FDI on the country economic welfare and benefits that it brings to host countries. FDI makes up for the shortages of capital that result from insufficient internal savings, it may contribute to technological modernisation of an economy, and enhance the export capacity of an importing country. FDI also offers potential transfer of intangible assets such as know-how and management skills. It is most frequently associated with productivity spillovers, which are usually defined as "the influence of the presence of foreign-owned enterprises on productivity of local-owned enterprises" (Buckley et al. 2010:193). Similar conclusions can be found in the OECD report (OECD 2002:16), which notes that the presence of foreign enterprises may greatly assist economic development by mobilising domestic competition. By the same token, it may lead to higher productivity, lower prices and more efficient resource allocation. FDI is also claimed to be the key driver of financial stability, increased well-being of societies and international economic integration.

A large portion of the studies demonstrating the impact of FDI on the host country focus on the analysis of developing countries (Nunnenkamp 2002; Sumner 2005; Wacker 2011; Shukla 2013), and emerging markets (Globerman et al. 2006; Zhang et al. 2010; Hanousek et al. 2011; Arbatli 2011; Kamaly 2014). There are much fewer studies devoted to highly developed countries (Agiomirgianakis et al. 2006; Koojaroenprasit 2012). As most of them point to positive effects of FDI inflow into economies and regions, many countries offer attractive conditions to foreign investment, treating it as a transfer medium for scientific and technological progress and an economic development factor.

The review of literature on FDI effects for the host country shows they may go in different directions. They depend on a wide range of factors connected with the features of the investing company, the development stage of the host country, and the local environment. Thus, one should be very cautious in assessing FDI effects and always consider circumstances specific to a given region and to a particular host country, as in many instances its outcomes may not be positive. Nevertheless, despite sceptical voices, the vast majority of opinions highlight numerous benefits implied by the inflow of foreign capital. That is why both developed and developing countries compete in creating favourable conditions for FDI location decisions.

Investment Attractiveness and Its Determinants

A great deal of research (theory and empirical studies) on FDI demonstrates that the location decisions made by investors are influenced not only by determinants connected to the reasons behind FDI, but also by determinants resulting from the investment attractiveness of the host country. In specialised literature, the latter is defined in different ways. Usually it is conceptualised as a set of advantages or shortages specific to the investment location. In other words, investment attractiveness is a combination of location-based (country, region) benefits that can be achieved as a result of economic operations due to specific features of the place where business is conducted. The report of Ernst&Young (2009), in turn, defines it as a compilation of an image of a given area and investors' confidence.

We may also speak of potential and real investment attractiveness. The first one represents a set of regional location advantages that impact the accomplishment of investor's goals (e.g. low cost of running a business, high revenue from sales, net profitability and competitiveness of a particular investment). The real attractiveness is about regional capacity to produce "client-investor satisfaction and absorption of financial and in-kind capital that takes the form of an investment. It can be measured with the efficiency of outlays in the form of financial, in-kind, human and natural capital" (Godlewska-Majkowska 2011:4).

Investment attractiveness is a term often interchangeably used with that of investment climate. Some authors (e.g., Rymarczyk et al. 2008), however, do not consider them to be identical. Investment attractiveness should be used only in the context of attracting new investors to a particular region. Investment climate, in turn, does not focus on just attracting investment projects, but is also linked with retaining them and with positive experiences of running a business. In other words, it should be understood as "a specific collection of objective circumstances decisive for the convenience of doing business in the region, smooth investment process, and the possibility to repeat the investment having collected some knowledge and experiences" (Rymarczyk et al. 2008:18).

Investment attractiveness is measured differently with, for instance, the capacity of output markets, the price of labour and other cost elements, favourable tax schemes, restricted competition, location, easy access and the possibility to enter the neighbouring markets, financial conditions offered to foreign investors, legal regulations addressed to foreign businesses, or special privileges for foreign investors. All of them should be available on the same terms to all businesses, regardless of their size or country of origin. Besides, these benefits are usually specific and typical of only one particular region and can be exercised within it.

As we have already mentioned, an area possessing location advantages appreciated by investors attracts investment projects and, by virtue of that fact, may improve the social and economic potential of a given region or country. Capital inflows may stimulate development, help overcome barriers to development or reinforce the existing competitive advantages.

The list of motivations behind an FDI decision is rather long. Areas attractive to investors are those which help to reduce investment outlays and operating expenses, which facilitates profit maximisation and limits potential risk of failure. It means, some regions represent advantages (connected e.g. with the size of the market, developed infrastructure, human capital, etc.) and offer better conditions for investment than others.

The investment attractiveness of a country is differently perceived by firms which are guided by diverse motivations in making the location decision and expect different effects of foreign expansion (in short- and long-term). The eclectic paradigm presented by Dunning (1979, 1981) includes the likely interaction among ownership advantages, internalisation and location advantages in guiding a firm's FDI decisions.[2] In later studies Dunning (2000) divided the reasons behind FDI into four groups: market seeking, resource seeking, efficiency seeking, and

---

[2]The OLI (*Ownership, Location, Internalisation*) theory explains that the FDI decision is a result of meeting three conditions: 1) a firm enjoys ownership advantages (oligopolistic advantages); 2) there are favourable location factors (host country advantages); 3) the advantage of internalisation over market transactions (exports, selling licenses). Advantages are not only necessary and decisive for internationalisation but they are complementary and reinforce one another.

strategic asset seeking, and he also stressed the importance of the political framework and business environment, i.e. institutions (Dunning 2003, 2004, 2006). Table 1 presents the FDI determinants as outlined by Dunning in the studies of 2006.

Researchers dealing with the subject of investment attractiveness conclude that the most relevant determinants of FDI inflow into a host country usually refer to: 1) market size (Mottaleb 2007) and its growth rate (Iamsiraroj and Doucouliagos 2015); 2) cost of labour (Bellak et al. 2008) and labour quality (Lin 2011); 3) infrastructure (Rehman et al. 2011), 4) openness to trade (Anyanwu 2012); 5) political risk (Asongu and Kodila-Tedika 2015); 6) quality of institutional system (Bartels et al. 2014); 7) corruption (Castro and Nunes 2013); 8) access to natural resources (Agosin and Machado 2007); 9) taxes (Feld and Heckemeyer 2008), special industrial parks (Guagliano and Riela 2005), and other investment incentives (Owczarczuk 2013).

From among all the above mentioned reasons conducive to FDI, investment incentives seem particularly interesting. In most countries they are coordinated by a dedicated Investment Promotion Agency. Investment incentives are used across both developed and developing world, with some notable moderation occurring in the European Union owing to the impact of State aid laws (Johnson and Toledano 2013). Most often governments offer investment incentives for places in the greatest need (Bartik 1991). It is also worth stressing that these incentives often represent very large sums of government spending and foregone revenue (Thomas 2007).

James (2009:1) defines investment incentives as "measurable economic advantages that governments provide to specific enterprises or groups of enterprises, with the goal of steering investment into favoured sectors or regions or of influencing the character of such investments". Thomas (2007:vii) describes investment incentives in a more explicit way and interprets them as "a subsidy given to affect the location of investment. The goal may be to attract new investment or to retain an existing facility". Generally, whenever the system of investment incentives is in place, it significantly impacts the investment climate in a given economy. It also contributes to an increased attractiveness of the host country.

Thus, public authorities, who hope that FDI inflows will improve the economic performance and the standard of living in the respective host country or region, may in principle choose one of the following three strategies of dealing with investors:

1) refrain from any specific activities and believe that the market will be the best to identify the desirable scale and structure of investment projects delivered by foreign capital;
2) try to attract all potential projects, irrespective of their size and industry;
3) attract only these FDI categories, which fit long-term development plans and structural transformations in the economy, meaning that the authorities favour certain categories of enterprises with foreign capital involvement.

Table 1 FDI determinants according to Dunning

I. Political framework of FDI
 – economic, political, and social,
 – regulations concerning market entry and establishment,
 – standards applicable to subsidiaries of multinational enterprises,
 – market and market structure policies (especially competition policy, mergers and acquisition),
 – bilateral international FDI agreements,
 – privatisation and price policy,
 – trade policy (customs duties and non-tariff barriers) and the exchange rate stability,
 – tax policy (including tax allowances),
 – regional/industrial policies.

II. Economic determinants
 1. For market-seeking firms
  – market size and per capita income,
  – market growth,
  – access to regional and global markets,
  – country specific consumer preference,
  – structure of markets,
  – psychic and institutional distance.
 2. For resource-seeking firms
  – land and building costs: land rents and rates,
  – cost and quality of raw materials, components, parts,
  – low cost of unskilled labour,
  – availability, quality and cost of skilled labour.
 3. For efficiency-seeking firms
  – cost of resources and assets listed in paragraph 2 adjusted for productivity of labour inputs,
  – other costs, e.g., transport and communication to/from and within the host economy,
  – membership of regional integration agreements conducive to promoting a more cost-effective inter-country division of labour,
  – quality of institutions facilitating the functioning of the market and market surveillance mechanisms.
 4. For asset or capability-seeking firms
  – quality of technological, managerial, relational and other generated assets,
  – physical infrastructure (ports, roads, power grids, telecommunication),
  – capacity of educational institutions that support (reinforce) entrepreneurship, competition and innovation at macroeconomic level,
  – growth/development oriented spirit, institutions and policies.

III. Business facilitation
 – incentives for entrepreneurship,
 – investment incentives and investment promotion schemes,
 – form and quality of the ownership system under binding law,
 – protection of intellectual property rights,
 – social amenities (bilingual schools, housing, quality of life, etc.),
 – pre- and post-investment services (e.g., one stop shopping),
 – good institutional infrastructure and support services, e.g. banking, legal, accounting,
 – social capital,
 – industry clusters in regions and development of links within networks,
 – legislation designed to reduce corruption, industrial crime, etc.

Source: Dunning (2006:206) after: Wawrzyniak (2010:90)

Support granted to investors may be helpful when the second strategy, and especially the third one, is selected as a viable option. We may list various forms of investment incentives (Columbia University 2013; OECD 2003):

1) regulatory—e.g. exemptions from specific regulations binding in the host country (connected with the environment, labour market, social insurance);
2) financial—e.g. providing physical infrastructure (e.g. roads, railways, harbours) or communication tailored to meet the needs of the investors; assistance in training workers where skilled labour is not available; relocation and expatriation support; administrative assistance; temporary wage subsidies; credits to investors; government preferential insurance; assistance in acquiring real estate (land or property sold below market prices);
3) fiscal—e.g. reduced taxes (tax holidays, reduced rates of corporate income tax, special tax-privileged zones); incentives for capital formation (special investment allowances, investment tax credits, reduced impediments to cross-border operation, withholding tax);
4) technical—they usually focus on technical matters relating to dissemination of information on investment opportunities and procedures and providing special services, and "aftercare" once an investor has already invested.

These technical and business support incentives can be divided between the key stages of a foreign investment lifecycle as illustrated in Table 2.

Among the types of incentives, fiscal incentives are widely used. However, regulatory incentives are also significant.

In spite of the fact that, as suggested by earlier considerations, there is a general belief that investment incentives to investors are relevant and efficient, in specialist literature there is no agreement about their positive impact upon FDI location decisions. Some researchers claim they may distort the investment decision making because "they are crowding out net supported investments and help to realize investments which would be profitable or are supporting investments realized even without government involvement" (Cedidlová 2013:109). Johnson and Toledano (2013) have devised an overview of many empirical studies which demonstrate that the impact of incentives upon investment decisions is often minimal. Authors give examples of surveys where the question: "Would you have invested even if incentives were not provided?" was answered "Yes" by the majority of investors (in some studies even by 98 % of respondents). In turn, James (2013) stresses that investment incentives are more important to highly mobile, efficiency seeking firms, focused on reducing costs for products destined for a global, rather than domestic market. Contrary to them, enterprises engaging in FDI to enter new markets or acquire natural resources (other resources or strategic assets) appear clearly less motivated by any incentives offered by the government. Besides, if some of the investment incentives (e.g. tax holidays) are only granted to a new investment, they may be biased in the opposite direction, discriminating against re-investments and investments that rely on long-lived depreciable capital (Morisset and Pirnia 2000). Thus, their efficiency seems questionable.

Table 2 Business support/technical services, by stage of investment

Phase	Type of service
Decision/pre-investment/pre-expansion stage	Information on markets
	Information on availability of supporting infrastructure
	Information on corporate taxation and incentives
	Information on strategic partners (distribution, legal support, recruitment support, etc.) and on relevant industry or sector
Entry stage	Information on procedures and regulations for doing business in this country (company registration, permits, labour regulations, etc.)
	Facilitating company registration, licensing (work permits, import/export permits, etc.)
	Introduction to legal, accounting and other professional services
	Soft landing services (e.g. schools, housing, safety)
Implementation stage	Finding suitable sites (e.g. land, office, factory)
	Facilitating building construction
	Access to utilities and infrastructure
	Finding key staff
Operation/after care stage	Complaint resolution (issues concerning tax, labour, customs, immigration, utilities)
	Information on finance
	Matchmaking (access to suppliers, buyers, finance)
	Assistance in upgrading (information on technology sources, terms of technology transaction)
	Access to utilities and infrastructure

Source: Johnson and Toledano (2013:21)

Many researchers also stress that the majority of investment incentives are costly tools of attracting FDI. In other words, their costs can exceed the resultant benefits (Perera 2012; Davis 2013; Johnson and Toledano 2013), which is why the incentive policy needs to be carefully considered. Moreover, it is also worth remembering that the receptiveness to investment incentives depends on the life-cycle stage of a firm and on how well the incentive matches its needs at that time (Johnson and Toledano 2013). Newly established firms might prefer incentives which help them reduce their initial expenses. Already established firms, whose aim is to further expand, may prefer tax-related incentives that affect profit.

The above considerations demonstrate that it is not easy to decide if and what investment incentives could be optimum from the point of view of the FDI host country. James (2010) provides a general guide for policymakers, who decide about the shape of an incentive policy, based on country conditions and goals. Table 3 summarises desirable short- and long-term incentive policies for various types of countries.

However, we should bear in mind that investment incentives may be decisive when the choice between two locations that offer similar conditions is made. That is

Table 3 Recommended investment incentive policies under various country scenarios

Scenario	Short-term policy	Long-term policy
Countries with poor investment climate	Investment incentives are ineffective and therefore the country loses tax revenues. Such revenues should instead be used to provide public goods. Reforms should also be introduced to put the tax system in order.	Such countries should reduce barriers to investment by, for example, simplifying investment procedures.
Countries facing tax competition	Incentives can be used in the short term to ensure that countries are not at a disadvantage relative to their neighbours.	Such countries should work on regional pacts to stop tax competition and promote their substantive differences (labour skills, infrastructure, and so on).
Countries seeking to diversify their economies.	Such countries can use incentives linked to investment growth (investment allowances, accelerated depreciation), but for a limited period based on clear prioritisation of sectors in line with FDI competitiveness.	Broader industrial policy strategies have to be followed, including a focus on sector targeting and promotion to attract investments.
Countries with unique advantages (natural beauty, natural resources)	General investment incentives to attract investments that exploit such advantages waste revenue unless they kick-start investment.	Barriers should be lowered for investments designed to exploit natural resources, improve access to land, and so on.

Source: James (2010:6)

true of countries from the same region at a similar level of economic development, e.g. Central and Eastern European countries. This is why many administrations feel that not offering incentives could put them at a disadvantage and they continue to offer support schemes (Tuomi 2012). They highlight the importance of governance as a factor conditioning the FDI process. Good governance means, *inter alia*, economic freedom, secure property rights, an honest and efficient public sector, a minimum of "dead-weight" regulations and restrictions on trade (Globerman et al. 2006).

On top of that, for the EU Member States we should also mention one additional investment incentive. EU membership allows the new EU Member States to attract European funds for investment projects in agriculture and infrastructure (Rădulescu and Druică 2011). For example, in recent years and in the years to come, Poland will be the biggest beneficiary of EU structural funds, which will additionally stimulate regional development, first and foremost, as a result of infrastructure investment projects (A.T. Kearney 2015). In the Czech Republic the inflow of EU funds helped to maintain the external balance and to make the banking sector perform relatively well (Éltető 2010).

European Union funds have been used to support various activities from restructuring to implementation of national-level innovations (Cywiński 2015). In most of the new EU Member States substantial amounts have been invested to support transport infrastructure, while only a relatively small portion of funds has been allocated to human capital programs.

As demonstrated by the above considerations, there is a plenitude of factors decisive for investment attractiveness. Their multitude and diversity usually make us narrow down the research framework to several selected ones. In our study, we covered only several out of all investment incentives, including state aid programmes and EU funds. Some of them have turned out to be statistically significant for the inflow of foreign direct investment into the new EU Member States. Detailed results of analyses are presented in the final part of the study.

Investment Attractiveness Assessment Based on Selected International Rankings

The new EU Member States differ largely when it comes to their economic performance, FDI absorption capacity and approach to investment incentives. Thus, they are differently perceived by foreign investors as well as in competitiveness and attractiveness rankings of international institutions. When analysing the results of the currently leading rankings, we may conclude that over the last several years, including the times of crisis and economic downturn, the new EU Member States, in particular the Visegrad Group countries (Hungary, Poland, the Czech Republic, Slovakia) have remained attractive investment locations.

According to The Global Competitiveness Report 2014–2015,[3] Poland, Latvia, Lithuania and Hungary are in transition from economies driven by increasing productivity to innovation-driven economies. Cyprus, Estonia, the Czech Republic, Slovakia, Malta, Slovenia are considered innovation-driven economies. The rest of the new Member States (Romania and Bulgaria) are considered efficiency-driven economies (The Global Competitiveness Report 2014–2015; 2015:11). Between 2004 and 2015 rankings of these countries were highly volatile. Only Poland markedly improved its Global Competitiveness Index ranking from 60 to 43, Czech Republic remained stable (+3). Slovakia (−32) and Hungary (−21) lost substantially. Taking the remaining the new Member States into account, Bulgaria (+5) improved its ranking the most, while Slovenia (−37) witnessed the deepest decline. Estonia (−9) is an example of a country, which has always been much ahead of other new Member States in the ranking in question. At present, it ranks 29. High ranking of Estonia is due to the increase in its economic potential

---

[3]The notion of competitiveness, as intended by the World Economic Forum, combines the 12 pillars of competitiveness with three stages of economic development of a given country: factor-driven economy, efficiency-driven economy, and innovation-driven economy. The main advantage of the ranking is its comprehensive approach to competitiveness. The method used in it focuses not only on the assessment of microeconomic environment, but also covers elements of business strategy and the business environment in combination with the evaluation of links with the global economy.

and development dynamics, in particular, technological progress and high quality of public institutions in this country. Its labour market, its productivity, competitiveness, as well as the structure and potential of human resources, the cost of labour, taxes and cost of insurance of the workforce, their education, etc., are all highly evaluated.

From among the Visegrad Group countries, the highest ranking positions in the competitiveness ranking in 2014–2015 are occupied by the Czech Republic and Poland, 37th and 43rd respectively, while Hungary and Slovakia rank 60th and 75th respectively (The Global Competitiveness Report 2014–2015; 2015:13–14). This means that the economic transformation has brought measurable results, as these countries have managed to achieve higher efficiency in many industries and improve the investment attractiveness of the region. At present, the areas where FDI is expected in these countries are creative industries, strategic services, and R&D (Owczarczuk 2013).

The high position of the Czech Republic should not come as a surprise since as a result of good understanding of market mechanisms and specialisation in innovation, the country occupies tops of rankings of investment attractiveness. In 2013, almost 26 % of research in the Czech Republic, more than 14 % in Hungary, 13 % in Poland and nearly 19 % in Slovakia were financed from abroad. Unquestionable assets of the Czech Republic are highly skilled labour and very well-developed infrastructure. Moreover, one of the crucial factors which attract FDI is a broad offer of investment incentives offered by the state. In 2012, state aid was extended to technology centres and business support services. On the other hand, it is claimed that the Czech Republic's competitiveness could have been more driven by the changes in its higher education system, where the Czech Republic features among the 10 lowest ranked EU economies.

It is also worth mentioning that both Poland and the Czech Republic offer a variety of incentives to FDI. Investors may avail themselves of multiannual assistance schemes, property tax exemptions, or choose to operate in special economic zones instead. Besides, Poland is the biggest beneficiary of structural funds among the new EU Member States. In the case of Poland it is also stressed that recent improvements have been made in terms of institutions, infrastructure, and education, and that the flexibility of the labour market increased. These key achievements "are steps in the right direction to boost the country's competitiveness" (The Global Competitiveness Report 2014–2015; 2015:24). Besides strengths, the report also highlights barriers faced and observed by foreign investors in Poland. The following dimensions have been assessed as poor in the ranking: transport infrastructure, some institutional aspects, such as the regulatory burden, rather inefficient legal framework for settling business disputes, and difficulties in obtaining information on government decisions for business. To bolster its innovative capacity, more attention should be paid to reinforcing its innovation ecosystem in close collaboration with the private sector.

In the discussed competitiveness ranking, the following new Member States received the least recognition: Slovakia (75th) and Slovenia (70th). In the case of both countries, the most problematic factors for doing business were: inefficient government bureaucracy, corruption, tax rates and regulations as well as restrictive labor regulations. In Slovenia, access to financing is also the main barrier to competitiveness.

Another competitiveness report published by the International Institute for Management Development in Lausanne shows that Lithuania and the Czech Republic achieve a higher value of the Global Competitiveness Index[4] than other countries among the new EU Member States. The above mentioned countries ranked 28 and 29 respectively out of 61 economies included in the study (IMD 2015). Further in the ranking we can find Estonia (31), Poland (33), Latvia (43), Slovakia (46), Romania (47), Hungary (48), and Slovenia (49). The last country was Bulgaria (55).[5] It is worth mentioning that the ranking of the Visegrad Group countries over the period 2010–2014 was stable and they occupied places in the range of 28–35. Only in 2015 Hungary dropped to a very distant place in the ranking, which may slightly negatively impact the perception of all the Visegrad Group. The ranking of Poland has not changed significantly during the last 6 years (rank 32–36).

As we have already mentioned, amongst the remaining new EU Member States, Estonia and Lithuania also reached high rankings in recent years. Both countries offer stable investment environment due to the ease of business operations, institutional order and innovation. When it comes to the most often identified assets of all the ranked countries, they include: cost competitiveness and dynamism of the economy, skilled workforce and workforce productivity, reliable infrastructure (IMD 2015).

The new Member States also rank high in the World Bank Group flagship report *"Doing Business"*. It suffices to say that several economies are among the top 30 in 2015 (Doing Business 2016, 2015): Estonia (rank of 16), Lithuania (20), Latvia (22), Poland (25), Slovakia (29), and Slovenia (also 29). In the case of Estonia and Slovakia, the authors of the report appreciated their efforts in facilitating preregistration and registration formalities (e.g. publication, notarisation, inspection, other requirements). Hungary and Latvia, in turn, changed their labour legislation, which also positively influenced the perception of these countries by the business community.

Studies by Ernst&Young show that Central and Eastern Europe is still the most attractive investment spot globally (E&Y attractiveness survey, Europe 2015). Investors even ranked the CEE region ahead of Brazil, Russia and India. Data presented in the E&Y report show that FDI inflows to the CEE region in 2014 increased by 9 % after years of decline. It may be due to the specific role which the CEE region plays as a workshop and back-office for the European market and an

---

[4]One of the most important and most commonly used synthetic indices which measure international competitive ability of countries. International Institute for Management Development classifies competitiveness factors by dividing them into: economic performance, government efficiency, business efficiency, infrastructure. In identifying the competitiveness of individual countries it uses national statistics, data from international and regional organisations and opinions of thousands of managers and several dozen partner institutes across the world.

[5]Cyprus and Malta were not included in the ranking.

integral part of many European value chains. CEE countries are the first choice for ca. 28 % investors, although Western Europe raises much higher interest as a potential investment location. Every second investor chooses it as the world's most attractive FDI destination (E&Y attractiveness survey, Europe 2015:7). The appeal of CEE countries has diminished by 14 points since 2008. That is most probably caused by the crisis in Ukraine and mutual sanctions imposed between Russia and the EU, which have damaged business, trade and confidence in CEE.

As we have mentioned above, there has been a significant difference in the perception of the attractiveness of individual countries in the region. Although Poland and the Czech Republic were voted the most attractive CEE countries, their overall attractiveness scores declined by six and four percentage points respectively. They have lost to countries such as Romania by up two points (EY's attractiveness survey, Europe 2014:5). The report also informs that Poland lost its leading position in the CEE region to Russia and slipped to the fifth position in terms of FDI job creation in Europe between 2009 and 2013. Despite these negative tendencies, Poland continues to be mentioned as the number one destination in the CEE region to specific groups of entrepreneurs. We mean here, e.g. international software companies, who invest in R&D projects.

The Report stresses important assets of Poland as a host country. They predominantly include: its size, gaining weight in Europe's economy and large public infrastructure projects. Besides, out of all the new EU Member States, Poland ranks the highest in sub-rankings where the number of FDI projects is the assessment criterion. According to experts, other countries are battling to replicate the Polish model. That is true, *inter alia*, for the Czech Republic and Hungary, where FDI inflows decreased recently. Data indicate that now the challengers for big, labour-intensive projects are found in South-Eastern Europe, e.g. in Romania. Bulgaria is attracting more interest, although it needs a better infrastructure and further reforms. However, the barrier to FDI increase in Bulgaria is posed by market interventions, red tape and corruption scandals (similar to Romania and Slovakia). On the other extreme, there are Estonia, Latvia and Lithuania, where the said problem does not exist. Baltic States are considered as "economic realists" and they have welded strong links to Scandinavia. Together they attracted a substantial body of projects in 2014, however, due to limited supply of labour they find it difficult to sign large-scale projects.

The attractiveness of a country to foreign investors may also be measured with the Baseline Profitability Index (BPI). It was used for the first time in 2013. Its estimates helped build a ranking published by foreignpolicy.com. The BPI index is calculated based on three principal criteria: the growth of an asset's value, the preservation of that value while the asset is owned, and the ease of bringing home the proceeds from selling the assets".[6] Thus, the BPI compares how local policies

---

[6]By the same token the authors of the portal are trying to tell how high rate of return can be achieved and how much profit there can be brought "home" by investors who invest their capital abroad.

and conditions would affect the same investment in different countries and ranks countries by their overall attractiveness as targets for a generic foreign investment. The ranking envisions a 5-year investment perspective.

Poland has been obviously doing very well as compared to other new EU Member States. Both in 2014 and in 2015 it ranked 14. It was followed by Lithuania and Estonia, 17 and 18 respectively, in the two last years. Both these countries overtook Poland (19) in the ranking in 2013 when they occupied 16 and 15 ranking position respectively. High BPI index in 2015 was also recorded for the Czech Republic (21), Latvia (24), Malta (25), and Hungary (28). Cyprus (89), Slovenia (61), and Bulgaria (46) scored the lowest. Over the years 2013–2015 Romania (+22; 31 place in 2015) and Slovenia (+15; 61 place in 2015) unquestionably improved their rankings while Bulgaria's ranking deteriorated (−18; 46 place in 2015).

The new EU Member States are also appreciated in the UNCTAD ranking when it comes to investment attractiveness. Again Poland performed the best compared to the rest of the group. Its major competitive advantages are: a large and rapidly developing internal market, an educated and flexible workforce, stable banking system, access to international local markets, and the availability of suppliers and partners. Report for 2014 also stresses that Poland adopted the "Programme to support investments of high importance to the Polish economy for 2011–2020", with the aim of increasing innovation and the competitiveness of the economy by promoting FDI in high-tech sectors (World Investment Report 2014:113). Most probably the above mentioned factors gave Poland, as the only member of the Visegrad Group, a place in the group of the top 15 attractive FDI locations in recent years (World Investment Report 2010, 2011, 2012, 2013, 2014).

Poland is also the only country among the new EU Member States included in the basket of 25 countries covered by the FDI Confidence Index.[7] This Index examines the overarching trends in FDI, on top of that, it is a forward-looking analysis of how political, economic, and regulatory changes will likely affect global FDI flows in the years to come. Poland occupied its highest, sixth ranking position in 2010, while in 2013 and 2015 it ranked 19th and 23rd, respectively. In 2014 Poland dropped out of the ranking altogether. Authors of the Report highlight the strategic location, large population, and economic stability of Poland as the major determinants of FDI inflows into the country. Apart from that, Poland is also likely to benefit from planned substantial improvements in its infrastructure. In the years to come, Poland will be the biggest beneficiary of the EU structural funds, which will additionally stimulate regional development. The report also stresses that Poland gains a lot from its interconnectedness with Germany, besides, its independent currency (still remaining outside of the Eurozone) facilitates the economy to adjust and retain its competitive position (A.T. Kearney 2015:16–17).

To sum up, we should also quote conclusions from the report of the Economist Intelligence Unit examining business potential of the new EU Member States. It

---

[7] The FDI Confidence Index is a regular survey of global executives conducted by A.T. Kearney.

reads, *inter alia*, that the rise in labour costs in China is set to bring investors' attention back to the CEE region, especially Poland. On top of that, the gap in growth dynamics between the countries of Asia and CEE narrows down, which additionally fosters the countries of this region. The Visegrad Group countries are actively supporting their manufacturing sectors with investment incentives and special economic zones. Poland is considered the country with development potential in the manufacturing sector, BPO/SSC services, and R&D. The potential is enhanced by the highest rate of absorption of EU resources (85 %) among the new EU Member States (Economist Intelligence Unit 2015:10).

The report for 2014 also stresses that in recent years investment climate in the CEE countries clearly improved. Authors believe that among factors that attract investment to the region in question, we should list "a low-cost but qualified labour force, proximity to developed markets and, in some cases, ample natural resource endowments" (Economist Intelligence Unit 2015:5). In the ranking for 2014 the top 30 countries recommended as investor-friendly (for 2014–2018) include Estonia (23), the Czech Republic (28) and Poland (29).

Examining Relationships Between Selected Determinants of Investment Attractiveness and FDI Inflow to the New EU Member States

As we have already mentioned in the first part of the chapter, investment attractiveness and the inflow of foreign direct investment to countries may result from various economic, social and territorial factors. To examine their relevance for the 13 new European Union Member States we used Pearson correlation coefficients and Spearman's rank correlation coefficient.

In the analysis we used a series of variables, which directly or indirectly determine investment attractiveness of countries. They were selected based on the review of theoretical and empirical works discussed in the first part of the chapter. These variables can be grouped in the following seven categories, which identify:

1) general economic performance of the country, e.g. GDP, GDP p.c.;
2) labour market situation, e.g. unemployment rate, employment rate, labour productivity (EUR per hour worked), people at risk poverty or social exclusion (% of total population), tertiary education (% of people at the age of 15–64);
3) development of transport infrastructure, e.g. goods transport by rail (thousands tonnes), by road (tonne-kilometre) and air transport of goods (tonnes);
4) innovativeness, np. gross domestic expenditure on R&D (% of GDP), enterprises engaged in any type of product or process innovation;
5) size of the domestic market and business partners, expressed by the size of population and number of enterprises;

6) availability of EU resources under the budget for 2007–2013, including the European Regional Development Fund (ERDF), the European Social Fund (ESF), and the Cohesion Fund (CF); and
7) state aid, in particular tax allowances, grants and support offered in special economic zones.

We used data from the years 2007 to 2013 for the Visegrad Group countries, i.e. for Poland, the Czech Republic, Hungary and Slovakia and for the nine remaining the new EU Member States, i.e. for the Baltic States (Lithuania, Latvia, and Estonia) and for Romania, Bulgaria, Malta, Cyprus, Slovenia, and Croatia. In the first stage, the change concerned 13 observations. In some categories of variables, this number was slightly smaller due to the lack of data, especially for Malta and Cyprus. Some of the variables are directly or indirectly linked with investment incentives offered by new EU Member States, in particular when using EU funds from the 2007 to 2013 budget. With respect to these data we also included Croatia, which became a fully fledged EU member on 1 July 2013 but benefited from the EU funds and offered various types of State aid under different pre-accession schemes. To examine their relevance for new EU Member States, we used Pearson correlation coefficients and Spearman's rank correlation coefficient.

The variables were contrasted with the cumulated value of foreign direct investment inflows to the above listed States in the period 2008–2014. Since data about FDI inflow to Malta manifestly differed from the rest of the sample, and distorted the results of analysis, we decided to exclude the country from the survey. Hence, we will present results for 12 new EU Member States excluding Malta.

We used data from Eurostat, UNCTAD (World Investment Report), World Bank, and additional data from statistical offices of the countries included in the study. We also used reports of private consulting companies (e.g. KPMG), and our own calculations.

The first step of analysis pertained to the identification of the strength of relationship between variables. For that purpose we used one of the most popular correlation coefficients, which is the Pearson correlation coefficient. Calculations were made using the SPSS 14 software. The results of these analyses are synthetically presented in Table 4.

Results in Table 4 indicate a statistically significant, strong relationship ($p = 0.01$) between selected factors, which determine investment attractiveness of the new EU Member States and the inflow of FDI. The relationship is particularly strong and similar (0.940–0.959) for all variables identifying the EU funds and State aid, excluding assistance offered under tax allowance schemes. Similarly, a high value of the correlation coefficient was observed for variables that describe the size of the domestic market expressed by the size of the population and the number of firms. A slightly weaker, but still statistically significant relationship, was obtained for the variable representing the advancement and intensity of using transport infrastructure in economy and business engagement in innovation. The remaining variables connected with overall investment attractiveness expressed

Table 4 Selected determinants of investment attractiveness and FDI inflow to new EU Member States—Pearson correlation coefficients

Independent variable	Pearson correlation coefficient	Significance (p-value)
EU funds	0.953	0.000
European Regional Development Fund	0.949	0.000
European Social Fund	0.959	0.000
Cohesion Fund	0.954	0.000
Non-crisis state aid	0.940	0.000
Tax exemptions	0.812	0.001
Grants	0.944	0.000
Population	0.946	0.000
No of enterprises (in the non-financial businesses)	0.928	0.000
Goods transport by rail	0.860	0.001
Goods transport by road	0.909	0.000
Air transport of goods	0.761	0.004
Enterprises engaged in any type of product or process innovation	0.748	0.005

Source: Authors' estimates using the SPSS software, based on UNCTAD, EUROSTAT and World Bank data

with GDP and labour market situation turned out to be irrelevant for the inflow of FDI into the countries included in the study.

In the second stage of analysis we used Spearman's rank correlation coefficient also referred to as the order correlation coefficient. It measures the strength and direction of associations between two characteristics by comparing the ranks (ranking orders) of two variables. The coefficient, unlike Pearson correlation coefficient and linear regression, measures a wider class of relationships, showing monotonic, not necessarily linear, relationship between the variables. It is also much more resilient to the presence of outliers in the sample (Sobczak 2000:249–251). Spearman's rank correlation coefficient has got several versions. In our study we used the formula applied in the SPSS 14 software:

$$r_s = \frac{cov(R_X, R_Y)}{\delta_{R_X} \cdot \delta_{R_Y}}$$

where:

$cov(R_X, R_Y)$—covariance of ranks for variables X,Y;
$\delta_{R_X} \cdot \delta_{R_Y}$—standard deviation of ranks for variables X,Y.
Results are presented in Table 5.

The results obtained in the Spearman's test partially confirm those obtained by using Pearson correlation coefficient. Relationship between FDI inflow into the new EU Member States and the selected determinants of investment attractiveness (in particular population and number of enterprises) turned out to be significant at the level of significance of 0.01. Slightly weaker, but still statistically significant

Table 5 Selected determinants of investment attractiveness and FDI inflow into the new EU Member States—Spearman's rank correlation coefficient

Independent variable	Spearman's rank correlation coefficient (r_s)	Significance (p-value)
EU funds	0.671	0.017
European Regional Development Fund	0.671	0.017
European Social Fund	0.685	0.014
Cohesion Fund	0.671	0.017
Non-crisis State aid	0.531	0.075
Tax exemptions	0.643	0.024
Grants	0.538	0.071
Population	0.832	0.001
No of enterprises (in the non-financial businesses)	0.804	0.002
Goods transport by road	0.655	0.029
Air transport of goods	0.650	0.022

Source: Authors' estimates using the SPSS software, based on UNCTAD, EUROSTAT and World Bank data

relationship, $p = 0.05$, was obtained for the variable representing the availability of the EU funds and transport infrastructure (in this part of the study, railway infrastructure turned out to be statistically insignificant). It is worth noting that for the Spearman's test the p-value for some variables was below the p-value for Pearson correlation coefficient. It means lower significance of the relationship according to Spearman for variables describing state aid (tax exemptions, grants and non-crisis state aid value). Although absolute values were replaced with order data, we did not arrive at any significant level of ranks for any of the remaining variables (GDP and GDP per capita, variables describing the labour market situation). The variable that characterises firms engaged in any type of product or process innovation was also insignificant.

In conclusion, we may state that some variables significantly impact on the inflows of FDI into the group of countries included in the study. A relationship was detected, first and foremost, in the case of certain factors that shape investment attractiveness, such as transport infrastructure, size of the domestic market, number of firms—potential suppliers, customers, business partners and the availability of subsidies and other forms of the EU assistance. Slightly weaker relationships with FDI inflows were identified for the variables decisive for the development of infrastructure, State aid and grants in Spearman test. Other relationships were not identified, e.g. with respect to the potential and development of countries expressed with GDP and GDP per capita.

All variables connected with the labour market proved insignificant. That should provide the basis for further and deepened quantitative analyses, especially when earlier works of the authors, which focused mainly around investment attractiveness of regions in Poland, demonstrated slightly different foreign investors' preferences. And thus, the key factor considered by foreign investors was production costs, including labour costs and resources but almost equally important were conditions of running the business, such as economic and social infrastructure. State attempts to impact the choice of investment locations by differentiating the intensity of State aid and other incentives offered in e.g. special economic zones, were usually secondary for investment decisions made by companies with foreign capital in Polish regions (Dorożyński et al. 2014, 2015). The study is consistent with the results of earlier works which validated the hypothesis on the existence of a statistically significant relationship between spending EU resources and the inflow of foreign direct investment into voivodeships in Poland (Dorożyński 2015).

Conclusions

The principal goal of the chapter was to identify factors decisive for investment attractiveness of the new EU Member States and to assess the impact thereof upon the scale of foreign direct investments inflow into these countries. Most of them underwent unprecedented political and economic transformations. Liberalisation of the provisions concerning foreign investments opened up their economies to external capital. At the same time, various incentives were put in place, e.g. state aid and special economic zones designed to encourage foreign capital investors to choose a particular location and to pursue business operations there. These processes were reinforced by the availability of additional resources from EU funds.

The general assessment of FDI inflow to the new EU Member States is positive. Available rankings of investment attractiveness present these countries as attractive and prospective investment locations for FDI. Our own studies in principle have confirmed these conclusions. They demonstrated that, besides general indicators that describe the size of the market (population, number of firms), investment incentives also turned out to be important for the inflow of foreign direct investment. That is particularly true of the EU resources, and other state aid schemes. Studies show that infrastructural investments, indirectly linked with the EU funds, also played a major role. The role of various factors decisive for attracting foreign capital to a country may become the subject of further in-depth analyses conducted based on quantitative methods.

References

Agiomirgianakis, G., Asteriou, D., & Papathoma, K. (2006). The determinants of foreign direct investment: A panel data study for the OECD countries. *Department of Economics Discussion Paper Series, 03*(06), 1–19.

Agosin, M., & Machado, R. (2007). Openness and the international allocation of foreign direct investment. *Journal of Development Studies, 43*(7), 1234–1247.

Anyanwu, J. C. (2012). Why does foreign direct investment go where it goes? New evidence from African countries. *Annals of Economics and Finance, 13*(2), 425–462.

Arbatli, E. (2011). *Economic policies and FDI inflows to emerging market economies*. IMF Working Paper. Middle East and Central Asia Department 11/192.

Asongu, S. A., & Kodila-Tedika, O. (2015). Conditional determinants of FDI in fast emerging economies: An instrumental quantile regression approach. *African Governance and Development Institute Working Paper* (15/003), pp. 1–24.

Bank for International Settlements (BIS). (2015).

Bartels, F. L., Napolitano, F., & Tissi, N. E. (2014). FDI in sub-Saharan Africa: A longitudinal perspective on location-specific factors (2003–2010). *International Business Review, 23*(3), 516–529.

Bartik, T. J. (1991). *Who benefits from state and local economic development policies?* W.E. Upjohn Institute for Employment Research, Kalamazoo, MI.

Bellak, C., Leibrecht, M., & Riedl, A. (2008). Labour costs and FDI inflows into Central and Eastern European countries: A survey of the literature and empirical evidence. *Structural Change and Economic Dynamics, 19*(1), 17–37.

Buckley, P. J., Clegg, J., & Wang, C. (2010). Is the relationship between inward FDI spillover effects linear? An empirical examination of the case of China. In P. J. Buckley (Ed.), *Foreign direct investment, China and the world economy* (pp. 192–215). London: Palgrave Macmillan.

Castro, C., & Nunes, P. (2013). Does corruption inhibit foreign direct investment? *Política/Revista de Ciencia Política, 51*(1), 61–83.

Cedidlová, M. (2013). The effectiveness of investment incentives in certain foreign companies operating in the Czech Republic. *Journal of Competitiveness, 5*(1), 108–120.

Contessi, S., & Weinberger, A. (2009). Foreign direct investment, productivity, and country growth: An overview. *Federal Reserve Bank of St. Louis Review, 91*(2), 61–78.

Cywiński, Ł. (2015, January 14). *EU cohesion policy incentives and knowledge intensive FDI inflows*. WSIiZ Working Paper Series WP, pp. 1–11.

Davis, C. (2013, August 12). *Tax incentives: Costly for states*. Drag on the Nation Institute of Taxation and Economic Policy.

Doing Business 2016. (2015). *Measuring regulatory quality and efficiency*. A World Bank Group Report.

Dorożyński, T. (2015). Fundusze unijne a napływ bezpośrednich inwestycji zagranicznych do Polski. In E. Małuszyńska, G. Mazur, & P. Idczak (Eds.), *Unia Europejska wobec wyzwań przyszłości. Aspekty społeczne, gospodarcze i środowiskowe* (pp. 163–177). Poznań: Wydawnictwo Uniwersytetu Ekonomicznego w Poznaniu.

Dorożyński, T., & Kuna-Marszałek, A. (2014). Investment attractiveness of Visegrad Group countries: Comparative analysis. In A. Zhuplev & K. Liuhto (Eds.), *Geo-regional competitiveness in Central and Eastern Europe, the Baltic Countries, and Russia* (pp. 239–288). Hershey, PA: IGI Global.

Dorożyński, T., & Kuna-Marszałek, A. (2016a). *Investment attractiveness: The case of the Visegrad Group countries*. Comparative Economic Research in Central and Eastern Europe 1 (in press).

Dorożyński, T., & Kuna-Marszałek, A. (2016b). The role of incentives in attracting FDI to the new EU Member States. *Journal of Management and Financial Sciences, 23*.

Dorożyński, T., Świerkocki, J., & Urbaniak, W. (2014). Attracting FDI to the region of Lodz by its local government. *Comparative Economic Research in Central and Eastern Europe, 17*(2), 101–118.

Dorożyński, T., Świerkocki, J., & Urbaniak, W. (2015). Incentives for attracting FDI: The case of the Lodz Region. *Gospodarka Narodowa, 1*, 147–168.

Dunning, J. H. (1979). Explaining changing patterns of international production: In defence of the eclectic theory. *Oxford Bulletin of Economics and Statistics, 41*(4), 269–295.

Dunning, J. H. (1981). *International production and the multinational enterprise*. London: George Allen and Unwin.

Dunning, J. H. (2000). The eclectic paradigm as an envelope for economic and business theories of MNE activity. *International Business Review, 9*(2), 163–190.

Dunning, J. H. (2003). The role of foreign direct investment in upgrading China's competitiveness. *Journal of International Business and Economy, 4*(1), 1–13.
Dunning, J. H. (2004). Determinants of foreign direct investment: Globalization-induced changes and the role of policies. In B. Tungodden, N. Stern, & I. Kolstad (Eds.), *Toward pro-poor policies. Aid, institutions and globalization*. Washington, DC: World Bank.
Dunning, J. H. (2006). Towards a new paradigm of development: Implications for the determinants of international business. *Transnational Corporation, 15*(1), 173–227.
Economist Intelligence Unit. (2015). Business environment ranking and index 2014.
Éltető, A. (2010). *Foreign direct investment in Central and East European Countries and Spain – A short overview*. ICEI WP 09/10, pp. 4–17.
Ernst&Young. (2009). *Reinventing European growth*. European Attractiveness Survey 2009.
Ernst&Young attractiveness survey. (2015). Europe 2015.
EY's attractiveness survey. (2014). Europe 2014.
Feld, L. P., & Heckemeyer, J. H. (2008). *FDI and taxation. A meta-study*. ZEW Discussion Paper 08–128, pp. 1–63.
Globerman, S., Shapiro, D., & Tang, Y. (2006). Foreign direct investment in emerging and transition European countries. In J. A. Batten & C. Kearney (Eds.), *Emerging European financial markets: Independence and integration post-enlargement* (pp. 431–459). Bingley: Emerald Group Publishing Limited.
Godlewska-Majkowska, H. (2011). Wprowadzenie. In H. Godlewska-Majkowska (Ed.), *Atrakcyjność inwestycyjna regionów jako uwarunkowanie przedsiębiorczych przewag konkurencyjnych. Wybrane fragmenty* (pp. 4–6). Warszawa: SGH.
Guagliano, C., & Riela, S. (2005). *Do special economic areas matter in attracting FDI? Evidence from Poland, Hungary and Czech Republic*. Working Paper ISLA 21.
Hanousek, J., Kočenda, E., & Maurel, M. (2011). Direct and indirect effects of FDI in emerging European markets: A survey and meta-analysis. *Economic Systems, 35*(3), 301–322.
http://imf.org
Iamsiraroj, S., & Doucouliagos, H. (2015). Does growth attract FDI? Kiel Institute for the World Economy. *Economics Discussion Papers, 18*, 1–41.
IMD Global Competitiveness Index. (2015).
Investment incentives: The good, the bad and the ugly. (2013). Background Paper for the Eight Columbia International Investment Conference, Vale Columbia Center on Sustainable International Investment, Columbia University.
James, S. (2009). *Incentives and investments: Evidence and policy implications. WB Group*. Washington, DC: Investment Climate Department.
James, S. (2010). Providing incentives for investment advice for policymakers in developing countries. *Investment Climate in Practice, 7*, 1–8.
James, S. (2013, September). *Tax and non-tax incentives and investments: Evidence and policy implications*. World Bank Investment Climate Advisory Services.
Johnson, L., & Toledano, P. (2013, November 13–14). *The good, the bad and the ugly. Assessing the costs, benefits and options for policy reform*. Background Paper for the Eighth Columbia International Investment Conference on Investment Incentives Columbia University.
Kamaly, A. (2014). Does FDI crowd in or out domestic investment? New evidence from emerging economies. *Modern Economy, 4*(5), 391–400.
Kearney, A. T. (2015). FDI Confidence Index.
Koojaroenprasit, S. (2012). The impact of foreign direct investment on economic growth: A case study of South Korea. *International Journal of Business and Social Science, 3*(21), 8–19.
Lin, F. (2011). *Labour quality and inward FDI: A firm-level empirical study in China*. The University of Adelaide School of Economics, Research Paper March, 2011–2012, pp. 1–29.
Morisset, J., & Pirnia, N. (2000, December). *How tax policy and incentives affect foreign direct investment: A review*. WB Policy Research Working Paper 2509.
Mottaleb, K. (2007). *Determinants of foreign direct investment and its impact on economic growth in developing countries*. MPRA Paper 9457, pp. 1–15.

Nunnenkamp, P. (2002). *Determinants of FDI in developing countries: Has globalization changed the rules of the game?* Kiel Institute for the World Economy, Kiel Working Paper 1122.

OECD. (2002). *Foreign direct investment for development maximising benefits, minimising costs* (pp. 1–32). France: OECD.

OECD. (2003). *Checklist for foreign direct investment incentive policies.*

OECD. (2008). *Benchmark definition of foreign direct investment.*

Owczarczuk, M. (2013). Government incentives and FDI inflow Into R&D – The case of Visegrad countries. *Entrepreneurial Business and Economics Review, 1*(2), 73–86.

Perera, O. (2012). *Rethinking investment incentives.* IISD commentary International Institute for Sustainable Development.

Rădulescu, M., & Druică, E. N. (2011). *FDIs and investment policy in some European countries after their EU accession. Challenges during the crisis.* http://www.revecon.ro/articles/2011-2/2011-2-10.pdf

Rehman, C. A., Ilyas, M., Alam, H. M., & Akram, M. (2011). The impact of infrastructure on foreign direct investment: The case of Pakistan. *International Journal of Business and Management, 6*(5), 268–276.

Rymarczyk, J., Błaszczyk, M., Michalski, B., Niemiec, M., Niemiec, W., & Wróblewski, M. (2008). *Klimat inwestycyjny Dolnego Śląska w ocenie bezpośrednich inwestorów zagranicznych.* Wrocław: oficyna wydawnicza arboretum.

Shukla, L. (2013). Foreign direct investment and developing countries: Its impact and significance. *Journal of Business and Management and Social Science Research, 2*(5), 75–81.

Sobczak, M. (2000). *Statystyka. Podstawy teoretyczne przykłady – zadania.* Lublin: Wyd UMCS.

Sumner, A. (2005). Is foreign direct investment good for the poor? A review and stocktake. *Development in Practice, 15*(3/4), 269–285.

The Global Competitiveness Report 2014–2015. (2015).

Thomas, P. K. (2007). *Investment incentives: Growing use, uncertain benefits, uneven controls.* Geneva: Global Subsidies Initiative.

Tuomi, K. (2012, June). *Review of investment incentives: Best practice in attracting investment.* IGC Working Paper, pp. 1–24.

Wacker, K. M. (2011). *The impact of foreign direct investment on developing countries' terms of trade.* Working Paper 2011/06. World Institute for Development Economics Research.

Wawrzyniak, D. (2010). Determinanty lokalizacji bezpośrednich inwestycji zagranicznych. *Gosp Nar, 4*, 89–111.

World Investment Report 2010. (2010).
World Investment Report 2011. (2011).
World Investment Report 2012. (2012).
World Investment Report 2013. (2013).
World Investment Report 2014. (2014).

Zhang, Y., Li, H., Li, Y., & Zhou, L.-A. (2010). FDI spillovers in an emerging market: The role of foreign firms' country origin diversity and domestic firms' absorptive capacity. *Strategic Management Journal, 31*, 969–989. doi:10.1002/smj.856.

Policies to Promote Eco-innovation: Results for Selected CEE Countries and Germany

Małgorzata Stefania Lewandowska

Abstract Eco-innovation should be identified as one of the main pillars for European countries, including those from the Central Eastern European (CEE) region. For this reason, the aim of this chapter is to present a comparative cross-country analysis of the relationship between eco-innovation and its main drivers for firms from selected CEE countries. The chapter provides a special insight into the role of public financial support and government regulations in stimulating eco-innovation performance. The empirical part is based on micro-data for CIS 2006–2008 for firms from Bulgaria, Czech Republic, Romania and Germany. The results of stepwise regression show that financial support for innovation activities has rather limited role in fostering eco-innovation, whereas existing environmental regulations are regarded by enterprises from CEE region as their most important driver. In Germany, country ranked higher in Eco-Innovation Scoreboard than the other above mentioned countries, the spectrum of equally important forces is much more enhanced. This leads to the conclusion that government efforts have to cover not only changes in existing environmental policies, but set the ground for the creation of a legal and institutional environment which promotes a model of green economy.

Keywords Central and Eastern Europe • Innovation and R&D • Factor analysis • Eco-innovation • Environmental regulations • CIS

Introduction

Acceleration of the phenomenon of global warming, declining natural resources, pollution control, as well as the recent financial crisis are among factors influencing the wider debate about what constitutes a "healthy economy". The proponents of Green New Deal (UNEP 2009) or Green Growth (OECD 2011) advocate more

---

M.S. Lewandowska, PhD (✉)
SGH Warsaw School of Economics, Warsaw, Poland
e-mail: mlewando@sgh.waw.pl

strict environmental regulations, expecting that this will facilitate promotion of low carbon, green economy (UNEP 2011), and contribute to economic growth.

In the heart of this dispute is the eco-innovation[1] concept, defined as "... the introduction of any new or significantly improved product (good or service), process, organizational change or marketing solution that reduces the use of natural resources (including materials, energy, water and land) and decreases the release of harmful substances across the life-cycle" (EIO 2010). This demonstrates a shift from the conventional understanding of eco-innovation as part of environmental protection, to a broader perception of being integrated in all industries.

The aim of this chapter is to present a comparative cross-country analysis of the relationship between eco-innovation and its main drivers within firms from selected Central Eastern European (CEE) countries.

The introduction presents the overall innovation performance and the eco-innovation performance of European Union Member States. It is then followed by the theoretical part that provides an insight into the role of eco-innovation driving forces in enhancing eco-innovation performance. The empirical part, based on micro-data from CIS 2006–2008, covers the results of stepwise regression analysis of main eco-innovation drivers (public financial support for overall innovation activity coming from local, government and European Union sources; existing and expected government regulations or taxes on pollution; government grants, subsidies or other financial incentives for environmental innovation; current or expected market demand from customers for environmental innovations and voluntary codes or agreements for environmental good practice within the sector of operations) and the eco-innovation performance of CEE countries. In geographic terms, priority is given to three EU Member States in this region: Bulgaria, Czech Republic and Romania. The results are compared with those for firms from Germany. In the last section, the conclusion of the chapter are presented.

The chapter contributes to extant literature by presenting insights into how to design the policy mix in order to foster the development of environmental-friendly innovation in CEE countries that are still lagging behind as compared with more advanced economies.

Overall Innovation Performance of CEE Countries

In terms of overall innovation performance, CEE countries are ranked low among European Member States. According to Innovation Union Scoreboard 2015 only Slovenia joined the group of *Innovation Followers*, with the overall innovation performance close to the EU average. Majority of countries from CEE region, including Croatia, Czech Republic, Estonia, Hungary, Lithuania and Poland, form

---

[1]The terms eco-innovation, environmental-friendly innovation, environmental innovation are used interchangeably in this chapter.

the group of *Moderate Innovators* with the innovation performance below the EU-27 average, whereas Bulgaria, Latvia and Romania are categorised as *Modest Innovators* (with innovation performance far below the EU-27 average). Although in the last 7 years the CEE countries, on average, are growing much faster than EU-15, the differences between these two groups in terms of overall innovation performance are still at a relatively high level (Innovation Union Scoreboard 2015).

Eco-innovation Performance of CEE Countries

As the transition to a resource-efficient, low-carbon economy is a central pillar of the Europe 2020 Strategy for the EU's economy for the next decade EC (2010), monitoring of eco performance of EU Member States is one of the key issues. Thus, the Eco-Innovation Scoreboard "Eco-IS", a tool to assess eco-innovation performance that complements other measurement approaches of innovativeness of EU countries has been introduced.[2] The indicators in the Eco-Innovation Scoreboard are divided into five components covering eco-innovation inputs (including early stage investments in clean technology), eco-innovation activities (such as the percentage of firms taking resource-efficiency measures), eco-innovation outputs (such as relevant patents), resource-efficiency performance, and socio-economic outputs (such as turnover, employment and exports). Indicators developed to reflect eco-innovation turnover and employment have covered areas of waste, recovery and recycling and, for the first time, repair, maintenance and rental services.[3]

The results of Eco-IS for years 2010–2013 show that—as in the case of data on general innovation performance derived from Innovation Union Scoreboard—there are striking differences between the EU15 and the New Member States in the overall eco-innovation performance. Top ranking EU countries for eco-innovation are members of the group of *Innovation Leaders*—Finland, Sweden, Germany and Denmark, followed by the United Kingdom, whose scores are relatively higher than the EU 28 average, whereas all CEE countries are lagging behind.

---

[2]The indicators in the Eco-Innovation Scoreboard are divided into five components covering eco-innovation inputs (including early stage investments in clean technology), eco-innovation activities (such as the percentage of firms taking resource efficiency measures), eco-innovation outputs (such as relevant patents), resource efficiency performance, and socio-economic outputs (such as data on turnover, employment and exports); for more information see: http://www.eco-innovation.eu.

[3]The 2013 version of the Eco-IS consists of 16 indicators from 9 different data sources, which were the same indicators used for the 2012 version; 13 indicators were updated, with most indicators having their latest values for the years between 2010 and 2012; for more information see: http://www.eco-innovation.eu.

Relationship Between Innovation Performance and Eco-innovation Performance

In order to investigate the potential relationship between overall innovation performance and eco-innovation performance of EU Member States, a linear regression model was constructed. Linear regression is an approach for modeling the relationship between a dependent variable y and one or more independent variables x.

A satisfactory level of coefficient of determination ($R^2 = 0.7234$) showing of how well the regression line approximates the real data, proves the existing relation between the investigated variables. Based on the data from the Innovation Union Scoreboard and Eco-Innovation Scoreboard for 2013 used in the regression model for the surveyed countries, we can distinguish two main groups: the first one where the level of both indicators is low, and the second one where both indicators are significantly higher. The first group consists of CEE countries, the second one consists of innovation leaders, both in terms of overall innovation performance, as well as eco-innovation indicators.

It should be remembered, however, that the findings can be influenced by many structural factors, such as the relative importance of different industrial sectors or the economic trends in each country (Eco-Innovation Scoreboard 2013), which were not taken into account here. Nevertheless, Fig. 1 confirms, that European Union is still divided, and the convergence process, both in terms of overall innovation performance, and eco-innovation, while progressing, is still far from being complete. Details of the data are summarised in Table 1, whereas the regression model is presented in Fig. 1.

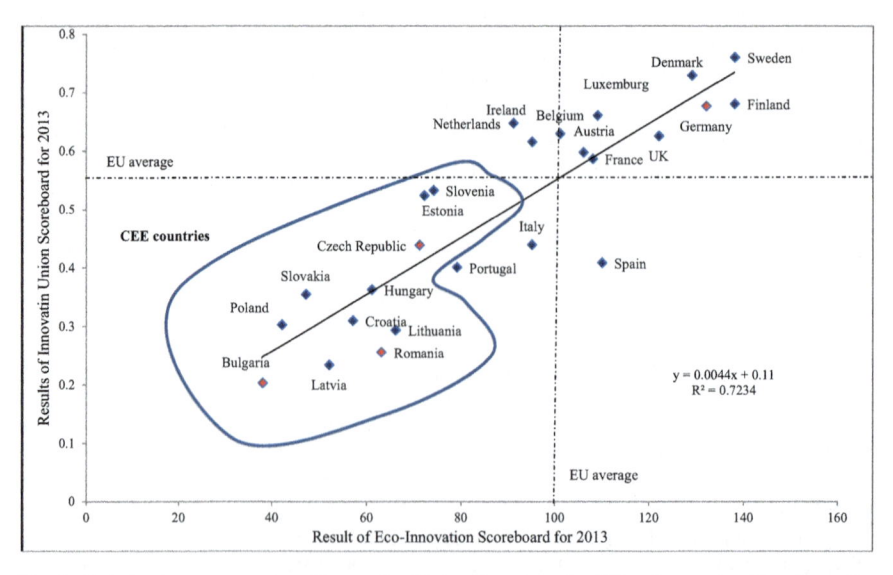

Fig. 1 Relation between results of Innovation Union Scoreboard and Eco-Innovation Scoreboard for year 2013. *Note*: Results for Malta, Greece and Cyprus were not taken into account. *Source*: Author's elaboration based on Eco-Innovation Scoreboard and Innovation Union Scoreboard for year 2013

Table 1 Comparison of results of Innovation Union Scoreboard 2013–2014 and Eco-Innovation Scoreboard for 2010–2013 for European countries

Country	Innovation Union Scoreboard results for 2013–2014				Eco-Innovation Scoreboard results for 2010–2013			
	SII 2013	SII 2014	SII growth rate 2008–2014 (%)	Country group	2010	2011	2012	2013
Finland	0.680	0.676	0.1	Innovation Leader	156	149	150	138
Sweden	0.680	0.740	0.3	Innovation Leader	128	142	134	138
Germany	**0.760**	**0.676**	**0.6**	**Innovation Leader**	**139**	**123**	**120**	**132**
Denmark	0.676	0.736	1.9	Innovation Leader	155	138	136	129
UK	0.729	0.636	1.7	Innovation Follower	103	105	101	122
Spain	0.625	0.385	−0.4	Moderate Innovator	101	128	118	110
Luxembourg	0.408	0.642	0.0	Innovation Follower	94	130	108	109
France	0.660	0.591	1.2	Innovation Follower	96	99	96	108
Austria	0.586	0.585	0.7	Innovation Follower	131	125	112	106
Belgium	0.597	0.619	1.1	Innovation Follower	114	115	118	101
Ireland	0.629	0.628	1.4	Innovation Follower	101	118	113	95
EU average	**0.554**	**0.555**	**1.0**		**100**	**100**	**100**	**100**
Italy	0.439	0.439	1.6	Moderate Innovator	98	90	92	95
Netherlands	0.647	0.647	1.8	Innovation Follower	110	109	111	91
Portugal	0.400	0.403	1.4	Moderate Innovator	72	81	84	79
Slovenia	0.532	0.534	2.6	Innovation Follower	75	109	115	74
Estonia	0.523	0.489	2.2	Moderate Innovator	56	74	78	72
Czech Rep.	**0.438**	**0.447**	**2.6**	**Moderate Innovator**	**73**	**91**	**90**	**71**
Lithuania	0.293	0.283	2.1	Moderate Innovator	45	52	53	66
Romania	**0.255**	**0.204**	**−2.3**	**Modest Innovator**	**52**	**67**	**78**	**63**
Hungary	0.362	0.369	1.3	Moderate Innovator	70	83	73	61

(continued)

Table 1 (continued)

Country	Innovation Union Scoreboard results for 2013–2014				Eco-Innovation Scoreboard results for 2010–2013			
	SII 2013	SII 2014	SII growth rate 2008–2014 (%)	Country group	2010	2011	2012	2013
Croatia	0.309	0.313	0.8	Moderate Innovator	0	0	0	57
Latvia	0.233	0.272	3.4	Modest Innovator	60	77	71	52
Slovakia	0.354	0.360	1.9	Moderate Innovator	48	52	54	47
Poland	0.302	0.313	1.4	Moderate Innovator	54	50	54	42
Bulgaria	**0.202**	**0.272**	**3.1**	**Modest Innovator**	**58**	**67**	**80**	**38**

Source: Own compilation based on Eco-Innovation Scoreboard (2013), Innovation Union Scoreboard (2015)
Note: There is no results for Cyprus, Greece and Malta. SII—Summary Innovation Index
Attention: In order to standardise the indicators, "Distance-to-reference" method is used, with the EU average being defined as the reference and set as a value of 100. Country specific figures of the single indicators are additionally weighted with the share of population in order to calculate an EU average which corrects for the bias of smaller Member States. Scores can be influenced by many structural factors, such as the relative importance of different industrial sectors or the economic trends in each country. http://database.eco-innovation.eu/indicators/view/269/1

Theoretical Background and Hypotheses Development

The growing global acceptance of the sustainable development (SD) and corporate social responsibility (CSR) concepts results in modifications in corporate and business strategies of firms. Engagement in SD/CSR activities also affects the firms' innovation strategies. Many scholars argue that environmental and social pressures offer new opportunities for innovative firms and that innovation is one of the important means by which firms can achieve both competitive advantage and sustainable growth.

Defining Eco-innovation

Green, sustainable or eco-innovation may be defined as the development of new products, processes, services and technologies that contribute to the development and well-being of human needs and institutions while respecting the worlds' natural resources and regenerative capacity (Gerlach 2003; Yoon and Tello 2009). This definition reflects the Corporate Social Responsibility (CSR) approach, and is consistent with the definitions of sustainable development that emphasise the integration of ecological, social and economic dimensions along with a sense of responsibility to existing and future generations.

As compared to "traditional" innovation, the environmental innovation have some major differences (Yarahmadi and Higgins 2012). Firstly, environmental innovation is not an open-ended concept, as it represents innovation that explicitly accentuates the reduction of environmental footprints, whether they are intended or not (OECD 2009). Secondly, an environmental innovation is not limited to innovation in product, process, marketing or organisational methods, but causes changes in social norms, cultural values and institutional structures. The importance of eco-innovation as one of the driver of firms' business model reconfiguration is also underlined in the literature (Szymura-Tyc and Bałoń 2011). Some researchers argue as well, that it requires a more intensive R&D cooperation with external partners (suppliers, Knowledge Business Intensive Services (KIBS) and universities) than other types of innovation (de Marchi 2012). However, a broad sourcing strategy reveals a level above which the propensity to introduce eco-innovation weakens (Ghisetti et al. 2015).

Determinants of Eco-innovation

Innovation theory stresses the importance of technology push and market/demand pull factors for the rationalisation of firms' innovation activities. Most scholars agree that technology push factors are especially important during the initial phase in developing a new product, whereas demand factors become more important during the diffusion phase (Pavitt 1984).

It should be stressed, however, that in the case of eco-innovation, the additional importance of regulation, environmental policy, institutional and political drivers is emphasised (Hemmelskamp 1999; Horbach and Rennings 2007).

Traditionally, environmental protection was treated as an additional cost imposed on the firm, which may reduce its competitiveness and productivity, as it obliges it to allocate some resources to pollution reduction, which is inefficient from the firms' business perspective (for a literature review see Palmer et al. 1995). This view was questioned by many scholars, particularly Porter (1991) and his co-author Claas van der Linde (Porter and van der Linde 1995b). Further debate on Porter's hypothesis is presented by Ambec et al. (2011). These authors argue that more severe, but correctly designed regulations, can "trigger innovation ... that may partially or more than fully offset the costs of complying with them" (Porter and van der Linde 1995a: 98). The determinants of eco-innovation are summarised in Table 2.

Table 2 Determinants of eco-innovation

Type of determinants	Characteristics
Technology push/supply side determinants	Technological capabilities (material efficiency, product quality, product assortment, energy efficiency); R&D activities; human capital endowment; appropriation problem and market characteristics.
Market pull/demand side	Expected increase in market share or penetration of new market segments. Social awareness of the need for clean production; environmental consciousness and preference for environmentally friendly products.
Regulatory push/institutional and political determinants	Implementation and institutionalisation of environmental policy instruments: economic and regulatory instruments. Regulatory design: stringency, flexibility, time frame, anticipation of future environmental regulations. Institutional structure: e.g. political opportunities of environmentally oriented groups, organization of information flow, existence of innovation networks, expected regulations.

Source: Own compilation based on Rennings (2000), Horbach (2008), Horbach et al. (2013)

Table 3 presents motivation to introduce an environmental innovation among European innovative industrial enterprises in the period of 2006–2008. Within the group of old Member States, the average fraction of indications for the importance of existing environmental regulations or taxes on pollution as drivers of eco-innovation attained the level of nearly 20 %, whereas within the group of CEE countries the score reached 36 %. There were 50 % of Hungarian enterprises indicating that motive as important, whereas only 9 % of Swedish enterprises regard this issue as an important driver for eco-innovation. These striking differences between two groups of countries (average fraction of 16 % and 26 %) are also visible in case of the role of environmental regulations or taxes expected to be introduced in the future. In case of remaining three other determinants: availability of government grants, subsidies or other financial incentives for eco-innovation, current or expected market demand from customers for environmental innovations and voluntary codes or agreements for environmental good practice within sector of operation, the differences between the two groups of countries are not that accentuated. Detailed results are presented in Table 3.

The chapter, apart from presenting a broader picture of eco-innovation driving forces, will particularly focus on the role of different policy measures for the firms' eco-innovation performance that include science, technology and innovation policy, environmental, as well as fiscal policy (Kemp and Pontoglio 2011; Rennings 2000). As for their taxonomy, we will follow the proposal of Edler and Georghiou (2007), who divide policy measures into these supporting the supply and the demand side. At the supply side, there are equity support; support for R&D in

Table 3 Motivation to introduce an environmental innovation within European industrial enterprises, fraction of innovative enterprises

Country	Existing environmental regulations or taxes on pollution	Environmental regulations or taxes expected to be introduced in the future	Availability of government grants, subsidies or other financial incentives for eco-innovation	Current or expected market demand from customers for environmental innovations	Voluntary codes or agreements for environmental good practice within sector of operation
Old Member States of European Union and other more developed economies					
Belgium	0.2640 (2)	0.1973 (4)	0.1091 (2)	0.1344 (9)	0.3092 (3)
Germany	**0.2153 (6)**	**0.2067 (3)**	**0.0624 (8)**	**0.1974 (4)**	**0.2105 (6)**
Finland	0.1840 (7)	0.1960 (5)	0.0839 (3)	0.3346 (1)	0.3017 (4)
France	0.2627 (3)	0.1644 (7)	0.0698 (6)	0.1775 (6)	0.2406 (5)
Italy	0.2535 (4)	0.1875 (6)	0.1340 (1)	0.1368 (8)	0.1539 (8)
Luxembourg	0.2431 (5)	0.2272 (1)	0.0690 (7)	0.2334 (2)	0.5715 (1)
Netherlands	0.1428 (8)	0.1213 (9)	0.0813 (5)	0.1822 (5)	0.1659 (7)
Portugal	0.3826 (1)	0.2133 (2)	0.0814 (4)	0.2330 (3)	0.4426 (2)
Sweden	0.0977 (9)	0.1297 (8)	0.0333 (9)	0.1544 (7)	0.1473 (9)
Average	0.1980	0.1607	0.0683	0.1833	0.2482
New Member States of European Union from CEE region					
Bulgaria	**0.0921 (10)**	**0.0558 (10)**	**0.0241 (10)**	**0.0352 (10)**	**0.0526 (10)**
Czech Republic	**0.4546 (2)**	**0.3184 (4)**	**0.0849 (4)**	**0.1591 (6)**	**0.2636 (5)**
Estonia	0.3085 (7)	0.2495 (6)	0.0720 (6)	0.2020 (4)	0.3277 (4)
Croatia	0.4302 (5)	0.3499 (2)	0.1113 (3)	0.2337 (3)	0.3643 (3)
Latvia	0.1940 (9)	0.1253 (9)	0.0624 (8)	0.1543 (7)	0.3768 (2)
Lithuania	0.4510 (3)	0.3412 (3)	0.1405 (1)	0.2700 (2)	0.1919 (8)
Hungary	0.5012 (1)	0.4199 (1)	0.0408 (9)	0.3663 (1)	0.3880 (1)
Poland	0.2885 (8)	0.1967 (8)	0.0648 (7)	0.1515 (9)	0.1564 (9)
Romania	**0.4181 (6)**	**0.2257 (7)**	**0.1148 (2)**	**0.1849 (5)**	**0.1954 (7)**
Slovakia	0.4378 (4)	0.2985 (5)	0.0686 (5)	0.1404 (9)	0.2417 (6)

(continued)

Table 3 (continued)

Country	Existing environmental regulations or taxes on pollution	Environmental regulations or taxes expected to be introduced in the future	Availability of government grants, subsidies or other financial incentives for eco-innovation	Current or expected market demand from customers for environmental innovations	Voluntary codes or agreements for environmental good practice within sector of operation
Average	0.3576	0.2581	0.0784	0.1897	0.2558

Attention: Each number in brackets indicates the ranking of frequency of indication for each of the eco-innovation driving force with selected countries (comparison in rows)
Source: Author's elaboration based on data from Eurostat, CIS 2006–2008

Table 4 Policy measures supporting eco-innovation in Bulgaria, Czech Republic, Romania and Germany

Group of policy measures	Max. number of policy types	Bulgaria	Czech Republic	Romania	Germany
Supply side measures					
Equity business support	2	2	–	–	2
Support for R&D in public sector and industry	3	3	1	–	3
Fiscal measures	2	1	–	–	–
Education, training	4	2	–	1	2
Networks and partnership promotion	4	2	3	3	4
Number of policy types supporting supply side	15	10 (66 %)	4 (27 %)	4 (27 %)	11 (73 %)
Demand side measures					
Regulations and standards	2	2	2	2	2
Public procurement	3	1	1	1	–
Technology transfer	2	–	1	2	2
Support of private demand	4	1	2	1	2
Number of policy types supporting demand side	11	4 (36 %)	6 (54 %)	6 (54 %)	6 (54 %)
Total number of policy types	26	14 (54 %)	10 (38 %)	10 (38 %)	17 (65 %)

Source: Author's elaboration based on EIO (2012:55–56)

public sector and industry; fiscal measures; education, training and mobility; promoting networks and partnership. The demand side of policy measures consists of regulations and standards; public procurement; technology transfer; financial or fiscal support for technology adopters and support of private demand.

Table 4 presents the comparison of different policy measures concerning eco-innovation in four investigated countries. Based on the obtained results we can conclude, that the overall spectrum of policy measures supporting eco-innovation is not fully exploited among countries from CEE region, while Germany seems to use much more diversified spectrum of these measures. Only support for cooperation in Czech Republic, Romania and Germany (with Bulgaria lagging behind), regulations and standards seem to be used similarly among all countries under study.

Hypotheses Development

The particular emphasis of this part of research will be given to the role of public financial support for overall innovation activity coming from local, government and European Union sources; government grants, subsidies or other financial incentives for environmental innovation and existing government regulations, or taxes on pollution in accelerating firms' eco-innovation performance.

Public Financial Support as an Eco-innovation Driver

Rationale to justify government intervention in firms' innovative activity is based on the presumed existence of market failure and draws on economic theories (Arrow 1962; Nelson 1959), which suggests, that a firm will underinvest in innovation activities, if it is not able to capture and appropriate all potential benefits from investment in R&D (Luukkonen and Niskanen 1998). It is generally expected by the policy makers that increasing public support for R&D results in *additionality*, which can be defined as the change in financed firms' R&D spending, behaviour or performance that will not occur without the public programme or subsidy (Buisseret et al. 1995). Whereas *input additionality* focuses on the degree to which public effort enhances private R&D spending, *output additionality* deals with its leverage effect on a firm's innovation performance (Luukkonen 2000). Garcia and Mohnen (2010) have found that support from the central government increases the intensity of R&D activities, as well as the share of innovative products in total sales. However, in the case of simultaneous central government and EU support, the latter source of support decreases in significance.

The government intervention not only influences innovation performance directly, but also indirectly, by improving the firm's knowledge of the market and its relations with third parties (Norman and Klofsten 2010). This gives rise to a concept of *behavioural additionality*, first introduced by Buisseret et al. (1995) that aims to measure the changes in the ways firms conduct R&D as a result of government intervention.

There is no yet much research concerning *additionality* issue in Central and Eastern European countries. Grabowski et al. (2013) assessing the efficiency of public support in Turkey and Poland, based on data for CIS 2008 and 2010, found out that government support contributes to higher innovation spending by firms (*input additionality*), and this in turn improves their chances to introduce product innovations, although support from local government proved to be less efficient than the support from central government or the European Union. As for Poland, they found grants for investment in new machinery and equipment and human resources to contribute significantly less to innovation performance than support for R&D activities in investigated manufacturing firms. Opposite results were obtained by Weresa and Lewandowska (2014) who investigated support of innovative activities with funds coming from the European Union among Polish big and medium-sized industrial enterprises. Based on Polish CIS 2010 data they found out the existence of *input additionality*, but only in case of expenditures on machinery and equipment, with a negative relationship between support and expenditures on external R&D. The *output additionality* has not been proven, meaning that there is no direct connection between EU funds and the increase of innovation performance measured by the turnover of innovative products in total sales. The analysis indicated the existence of the *cooperation additionality* with institutional partners.

For the purpose of this chapter the notion "*eco-output additionality*" will be coined, defined as "enhanced firms' eco-innovation performance resulting from public financial support". Although the importance of eco-innovation for EU economic growth is underlined, the attempts to shift the course of entire R&D programmes towards a more environmental or eco-innovation focus are still rare among majority of countries. Additionally, in most countries there still exist separation between innovation policy and environmental policy, due to the fact that innovation policy is usually directed by the ministries for trade and industry and science and technology, whereas environmental policy is usually developed by environment ministries (OECD 2009).

Even despite these existing disparities, we will suppose that public financial support, if directed towards enhanced innovation performance, will result, at least to some extent, in *eco-output additionality*, thus the first hypothesis is formulated:

Hypothesis 1. *Public financial support for innovation activities from local (H1a), government (H1b), EU authorities (H1c) results in eco-output additionality and thus generates firms' eco-innovation performance.*

The government has a wide range of tools at its disposal that can support companies, such as deferred tax payments, tax deductions, grants, preferential loans for R&D activities, and establishing technology labs and innovation clusters. However, grants are not without drawbacks, arising from information asymmetries between the investors and government agencies, costly administrative procedures, corruption and often from political pressure (Czarnitzki et al. 2011). Tax incentives directed at stimulating R&D (delayed tax payments, tax allowances and payroll withholding credit for R&D wages, preferential rates on royalty income and other income associated with knowledge ownership) can act as market tools aimed at lowering marginal costs of R&D activities. Such an approach to the problem of financing innovation can be more effective than direct support for R&D (OECD 2012). This is because no arbitrary decisions need to be made about the distribution of support among specific economic sectors, industries, and firms. As a result, more firms are encouraged to undertake innovative activities (Bloom et al. 2002). Policy makers are convinced that greater public support for R&D activities will lead to an increase in R&D investments, which, in turn, will result in an increase in innovation performance. An example of how the *additionality* effect can be estimated is included in the works of Halpern (2010), who investigated Hungarian firms and found a positive relationship between subsidies and both the level of R&D expenditure and innovation performance. In this research we will suppose that financial support which directly influences eco-innovation will have more impact on the eco-innovation performance than the public financial support that is directed towards innovation activities as a whole. Thus, the second hypothesis is proposed:

Hypothesis 2. *Grants, subsidies and tax incentives supporting intentionally eco-innovation have a stronger impact on the firms' eco-innovation performance than public financial support directed towards general innovation activities.*

Environmental Regulations as Eco-innovation Drivers

In the case of eco-innovation, economic returns on research and development in environmental technology are lower than its social return, hence firms are not strongly determined to invest in such innovation. It is important and worth underlining that eco-innovation can produce positive spillovers in both introduction and diffusion phase, which requires even more investment from the firm. This „double externality" problem reduces the will to invest in eco-innovation and is considered as an additional key determinant for the introduction of eco-regulation (Kemp 2000), which in the broad sense "is a policy with a strictly controlled purpose that is formulated by public authorities without the involvement of private agents" (Paraskevopoulou 2012).

The existing literature stresses the central role of environmental standards and policies in encouraging the adoption of eco-innovation (Beise and Rennings 2005). An extensive body of literature positively tests the hypothesis on the important impact of regulation on the introduction eco-innovation in firms (Frondel et al. 2008; Rennings and Rexhäuser 2011). Also Belin et al. (2011) in their cross-country comparison of the drivers of eco-innovation, based on CIS data, found environmental regulatory stringency and cost-saving motives to be the most important drivers of eco-innovation. Thus, environmental regulations, while being rather traditional tools, create the conditions that motivate firms to shift their efforts towards green practices (Kemp 2011). Hence, in line with this reasoning, the following hypothesis is submitted for empirical verification:

Hypothesis 3. *Out of all measures of eco-innovation policy, those related to existing environmental regulations or taxes on pollution have the highest impact on the introduction of eco-innovation.*

Sample Description, Variables Operationalisation, Methods Applied

Analysis of eco-innovation drivers is based on firm-level anonymised data from the Community Innovation Survey (CIS) for 2006–2008, covering firms from Bulgaria, Czech Republic, Romania and Germany.[4]

---

[4]CIS 2008 micro data for 16 European countries (namely: BG-CY-CZ-DE-EE-ES-HU-IE-LT-LV-PT-RO-SI-SK-NO) obtained based on the *"Contract on the use of Community Innovation Survey*

The Community Innovation Survey (CIS) is a survey on innovation activity of enterprises covering EU Member States and candidate countries, Iceland and Norway. The CIS 2008 was based on a common survey questionnaire and methodology, with reference to the Oslo Manual (2005), as to get comparable, harmonized and high quality statistical results. The CIS is designed to obtain information on firms' innovation activities, as well as their expenditures for process and product innovations, public financial support for innovation activities, sources of information and cooperation within innovation projects, innovation objectives. The CIS also contains data on the introduction of organisational and marketing innovations, as well as eco-innovations. The target population of the CIS 2008 were small, medium and large enterprises from NACE sections A to N. In most countries the survey was carried out on the entire population (census). In order to extrapolate results to the whole target population, weighting factors were calculated based on the ratio of the number of enterprises or the number of employees in the realised sample and the total number of enterprises or employees in each layer of the reference population (CIS 2008).

CIS 2006–2008 exceptionally included set of 15 questions on environmental innovation, covering both types of eco-innovation potentially introduced by the firm, as well as their drivers. According to CIS definition: "An environmental innovation is a new or significantly improved product (good or service), process, organizational method or marketing method that creates environmental benefits compared to alternatives. The environmental benefits can be the primary objective of the innovation or the result of other innovation objectives. The environmental benefits of an innovation can occur during the production of a good or service, or during the after sales use of a good or service by the end user (CIS 2008).

For the purpose of this research, firms from branches with potentially higher impact on environment were extracted from each country sample. These were: enterprises from NACE section B (mining and quarrying); section C (manufacturing); section D (electricity, gas, steam and air conditioning) and section H (transportation and storage).

The Chi-square test with column proportions (Bonferroni method) was applied to verify statistically significant differences between country sub-samples. Within the refined sub-samples there are 16 % of firms from Bulgaria; 35 % of firms located in Czech Republic; 18 % of Romania-based firms and 39 % of firms in Germany that introduced product innovation, and 17 %, 39 %, 23 % and 36 % of firms, (respectively, in countries under study) of those that implemented process innovation. In all of the analysed countries the minority of firms implemented organisational innovation (16 %, 42 %, 25 % and 43 % of firms, respectively). Also fewer firms implemented marketing innovation (11 %, 37 %, 23 % and 43 %, respectively). Small firms constitute 74 % of the Bulgarian, 34 % of the Czech, 36 % of the Romanian and 38 % of the German samples. Regarding medium and

---

(CIS) micro data for research purposes – CIS/2012/13" signed on 18.10.2012 between European Commission Eurostat, Unit B1 and the Warsaw School of Economics.

Table 5 Sample description of enterprises from Bulgaria (n = 10,742), Czech Republic (n = 3470), Romania (n = 6034) and Germany (n = 3940) from selected NACE, that in 2006–2008 introduced at least one type of eco-innovation

Sample characteristics		Bulgaria (BG) (n = 10,742)		Czech Republic (CZ) (n = 3470)		Romania (RO) (n = 6034)		Germany (DE) (n = 3940)	
		n	%	n	%	n	%	n	%
Product innovation		1712	15.9b	1216	**35.0a**	1110	18.4b	1529	**38.8a**
Process innovation		1850	17.2b	1351	**38.9a**	1399	23.2b	1408	**35.7a**
Organisational innovation		1743	16.2c	1450	**41.8a**	1532	25.4b	1693	**43.0a**
Marketing innovation		1196	11.1d	1283	37.0b	1412	23.4c	1694	**43.0a**
Enterprise as part of capital group		813	7.6d	1398	40.3b	723	12.0c	1738	**44.1a**
NACE	B	153	**1.4a**	111	**3.2a**	166	**2.8a**	87	**2.2a**
	C	8942	**83.3a**	2792	80.4a	5070	**84.0a**	3283	**83.4a**
	D	104	1.0c	176	**5.1a**	144	2.4a.b	161	4.1b
	H	1543	**14.4a**	391	11.3b	654	10.8b	409	10.6b
Size	Small	7893	**73.5a**	1195	34.4b	2172	36.0b	1503	38.1b
	Medium	2415	22.5d	1370	39.5b	2829	**46.9a**	1350	34.3c
	Large	434	4.0c	905	**26.1a**	1033	17.1b	1087	**27.6a**
Target market	Local/regional	7742	**72.1a**	2141	61.7b	2638	43.7d	2077	52.7c
	National	6836	63.6b	2624	**75.6a**	2744	45.5c	2916	**74.0a**
	EU. EFTA. EU CC	2881	26.8d	2265	**65.3a**	2602	43.1c	2304	58.5b
	All other countries	1266	11.8c	995	28.7b	765	12.7c	1532	**38.9a**

Note: Each letter (a, b, c, d) denotes a subset of categories whose column proportions (Bonferroni method) do differ significantly from each other at the 0.05 level (differences in lines between results for four samples)
Source: Own calculations in SPSS 21 based on anonymised micro data from CIS 2008 for Bulgaria, Czech Republic, Romania and Germany

large enterprises, there are 23 % and 4 % of them, respectively, in the Bulgarian, 40 % and 26 % in the Czech, 47 % and 17 % in the Romanian, and 34 % and 28 % percent in the German samples. In all surveyed countries the majority of firms are from NACE C, followed by H, D and B. The domestic (national) market was the most important target market for the analysed firms, followed by European market (EU/EFTA). The other than the EU/EFTA markets were the least important ones for firms in each country sample (see Table 5 for further details).

Detailed operationalisation of variables used in the study is based on the definitions derived from CIS 2008 and is presented in Table 6.

Table 6 Description and construction of variables

Variable	Description and construction of variables
Variable—"Eco innovation drivers"	
LocSupp	"1" if the firm during 2006–2008 received public financial support for innovation activities from local or regional authorities (including financial support via tax credits or deductions, grants, subsidised loans, and loan guarantees. Excluding research and other innovation activities conducted entirely for the public sector under contract); "0" otherwise
GovSupp	"1" if the firm during 2006–2008 received public financial support for innovation activities from central government (including financial support via tax credits or deductions, grants, subsidised loans, and loan guarantees. Excluding research and other innovation activities conducted entirely for the public sector under contract); "0" otherwise
EUSupp	"1" if the firm during 2006–2008 received public financial support for innovation activities from European Union (including financial support via tax credits or deductions, grants, subsidised loans, and loan guarantees. Excluding research and other innovation activities conducted entirely for the public sector under contract); "0" otherwise
EnReg	"1" if the firm during 2006–2008 introduced eco innovation in response to existing environmental regulation or taxes on pollution; "0" otherwise
EnRegExp	"1" if the firm during 2006–2008 introduced eco innovation in response to expected environmental regulations or taxes; "0" otherwise
EnGra	"1" if the firm during 2006–2008 introduced eco innovation in response to availability of government grants, subsidies or other financial incentives for environmental innovation; "0" otherwise
EnDem	"1" if the firm during 2006–2008 introduced eco innovation in response to market demand from customers for eco innovation; "0" otherwise
EnAgr	"1" if the firm during 2006–2008 introduced eco innovation in response to voluntary codes or agreements within sector; "0" otherwise
Variable—"Introduction of eco innovation"	
EcoMat	"1" if the firm during 2006–2008 introduced eco innovation resulting in reduced material use per unit of output; "0" otherwise
EcoEn	"1" if the firm during 2006–2008 introduced eco innovation resulting in reduced energy use per unit of output; "0" otherwise
$EcoCO_2$	"1" if the firm during 2006–2008 introduced eco innovation resulting in reduced CO_2 production by enterprise; "0" otherwise
EcoSub	"1" if the firm during 2006–2008 introduced eco innovation resulting in reduced materials with less polluting substitutes; "0" otherwise
EcoPol	"1" if the firm during 2006–2008 introduced eco innovation resulting in reduced soil, water, noise or air pollution; "0" otherwise
EcoWat	"1" if the firm during 2006–2008 introduced eco innovation resulting in recycled waste, water, materials; "0" otherwise
EcoEnEndU	"1" if the firm during 2006–2008 introduced eco innovation resulting in reduced energy use by the end user; "0" otherwise
EcoPolEndU	"1" if the firm introduced eco innovation resulting in reduced air, water, soil or noise pollution by the end user; "0" otherwise
EcoRecEndU	"1" if the firm introduced eco innovation resulting in improved recycling of product after use; "0" otherwise

Note: Definitions are taken directly from the CIS 2006–2008 questionnaire
Source: Author's elaboration based on questionnaire CIS 2006–2008

Results of an Analysis

The explorative character of this part of the chapter influenced the data analysis methods. To answer the research questions exploratory factor analysis (Oblimin rotation), stepwise regression and Z Fisher were used. Factor analysis of eco-innovation for Romanian enterprises[5] using Oblimin rotation (KMO = 0.872; x^2 (36) = 289,245.67; p < 0.001) allowed to determine two underlying factors which explain 65.46 % of the Variance. The first factor: "Environmental benefits from the production of goods within the enterprise" explains 35.88 % of the Variance (Crombach's α = .856), the second one: "Environmental benefits from the after sales use of goods by the end user" explains 29.58 % of the Variance (Crombach's α = .781). Similar results were obtained for samples from other investigated countries. Details of the analysis are presented in Table 7.

In the following part, all the hypotheses H1–H3 will be tested separately for the extracted two groups of variables: "Environmental benefits from the production of goods or services within the enterprise" and for the group of "Environmental benefits from the after sales use of goods or service by the end user".

Based on the results of stepwise regression we can argue that public financial support for innovation activities from local authorities does not have statistically significant impact on the introduction of eco-innovation within surveyed countries, whereas public financial support from government authorities is an important factor

Table 7 Rotated Component Matrix for eco-innovation introduced within Romanian enterprises

	Environmental benefits	
Components[a]	From the production of goods within the enterprise *EcoEnt*	From the after sales use of goods by the end user *EcoEndU*
EcoMat	0.828	
EcoCO$_2$	0.786	
EcoWat	0.728	
EcoPol	0.666	
EcoSub	0.580	
EcoEn	0.566	
EcoEnEndU		0.854
EcoRecEndU		0.839
EcoPolEndU		0.629

Extraction Method: Principal Component Analysis
Note: The results for Bulgaria, Czech Republic and Germany were very similar. Available on the request from the author
Source: Own calculations in SPSS 21 based on anonymised micro data from CIS 2008 for Romania
[a]Rotation converged in five iterations

---

[5]Results for Bulgarian, Czech Republic and German enterprises were very similar and are available on request from the corresponding author.

for the introduction of eco-innovation with the environmental benefits from production in Czech Republic and Germany. Public financial support from European Union is important only among Bulgarian firms. Based on these results we can argue that for the introduction of eco-innovation with environmental benefits within the firm, **hypothesis H1a** has been **rejected for all surveyed countries**, H1b has been **supported for Czech Republic** and **Germany** and H1c has been **supported** only in case of **Bulgarian firms**.

Government grants, subsidies of other financial incentive designed specially to spur eco-innovation, while they do have positive and statistically important impact, they do not occur to be more influential than public financial support for overall innovation performance. Thus, **hypothesis H2** in case of eco-innovation with environmental benefits within the enterprise has been **rejected for all surveyed countries**.

Out of five driving forces directly connected with eco-innovation that can have potential impact on its introduction, these related to existing regulations are ranked the highest in two countries. Thus, **hypothesis H3** can be **supported** for **Bulgaria** and **Romania**. Apart from analysing the policy drivers, due to the construction of CIS questionnaire, it was also possible to observe the impact of expected regulations or taxes, market demand for eco-innovation, as well as voluntary codes or arrangements within the sector on the introduction of eco-innovation.

As for expected market regulations, in all surveyed countries they have significantly important impact on the introduction of eco-innovation. Also voluntary codes or arrangements within the sector and market demand for innovation are important eco-innovation drivers.

In the case of Bulgaria, the analysis of the whole spectrum of eco-innovation drives shows that their importance, although having a statistically significant impact, does not play as important a role as do the existing environmental regulations. Very similar results were obtained for Romanian enterprises. It is different in case of Czech Republic, where voluntary codes or agreements within sector, as well as expected regulations play an equally important role as regulations. It is very similar to the results obtained for Germany, where the spectrum of equally important factors for the introduction of eco-innovation is even larger.

In the case of the group of innovation with environmental benefits from the after sales use of goods or service by the end user, the results show that the impact of financial support, as well as regulations is a bit more limited as compared with the above mentioned results for the first group. For the financial support coming from government authorities as the driver of eco-innovation (**H1b**), the relationship is found only in case of **Germany**, whereas **H1c**, suggesting the positive impact of public financial support from EU is supported only for **Bulgaria**. All other **hypotheses (H1a; H2 and H3)** are **rejected for all surveyed countries**. The results of stepwise regression are presented in Table 8, whereas Table 9 contains the summary of hypotheses verification.

Table 8 Driving forces of eco-innovation and their hierarchy within Bulgarian, Czech, Romanian and German enterprises, results of stepwise regression

Eco-innovations and their driving forces		Bulgaria n = 10,742		Czech Republic n = 3470		Romania n = 6034		Germany n = 3193	
		Beta	p	Beta	p	Beta	p	Beta	p
Environmental benefits from the production of goods or services within the enterprise and the hierarchy of their driving forces for each analysed country, including *eco-output additionality* (results for the combined group: *EcoMat, EcoEn, EcoCO₂, EcoSun, EcoPol, EcoWat*)									
EcoEnt	Public support from local authorities	−0.002d	.880	0.019c	.348	−0.005d	.776	0.021c	.192
	Public support from government authorities	0.011d	.439	**0.056b**	.007	0.035d	.067	**0.043c**	.008
	Public support from European Union	**0.055c**	.000	0.007c	.754	−0.005d	.775	0.023c	.160
	Government grants, subsidies	**0.092c**	.000	**0.066b**	.002	**0.065c**	.002	0.011c	.485
	Existing environmental regulations or taxes	**0.376a**	.000	**0.254a**	.000	**0.370a**	.000	**0.149a**	.000
	Expected environmental regulations or taxes	**0.189b**	.000	**0.205a**	.000	**0.154b**	.000	**0.196a**	.000
	Market demand for eco-innovations	**0.056c**	.000	**0.094b**	.000	**0.200b**	.000	**0.206a**	.000
	Voluntary codes or agreements within sector	**0.173b**	.000	**0.203b**	.000	**0.118c**	.000	**0.193a**	.000
Environmental benefits from the after sales use of goods or service by the end user and the hierarchy of their driving forces for each analysed country, including *eco-output additionality* (results for the combined group: *EcoEnEndU, EcoPolEndU, EcoRecEndU*)									
EcoEndU	Public support from local authorities	0.020b.c	.176	0.032b.c	.135	0.022c	.284	0.025c	.134
	Public support from government authorities	0.002c	.892	−0.002c	.945	0.026c	.230	**0.045c**	.006
	Public support from European Union	**0.060b**	.000	0.024c	.287	−0.025c	.238	0.030c	.066
	Government grants, subsidies	**0.062b**	.000	**0.113b**	.000	**0.112b**	.000	0.014b	.391
	Existing environmental regulations or taxes	**0.230a**	.000	**0.125b**	.000	**0.188a**	.000	**0.106b**	.000
	Expected environmental regulations or taxes	**0.152b**	.000	**0.212a**	.000	**0.160b**	.000	**0.183a**	.000
	Market demand for eco innovations	**0.227a**	.000	**0.172a**	.000	**0.219a**	.000	**0.238a**	.000
	Voluntary codes or agreements within sector	**0.120b**	.000	**0.124b**	.000	0.042d	.111	**0.152a**	.000

Note: Each letter (a,b,c,d) denotes a subset of categories whose column proportions (Z Fisher method) do differ significantly from each other at the 0.05 level (differences in lines between results for four samples)

Source: Own calculations in SPSS 21 based on anonymised micro data from CIS 2008

Table 9 Summary of results for the tests of hypotheses

Hypothesis	Bulgaria	Czech Rep.	Romania	Germany
Environmental benefits from the production of goods or services within the enterprise				
H1a: *Public financial support for innovation activities from local authorities results in eco-output additionality and thus generates firms' eco-innovation performance.*	Rejected	Rejected	Rejected	Rejected
H1b: *Public financial support for innovation activities from government authorities results in eco-output additionality and thus generates firms' eco-innovation performance.*	Rejected	(+)**	Rejected	(+)**
H1c: *Public financial support for innovation activities from EU authorities results in eco-output additionality and thus generates firms' eco-innovation performance.*	(+)***	Rejected	Rejected	Rejected
H2: *Grants, subsidies and tax incentives supporting intentionally eco-innovation have a stronger impact on the firms' eco-innovation performance than public financial support directed towards general innovation activities.*	Rejected	Rejected	Rejected	Rejected
H3: *Out of all measures of eco-innovation policy, those related to existing environmental regulations or taxes on pollution have the highest impact on the introduction of eco-innovation.*	(+)***	Rejected	(+)***	Rejected
Environmental benefits from the after sales use of goods or services by the end user				
H1a: *Public financial support for innovation activities from local authorities results in eco-output additionality and thus generates firms' eco-innovation performance.*	Rejected	Rejected	Rejected	Rejected
H1b: *Public financial support for innovation activities from government authorities results in eco-output additionality and thus generates firms' eco-innovation performance.*	Rejected	Rejected	Rejected	(+)**
H1c: *Public financial support for innovation activities from EU authorities results in eco-output additionality and thus generates firms' eco-innovation performance.*	(+)***	Rejected	Rejected	Rejected
H2: *Grants, subsidies and tax incentives supporting intentionally eco-innovation have a stronger impact on the firms' eco-innovation performance than public financial support directed towards general innovation activities.*	Rejected	Rejected	Rejected	Rejected
H3: *Out of all measures of eco-innovation policy, those related to existing environmental regulations or taxes on pollution have the highest impact on the introduction of eco-innovation.*	Rejected	Rejected	Rejected	Rejected

Note: Significant at ***$p < 0.001$; **$p < 0.01$; *$p < 0.05$
Source: Author's elaboration based on the research results

Discussion and Conclusions

This chapter discusses the relationship between public financial support and environmental regulations with eco-innovation performance and provides evidence on the importance of these driving forces for eco-innovation activity of firms originating from Bulgaria, Czech Republic, Romania and Germany.

The results for Bulgaria indicated *eco-innovation additionality* of public financial support from European Union in case of both groups of eco-innovation with a simultaneous lack of impact of resources from local and government authorities. The positive impact of funds from the EU may be related to the sample structure, dominated by small enterprises. Research shows that financial support *additionality* is much more visible within this group of firms, and the crowding out effect of private funds is less frequent (Kemp 2011). The limited role of financial support may result from the fact that the innovation process cannot be reduced to linear relationships only, and that the effects may be postponed in time. Other reason, while looking at the case of Romania, may be the still insufficient level of such aid directed towards eco-innovation, as well existing barriers to absorption of European funds by enterprises (Cace et al. 2011).

On the other hand, the positive impact of support from government authorities in Czech Republic and Germany (for both groups of innovation) may reflect the shift in the innovation policy towards environmentally-friendly innovation in the aforementioned countries.

It also seems that the potential of grants and subsidies directed towards eco-innovation is not fully exploited by CEE-based firms. It may be caused by many drawbacks of this stimuli, mentioned already in the theoretical part. The results of other studies reveal the fact of increased impact of environmental policies, when combining regulations and taxes with subsidies, particularly for the adoption of innovations to reduce CO_2 emissions (Veugelers 2012). This complementarity between policy instruments may be the way to leverage the impact of subsidies directed towards CEE enterprises to a greater extent.

Based on the obtained results, we can argue that eco-innovation cannot be considered only as a systematic reply to regulation. The positive impact of demand for eco-innovation reflects the findings of many authors including Doran and Ryan (2012). At this point we should remember, however, that the CIS questionnaire does not specify whether the demand comes from individual customers or other enterprises. It may also be created by the government itself. More precise questions may be helpful for investigating this issue further.

Based on the obtained results we can argue that the spectrum of driving forces of innovation with environmental benefits from the after sales use of a good or service by the end user—is much broader than in the case of innovation with environmental benefits from the production of goods or services within enterprise. One of the reasons may be the fact that firms' involvement in value chains advances corporate learning through mutual knowledge flows, including the knowledge of eco-innovation. It is beneficial for companies, as the knowledge transmitted along the value chain is less apparent and, consequently, more difficult to be imitated (Carter and Rogers 2008).

But it should be underlined that customer demands and public pressure, while essential for eco-innovation (Horbach 2008), will in themselves not provide sufficient motivation for eco-innovation (Rennings 2000). Only a wider policy, based on several sources of incentives may be sufficiently influential to convince firms to introduce eco-innovation and follow the path of sustainable growth.

The breadth of results of this chapter opens up research avenues for in-depth analyses on each of the eco-innovation separately (reduction of energy use, air, water, or soil pollution), as well as the relationship between them and their driving forces. Also the complementarity impact of different eco-innovation driving forces should be taken into account in the future research.

It should be underlined, based on the results of empirical part, that every decision-making body, both at the government or EU level, has competences to contribute to fostering eco-innovation performance. However, there is a striking need to coordinate it and add proper direction (Costantini et al. 2015). Results show that eco-innovation is affected by multiple policies, which suggests that its better coordination and its final objective of sustainability should be a major governance challenge for single EU countries, as well as for the European Union as a whole (Flanagan et al. 2011). This provides an opportunity to work out a model of policy intervention with societal and environmental value added that will lead to the fulfilment of Strategy 2020, which in turn requires a forward-looking process of adaptive policy making (Borrás and Edquist 2013).

Even though this study reinforces the importance of different eco-innovation drivers and is based on a huge sample of firms from four countries, it clearly has its limitations. It covers only a single-period CIS panel, which reduces the opportunities to assess long-term trends of causal effects under study. The statistically significant differences among the surveyed samples might also bias the results of the study to some extent, especially due to differences in firms' size structure, intensity of introduction of other types of innovation, or sales target markets. Also the complementarity of eco-innovation driving forces and policy interaction effects was not investigated. It should be underlined, however, that the presented analysis which is based on representative samples of Bulgarian, Czech, Romanian and German enterprises, does to a high extent reflect the actual casual relationships between eco-innovation and their drivers in the context of the overall innovation performance of the aforementioned countries.

Acknowledgment This chapter was supported with funds provided by the Polish Ministry of Science and Higher Education for the World Economy Research Institute—a unit of the Collegium of the World Economy at the Warsaw School of Economics.

References

Ambec, S., Cohen, M. A., Elgie, S., & Lanoie, P. (2011). *The Porter hypothesis at 20: Can environmental regulation enhance innovation and competitiveness?* Discussion paper, Resources for the Future, Washington, DC.

Arrow, K. J. (1962). Economic welfare and the allocation of resources for invention. In R. R. Nelson (Ed.), *The rate and direction of inventive activity: Economic and social factors* (National Bureau of Economic Research, Conference Series, pp. 609–625). Princeton: Princeton University Press.

Beise, M., & Rennings, K. (2005). Lead markets and regulation: A framework for analyzing the international diffusion of environmental innovations. *Ecological Economics, 52*(1), 5–17.

Belin, J., Horbach, V., & Oltra, V. (2011). *Determinants and specificities of eco-innovations – An econometric analysis for the French and German industry based on the Community Innovation Survey.* Cahiers du GREThA, no. 2011–17.

Bloom, N., Griffith, R., & Van Reenen, J. (2002). Do R&D tax credit works? Evidence from a panel of countries 1979–1997. *Journal of Public Economics, 85*, 1–31.

Borrás, S., & Edquist, C. (2013). The choice of innovation policy instruments. *Technological Forecasting and Social Change, 80*(8), 1513–1522.

Cace, C., Cace, S., & Nicolaescu, V. (2011). Absorption of the structural funds in Romania. *Romanian Journal of Economic Forecasting, 2*, 84–105.

Cameron, T. J., Buisseret, H., & Georghiou, L. (1995). What difference does it make? Additionality in the public support of R&D in large firms. *International Journal of Technology Management, 10*(4–6), 587–600.

Carter, C. R., & Rogers, D. S. (2008). A framework of sustainable supply chain management: Moving toward new theory. *International Journal of Physical Distribution and Logistics Management, 38*(5), 360–387.

CIS. (2008). *Community Innovation Survey 2006–2008.* Accessed April 10, 2014, from http://epp.eurostat.ec.europa.eu

Costantini, V., Crespi, F., & Palma, A. (2015). *Characterizing the policy mix and its impact on eco-innovation in energy-efficient technologies.* SEEDS Working Paper Series, 11/2015.

Czarnitzki, D., Hanel, P., & Rosa, J. M. (2011). Evaluating the impact of R&D tax credits on innovation: A microeconometric study on Canadian firms. *Research Policy, 40*(2), 217–229.

De Marchi, W. (2012). Environmental innovation and R&D cooperation: Empirical evidence from Spanish manufacturing firms. *Research Policy, 41*, 614–624.

Doran, J., & Ryan, G. (2012). *Regulation and firm perception, eco-innovation and firm performance.* MPRA Paper, 44578. http://mpra.ub.uni-muenchen.de/44578

EC (European Commission). (2010). *Europe 2020 – A European strategy for smart, sustainable and inclusive growth.* Accessed October 1, 2014, from http://ec.europa.eu/europe2020

Eco-Innovation Scoreboard. (2013). www.eco-innovation.eu

Edler, J., & Georghiou, L. (2007). Public Procurement and Innovation: Resurrecting the demand side. *Research Policy, 36*, 949–963.

EIO. (2010). *Methodological report.* Eco-innovation observatory. Funded by the European Commission, DG Environment, Brussels.

EIO. (2012). *The eco-innovation gap: An economic opportunity for business.* Eco-innovation observatory. Funded by the European Commission, DG Environment, Brussels.

Flanagan, K., Uyarraa, E., & Laranja, M. (2011). Reconceptualising the policy-mix for innovation. *Research Policy, 40*, 702–713.

Frondel, M., Horbach, J., & Rennings, K. (2008). What triggers environmental management and innovation? Empirical evidence for Germany. *Ecological Economics, 66*(1), 153–160.

Garcia, A., & Mohnen, P. (2010). *Impact of government support on R&D and innovation.* Unu-Merit Working Paper, 2010-034.

Gerlach, A. (2003). Sustainable entrepreneurship and innovation. Center for Sustainability Management, University of Lüneburg. In Proceedings from the 2003, Conference on Corporate Social Responsibility and Environmental Management, Leeds, UK.

Ghisetti, C., Marzucchi, A., & Montresor, S. (2015). The open eco-innovation mode. An empirical investigation of eleven European countries. *Research Policy, 44*, 1080–1093.

Grabowski, W., Pamukcu, T., Szczygielski, K., & Tandogan, S. (2013). *Does government support for private innovation matter? Firm-level evidence from Turkey and Poland*. CASE Network Studies & Analysis 458.

Halpern, L. (2010). *R&D subsidies and firm performance in Hungary*. Micro-Dyn Working Paper, 38/10.

Hemmelskamp, J. (1999). *The influence of environmental policy on innovative behavior – An econometric study*. Fondazione Eni Enrico Mattei Working Paper No. 18.99, Milan.

Horbach, J. (2008). Determinants of environmental innovation – New evidence from German panel data sources. *Research Policy, 37*(1), 163–173.

Horbach, J., & Rennings, K. (2007). *Panel-survey analysis of eco-innovation: Possibilities and propositions, deliverable 4 and 5 of MEI (measuring eco-innovation) project*. Mannheim: MEI (Measuring eco-innovation) project.

Horbach, J., Oltra, V., & Belin, J. (2013). Determinants and specificities of eco-innovations compared to other innovations: An econometric analysis for the French and German industry based on the community innovation survey. *Industry and Innovation, 20*(6), 523–543. doi:10.1080/13662716.2013.833375.

Innovation Union Scoreboard. (2015). ec.europa.eu/.../innovation/.../scoreboards/.../ius-2015.

Kemp, R. (2000, June 19). *Technology and environmental policy: Innovation effects of past policies and suggestions for improvement*. Paper for OECD workshop on Innovation and Environment, Paris.

Kemp, R. (2011). Ten themes for eco-innovation policies in Europe. *S.A.P.I.EN.S., 4*(2). http://sapiens.revues.org/1169

Kemp, R., & Pontoglio, S. (2011). The innovation effects of environmental policy instruments — A typical case of the blind men and the elephant? *Ecological Economics, 72*, 28–36.

Luukkonen, T. (2000). Additionality in EU framework programmes. *Research Policy, 29*(6), 711–724.

Luukkonen, T., & Niskanen, P. (1998). *Learning through collaboration. Finnish participation in EU framework programmes*. VTT, Group for Technology Studies, Espoo.

Nelson, R. R. (1959). The simple economics of basic scientific research. *Journal of Political Economy, 49*, 297–306.

Norman, C., & Klofsten, M. (2010). Financing new ventures: Attitudes towards public innovation support. *New Technology-Based Firms in the New Millennium, 8*, 89–110.

OECD and Eurostat. (2005). *Oslo Manual. Guidelines for collecting and interpreting innovation data* (3rd ed.). Paris: OECD Publishing. Joint publication by OECD and Eurostat.

OECD. (2009). *Eco-innovation in industry: Enabling green growth*. Paris: OECD.

OECD. (2011). *Towards green growth*. Paris: OECD.

OECD. (2012). *Tax incentives for research and development. OECD science technology and industry outlook 2012*. Paris: OECD.

Palmer, K., Oates, W. E., & Portney, P. R. (1995). Tightening environmental standards: The benefit-cost or the no-cost paradigm? *Journal of Economic Perspectives, 9*(4), 119–132.

Paraskevopoulou, E. (2012). Non-technological regulatory effects: Implications for innovation and innovation policy. *Research Policy, 41*, 1058–1071.

Pavitt, K. (1984). Sectoral patterns of technical change: Towards a taxonomy and a theory. *Research Policy, 13*, 343–373.

Porter, M. (1991, April). America's green strategy. *Scientific American, 264*(4).

Porter, M. E., & van der Linde, C. (1995a). Towards a new conception of the environment-competitiveness relationship. *Journal of Economic Perspective, 9*(4), 97–118.

Porter, M. E., & van der Linde, C. (1995b). Green and competitive. Ending the stalemate. *Harvard Business Review, September–October*, 120–134.

Rennings, K. (2000). Redefining innovation – Eco-innovation research and the contribution from ecological economics. *Ecological Economics, 32*(2), 319–332.

Rennings, K., & Rexhäuser, S. (2011). Long-term impacts of environmental policy and eco-innovative activities of firms. *International Journal of Technology Policy and Management, 11*(3), 274–290.

Szymura-Tyc, M., & Bałoń, M. (2011). Ekoinnowacja jako przesłanka rekonfiguracji modelu biznesu. Zeszyty Naukowe. *Uniwersytet Ekonomiczny w Poznaniu, 169*, 256–265.

UNEP. (2009, March). *United Nations environment programme. Global green new deal.* Policy Brief.

UNEP. (2011). *Towards a green economy: Pathways to sustainable development and poverty eradication*. http://unep.org/greeneconomy/

Veugelers, R. (2012). Which policy instruments to induce clean innovating? *Research Policy, 41*, 1770–1778.

Weresa, M. A., & Lewandowska, M. S. (2014). Innovation system restructuring in Poland in the context of EU membership. In M. A. Weresa (Ed.), *Poland competitiveness report 2014: A decade in the European Union* (pp. 171–191). Warsaw: Warsaw School of Economics.

Yarahmadi, M., & Higgins, P. G. (2012). Motivations towards environmental innovation. A conceptual framework for multiparty cooperation. *European Journal of Innovation Management, 15*(4), 400–420.

Yoon, E., & Tello, S. (2009). Drivers of sustainable innovation. *Seoul Journal of Business, 15*(2), 85–115.

CEE Countries as a Business Process Outsourcing Destination

Patryk Dziurski

Abstract Business process outsourcing (BPO) is a relatively new economic phenomenon. The first BPO projects were implemented in the early 1990s of the last century. Around that time, American companies started collaborating with Indian IT companies. Ever since, the BPO market has been growing rapidly at considerable growth rates. In view of these developments, business process outsourcing has clearly become an important topic that requires dedicated in-depth analyses.

The author formulates two aims of the chapter. The first one is to identify global business process outsourcing destinations and compare two major locations, Central and Eastern Europe and Middle East and North Africa. The second aim is to indicate key challenges which BPO providers in Central and Eastern Europe are currently facing.

Four major global BPO destinations have been identified: (1) Asia Pacific, (2) Central and Eastern Europe, (3) Latin America and (4) Middle East and North Africa. Several challenges can be identified, such as specialisation, automation, public institution outsourcing and freelance outsourcing.

Keywords Outsourcing • Offshoring • Central and Eastern Europe • Business process outsourcing • BPO

Introduction

Outsourcing can be defined as the transfer of any task outside of the organisation, while business process outsourcing (BPO) pertains to transferring business processes. Once managers identify processes in the company, they can then indicate those which are not related to core operations and, based on economic analysis, they decide what can be transferred to third parties.

Business process outsourcing is a relatively new economic phenomenon. The first BPO projects were executed in the early 1990s. Then American companies started collaborating with Indian IT companies. Since then BPO market is growing

---

P. Dziurski (✉)
SGH Warsaw School of Economics, Warsaw, Poland
e-mail: patryk.dziurski@doktorant.sgh.waw.pl

rapidly at a considerable growth rate. Consequently, business process outsourcing is an important topic and all in-deep analyses are desirable.

The author formulates two aims of the chapter. The first aim is to identify global business process outsourcing destinations and compare two major locations (Central and Eastern Europe and Middle East and North Africa). The second aim is to indicate key challenges faced by BPO providers in Central and Eastern Europe.

The Essence of Outsourcing

According to the *Harvard Business Review*, outsourcing has been one of the most important management concepts for the past 75 years (Gay and Essinger 2002). Majchrzak (2012) points out that General Motors initially used outsourcing in delivering car components, but the first outsourcing contract was signed in 1963 between Electronic Data System and Frito-Lay. However, outsourcing was used even earlier than that. In the Middle Ages, royal families delegated education to monks and Napoleon outsourced ammunition deliveries to private companies (Grudzewski and Hejduk 2004). Despite the fact that outsourcing is a relatively new concept, it was actually present in the business reality well before it was named and described by scholars. Mass interest in outsourcing arose in the 1970s of the last century (Trocki 2001). Since then outsourcing has constantly been evolving. More and more companies decide to transfer some of their functions to third parties, which are specialised in one or few areas.

Outsourcing can be defined as a transfer of any task outside of the organisation (Power et al. 2008). The opposite of outsourcing is insourcing, which means that managers are incorporating an external function into their organisational structure (Trocki 2001). Outsourcing refers to outside-resource-using (Majchrzak 2012). Resources, tangible as well as intangible, which are identified as core competencies, should be kept in-house in order to gain and sustain a permanent source of competitive advantage. Other resources (non-core competences), depending on economic analyses, can be outsourced or kept in-house (Romanowska 2009). Companies outsource non-core competencies, when the cost of owning them is higher than cost of buying.

Outsourcing is an umbrella term including onshoring, nearshoring and offshoring. Differences between those terms are presented in Table 1. The table is not exhaustive; more delimitation propositions are presented in papers of Carmel and Tjia (2007), Majchrzak (2012), as well as Zarzycka and Michalak (2013).

Outsourcing is a project involving both the client and the provider, whereby parties should closely work together (Power et al. 2008). It is not only a one-time transaction, but it is a long-term collaboration. At the client side, Lacity et al. (2009: 142) correctly state that "outsourcing is not about giving up management, but managing in a different way" and creating durable relations. At a provider's side, client's cost savings, which can be crucial at the beginning of collaboration, are not

Table 1 Outsourcing and interconnected terms

Geographical location of outsourced function		
In-country localisation	Out-country localisation; close physical proximity	Out-country localisation; far physical proximity
Onshoring	Nearshoring	Offshoring

Source: Micek et al. (2009)

sufficient to sustain a long-term relationship. Clients, especially after the first period of collaboration, require high quality service (Colliers International 2014), which can be accomplished by maintaining close interrelations between both sides. Clients, as well as providers, have to take into consideration long-term benefits instead of short-term profits (Phelps and Fleischer 2002), or otherwise outsourcing may not be beneficial. Mucisko and Lum (2005) show that 70 % of outsourcing clients had negative experiences with outsourcing. Atesci et al. (2010: 277) point out that "there have been several well-known success stories in the history of this topic (...) Yet, outsourcing deals frequently fail and instead of bringing expected advantages, the clients end up in messier situation than before they began".

Companies, which transferred some of their functions outside of their boundaries, can gain multiple benefits—from operational to strategic gains (Lacity and Rottman 2008). Lacity et al. (2008) report that in most instances companies achieve operational benefits and only some of them gain strategic ones. The 2004 Outsourcing World Submit states that a significant part of companies decide to do outsourcing due to cost reduction (40 % of respondents). Most of motives referred to potential operational gains and only two of them (to improve focus and innovation) referred to strategic benefits (Corbett 2004). Trocki (2001) indicates that outsourcing has been seen as a method of cost reduction, at first. Subsequently, it has been used as an effective way of limiting the technological risk. Next, outsourcing has helped managers to focus on their core operations. More recently, outsourcing has been considered as a strategic operation, what is supported by conclusions of Lacity et al. (2008). Many companies treat outsourcing as a strategic operation, but also many companies used it mainly for cost reduction, particularly at the beginning of the collaboration, as mentioned above.

Laudicina et al. (2014), consultants at A.T. Kearney, present a different approach to outsourcing evolution. They identified three waves of outsourcing which appeared sequentially, but recently they "are all acting on concert" (Laudicina et al. 2014: 1). The first wave (offshoring) started in the early 1990s to offshore information technology projects to Ireland and India (Szukalski 2007), which was strengthening in the late 1990s by intercontinental telecommunication improvement. The second wave is outsourcing (as named by A.T. Kearney), which begun in the mid-2000s. Outsourcing projects, which were previously the firm's own offshore investments, started being executed by specialised third parties (offshore, as well as onshore). The third wave started recently and it is referred to the automation and "no location" approach. Technological advancement has enabled replacement of human beings by machines (e.g. voice machine in call centres) in simple performing tasks. Additionally, freelance outsourcing is emerging (Laudicina et al. 2014). Standardisation and precise description of many in-house jobs flourished companies' offshoring to low-cost developing countries, then outsourcing to third parties and now it has enabled them to automatise increasing number of tasks. A client's geographical expansion and perceiving BPO as a strategic operation allow for global destinations, as well as different forms of outsourcing (e.g. business process outsourcing, knowledge process outsourcing) to emerge, which is going to be discussed in the ensuing part.

Definition of Business Process Outsourcing

Business process outsourcing (BPO) "is a subset of outsourcing that involves contracting of operations and responsibilities of specific business functions (or processes) to a third-party service provider" (von Rosing et al. 2015: 657–658). In other words, BPO is about transferring non-core business processes to a service provider (Duening and Click 2005). Business process outsourcing has many similarities with a strategic outsourcing. Building and sustaining long-term relationships is an essential prerequisite to succeeding within both processes. Clients have to correctly describe all processes, while a provider is obliged to constant improvement (PARP 2010). Different kinds of processes can be identified in companies: those well established, like procurement, as well as those newly emerging, such as social media management. Nonetheless, seven common business process categories are often being distinguished (Halvey and Melby 2007):

- human resources,
- finance and accounting,
- investments and assets management,
- procurement,
- logistic,
- real estate management,
- miscellaneous.

Business process outsourcing can apply to all of these processes. However, Borman (2006) indicates that BPO best suits processes, which are well defined, easily described, self-contained, easy measurable, modular and IT-enabled.

Business process outsourcing is often divided into two types: (1) back office outsourcing, which includes processes such as pay rolling, billing etc.; (2) front office outsourcing, which includes processes such as tech service, post sale service etc. (von Rosing et al. 2015). Another BPO classification is based on the type of process. For instance, business process outsourcing includes:

- ITO or ITES-BPO (information technology outsourcing or information technology enabled services)—a type of centre contracts IT operations, such as

- software, network and server management, as well as preparing engineering projects (Szukalski 2008);
- KPO (knowledge process outsourcing)—a type of centre contracts processes, which involve advanced knowledge and high qualification (Majchrzak 2012), like advanced market analysis;
- R&D (research and development)—a type of centre involves products/service development or improvement of existing ones (Żuchniewicz et al. 2014);
- RPO (recruitment process outsourcing)—a type of centre contracts recruitment processes;
- Call/Contact centre—an entity specialised in front office processes, which require contacts with payer's clients in the filed of e.g. tech assistance, complaint services and market research;
- OFC (offshore financial centre)—a type of centre that contracts financial services (Majchrzak 2012), which has been firstly involved in taxation processes (Halvey and Melby 2007), then in more advanced activities such as financial analysis and planning and management financial resources (ABSL 2010).

It seems that all types of BPO are well distinguished, however overlaps can appear (e.g. financial analysis can be contracted by KPO and OFC). Moreover, presented classification is not universal. In a lot of research, ITO is not included as a subset of BPO, but it is indicated as a different form of outsourcing (e.g. Atesci et al. 2010; Colliers International 2014; Lacity et al. 2009). It is worth pointing out that "the line between IT and BPO is blurring as players offer bundled and specialised services to their clients and develop skills in niche domains such as healthcare and telecommunications, where sector-specific knowledge is crucial" (Laudicina et al. 2014: 4). Additionally, BPO projects are executed by third parties, which are not capital-related with clients (named BPO centres or ITO centres), or in shared service centres (SSC), which are independent companies separated from the parent firm (Majchrzak 2012; Micek et al. 2009). This distinction is taken into account in some studies, as well. The used of a variety of classifications in extant research, however, impaired comparisons and analyses of dynamics across different studies.

Methodology

The Author's research focuses on global business process outsourcing destinations. To meet the previously stated two aims of the chapter, the Author applies an appropriate methodology. The research method is a critical analysis of academic, as well as business literature (desk research) supported by the author's own observations.

Selecting an outsourcing location for clients, as well as providers, is one of the most challenging decisions. Generally, providers and clients make their decisions based on location attractiveness. Additionally, clients take into consideration provider attractiveness. Several frameworks for selecting BPO destinations have been developed in the existing academic and professional literature (Oshri et al. 2009). Details of proposals are very differentiated. Some proposals are more detailed (e.g. Laudicina et al. 2014; Carmel 2003; Farrell 2006) than others (e.g. Żuchniewicz et al. 2014; Colliers International and A.T. Kearny 2010; Cushman & Wakefield 2013, 2015) in terms of the number of included factors. Some similarities can be observed; "all of these frameworks consider costs, business environment, availability of labour resources, and specific skills" (Oshri et al. 2009: 33). In the paper, the comparison of global BPO destinations consists of three characteristics: the closest markets, scale of operations and core competencies. The comparison of CEE and Middle Eastern and North African countries is conducted based on a six-factor framework proposed by Farrell (2006) and supported by Oshri et al. (2009). It consists of the following categories: costs, availability of skills, environment, quality of infrastructure, risk profile, market potential.

Global BPO Destinations

Von Rosing et al. (2015) report that global business process outsourcing market surpassed $950 billion in 2014–2015; the expected average growth rate to 2018 is 5 % year-to-year. The largest part of the market is the IT-related segment (IT professional segment; IT infrastructure; other IT service) which accounts for $578 billion; the BPO-related segment accounts for $262 billion. According to Cushman & Wakefield (2015), the BPO market is worth over $100 billion in annual contract value; its growth rate exceeds 5 %.

A lot of different BPO location rankings (or, more generally, outsourcing location rankings which contain business process outsourcing, as well) are prepared and published. International corporations, such as A.T. Kearney, Colliers International, Jones Lang LaSalle and Cushman & Wakefield, have published most of them. Some analyses are not done on a regular basis. A.T. Kearney, and recently also Cushman & Wakefield prepare regular analyses.

In 2014 A.T. Kearney published the sixth edition of the Global Service Location Index (GSLI). Countries ranked in the GSLI have been evaluated against 43 measurements across three main categories: financial attractiveness—40 % of the total weight in the index, people and skills availability—30 % of the total weight in the index, and business environment—30 % of the total weight in the index (Laudicina et al. 2014). In 2013 Cushman & Wakefield prepared the first BPO Location Index, which was reiterated in 2015 as the BPO and Shared Service Location Index. Authors have evaluated countries based on the same 17 measurements grouped in three major categories: conditions—30 % of the total weight in the index, risk—20 % of the total weight in the index, costs—50 % of the total weight in the index; they noted that weight of specific measurements changed compare to 2013 index (Cushman & Wakefield 2013, 2015). In both rankings the main emphasis has been

Table 2 Analysis of business process outsourcing destinations

Examples of destinations	Asia Pacific	Latin America	Central and Eastern Europe	Middle East and North Africa
GLSI 2015[a]/ BPO and Shared Service Location Index 2015[b]	India 1[a]/20[b]; China 2/10; Malaysia 3/6; Indonesia 5/-[c]; Thailand 6/-[c]; Philippines 7/2; Sri Lanka 16/12; Bangladesh 26/-[c]	Mexico 4/24; Brazil 8/8; Chile 13/14; Costa Rica 24/21	Bulgaria 9/3; Poland 11/18; Lithuania 15/11; Romania 18/4; Latvia 23/-[c]; Czech Republic 33/17; Hungary 31/9; Slovakia 35/-[c]	Egypt 10/-[c]; Tunisia 28/-[c]; Morocco 34/13; Mauritius 36/-[c]
The closest markets	Japan; Korea; Australia; China; India	USA; Canada	Western Europe	Western Europe
Scale of operations	Global markets	North America markets	European markets	European markets
Core competencies	– Low costs – English language proficiencies – Providers' maturity – Large poll of skilled labour	– Spanish language proficiencies – Cultural affinity with North America – Large poll of skilled labour	– European languages proficiencies – Educated workforce – Good infrastructure	– Low costs – Relationships with ex-colonizers

Source: Own elaboration
[a]Country position in the ranking of A.T. Kearney Global Services Location Index™ 2014 (see more: Laudicina et al. 2014)
[b]Country position in the ranking of BPO and Shared Service Location Index 2015 (see more: Cushman & Wakefield 2015)
[c]Country is not classified in the ranking of BPO and Shared Service Location Index 2015

put on financial aspects, but A.T. Kearney has concentrated more on the general business environment and Cushman & Wakefield has rather focused on macroeconomics aspects.

Taking into account the most valuable BPO location indices (A.T. Kearney Global Services Location Index™ 2014 and the BPO and Shared Service Location Index 2015), the author points out that four global BPO centres emerged: Asia Pacific, Central and Eastern Europe, Latin America and Middle East and North Africa. Detailed characteristics of the said regions are presented in Table 2.

The leader of global business process outsourcing is Asia Pacific with the greatest number of countries in many rankings, including India with around 43 % of share in the global BPO market (Oshri et al. 2009). The region offers a significant diversity: from emerging new destinations (e.g. Bangladesh) with low labour costs and specialisation in simple processes through established players (e.g. Malaysia and Philippines) with good economics and business fundamentals to mature localisations (e.g. India) specialising in more advanced processes such as voice services (Laudicina et al. 2014), advanced business analysis (Kubicka 2010) and KPO (Jorek et al. 2009).

The next three destinations are smaller than Asia Pacific. Latin America is an established location for BPO projects from North America and specialised in not-advanced processes as well as knowledge-intensive tasks (Jorek et al. 2009). The next important destination is Middle East and North Africa with increasing significance. The fourth location is Central and Eastern Europe. According to Colliers International (2014), 30 % of the top 100 global outsourcing companies are located in the CEE. According to Żuchniewicz et al. (2014) more than 1000 centres are located in the CEE region. In 2014 companies operating in the outsourcing industry in Europe employed 3.8 million people; sector was worth 67 billion euros; 17.9 % accounted for BPO with 3.6 % annual growth (Blanaru 2015). Significant numbers of companies operating in CEE are specialised in IT-related processes (46 % of overall employment). Fewer companies are focusing on financial services—23 % of overall employment, energy and industrial—18 % of overall employment—and professional services sector—13 % of overall employment (Żuchniewicz et al. 2014). Companies in Central and Eastern Europe, as well as in Middle East and North Africa are main partners for companies form Western Europe in executing BPO projects (compare: Colliers International & A.T. Kearney 2010; Lacity et al. 2008). It looks that the CEE and Middle East and North Africa compete for projects from Western Europe.

In order to indicate similarities and differences between regions, a detailed analysis is required. Its results are presented in Table 3.

Comparative advantages for Middle East and North Africa mostly pertain to lower labour costs and a large pool of workforce. Additionally, in the Middle East (e.g. Pakistan) freelance outsourcing is emerging (Laudicina et al. 2014; Lacity et al. 2008). Moreover, comparative advantages are also related to good quality of infrastructure and government incentives. The main disadvantages of the region include political instability (increasing general risk since the Arab Spring), low attractiveness of local markets, or corruption and red tape. In contrast, countries in the CEE region have constantly improved conditions of doing business—a constant improvement in World Bank's Doing Business reports (see more: World Bank Group 2014, 2015). CEE countries mostly have a favourable share of well-educated people in the total population, but—interestingly—this percentage is lower than in the Middle East and North Africa. A huge advantage is access to people with desirable skills and proficiency in European languages. The supply of office space is at a high level with good quality standards. Physical proximity and cultural affinity to Western Europe are major pros, as well. It seems that the Middle East and North Africa are less developed than Central and Eastern Europe, but the distance is constantly decreasing. This development can be hindered by recent terrorism attracts, effects of the Arab Spring mainly causing general instability, and the evolution of the Islamic State. However, providers located in CEE countries have to strengthen their comparative advantage, look for new opportunities and minimise effects of treats.

Table 3 Characteristics of CEE and Middle East and North Africa countries

Category	Subcategory	Characteristics[a]	
		CEE countries[b]	Middle East and North Africa countries[c]
Costs	Labour cost	Average wages for skilled workers and managers lower than in Western Europe, USA and Canada, but higher than in North Africa and Middle East as well as Asia Systematic labour cost increase	Average wages for skilled workers and managers lower than in Western Europe, USA and Canada as well as CEE countries Systematic labour cost increase (but still lower compared to CEE countries)
	Infrastructure cost	Low cost of telecom networks, internet access and power Medium cost of office rent (higher in capitals and major cities)	Low cost of telecom networks, internet access and power Low cost of office rent
	Corporate taxes	Preferential tax policy Supporting new BPO investments	Preferential tax policy (higher incentives than in the CEE) Supporting new BPO investments
Availability of skills	Skill pool	Large and well-educated workforce with desirable skills, but fewer graduates compared to Asia and North Africa Lack of management skills	Large pool of under-educated people living in the rural area; the percentage of population that it being well-educated in higher than in the CEE region Lack of management skills
	Provider landscape	Well-developed local sector providing IT services and other business functions	Developing local sector providing IT services and other business functions
Environment	Governance support	Wide pool of business incentives Corruption and red tape as an issue	Wide pool of business incentives Corruption and red tape as an issue (higher than in the CEE region)
	Business environment	Cultural affinity with Western Europe and North America	Partial cultural affinity with Western Europe and North America, but relations with ex-colonisers remain strong
	Living environment	High attractiveness for expatriates	Low attractiveness for expatriates

(continued)

Table 3 (continued)

Category	Subcategory	Characteristics[a]	
		CEE countries[b]	Middle East and North Africa countries[c]
	Accessibility	High frequency (with good quality) of all type of transportation means Travel time and time differences is not an issue traveling within Europe	Medium frequency of all type of transcontinental transportation means Poor quality of intercontinental transportation means Travel time and time differences is not an issue traveling within Europe
Quality of infrastructure	Telecommunication and IT	Significant differences among CEE countries Constant improvement of quality of infrastructure	Good availability and quality of telecommunication and IT infrastructure
	Real estate	Availability of office space; constant expanding office space High standard of office space	Availability of office space; constant expanding office space High standard of office space
	Transportation	Developed and mostly well-maintained road, rail and air network Well-developed public transportation	Developed and mostly well-maintained road, rail and air network (only in outsourcing centres) Lack of public transportation (transport organised by companies itself)
	Power	Reliability of power supply	Reliability of power supply
Risk profile	Security	Low risk to terrorism Medium risk to fraud and crime	High risk to terrorism High risk to fraud and crime
	Disruptive events	Low risk to labour uprising Medium risk to political unrest and natural disasters	Low risk to labour uprising High risk to political unrest Low risk to natural disasters
	Regulatory risk	High stability Medium fairness and efficiency of legal framework	Medium stability Medium fairness and efficiency of legal framework
	Macroeconomic risk	Mostly good macroeconomic situation Capital freedom	Mostly medium macroeconomic situation Capital freedom
	Intellectual property risk	Medium standard of intellectual property protection	Low standard of intellectual property protection
Market potential	Attractiveness of local market	Lucrative local market	Low attractiveness of local market

(continued)

Table 3 (continued)

Category	Subcategory	Characteristics[a]	
		CEE countries[b]	Middle East and North Africa countries[c]
	Access to nearby markets	Easy access to other European countries and the EU trade partners	Easy access to other North Africa and Middle East countries (low attractiveness of those markets)

Source: Own elaboration
[a]It is a general characteristic of countries in analysed regions; differences between countries can occur
[b]CEE countries—Bulgaria, Czech Republic, Hungary, Latvia, Lithuania, Poland, Romania and Slovakia
[c]Middle East and North Africa countries—Egypt, Tunisia, Morocco, Mauritius, Jordan, United Arab Emirates, Pakistan

To sum up, four analysed regions have different expansion areas, besides the CEE, Middle East and North Africa. Each of the analysed regions has different core competencies, which allows them to gain different clients and develop different specialisation. However, one significant trend can be indicated, countries, becoming more mature, turn to executing more advanced processes and start focusing on knowledge process outsourcing.

Key Challenges in CEE Region

The Author identified four key challenges faced by providers in Central and Eastern Europe. The first huge challenge for providers is a technological change (compare: Żuchniewicz et al. 2014; Colliers International 2014; Laudicina et al. 2014). The positive aspect is that many providers have moved to executing more advanced processes—e.g. "software and service" projects; web/cloud platforms (Colliers International 2014), however it is not a direct result of technological change but a market requirement. Cost savings are not enough, clients require constant improvement in the service offering and adding value to them. As a result, more and more companies specialised in more advanced processes. They have been moved up the value chain and lured more complex jobs (Lacity and Rottman 2008; Żuchniewicz et al. 2014; Colliers International 2014). The negative side is that machines instead of people perform many basic BPO processes—e.g. monitor financial transaction, voice machine (Colliers International 2014; Żuchniewicz et al. 2014). It is also worth to point out that more advanced tasks can be automatised. For instance, the Watson IBM machine has learnt medical diagnosis (see more: http://www.ibm.com/smarterplanet/us/en/ibmwatson/. Accessed 25 June 2015).

It is highly likely, that localisations with a well developed and maintained IT infrastructure as well as high technological skills are going to be more significant in future; CEE has a chance to become the location that meets indicated prerequisites, but it requires constant improvement. On one hand, automation is going to reduce a number of physical staff, but on the other hand it is going to result in an execution of more complex and higher value-added services (compare: Żuchniewicz et al. 2014). It does not mean that all business processes are going to be automatised, some of them are going be to performed by human beings. Taking into consideration specialisation and automation trends, it is possible that "less complex and lower cost outsourcing services will migrate to cheaper locations within CEE such as Bulgaria or Romania. These services will most probably be replaced by higher value-added services" (Żuchniewicz et al. 2014: 7) in mature locations. Moreover, secondary and tertiary locations are gaining popularity within CEE countries such as Lublin, Bydgoszcz, Ostrava, Debrecen and Cracov (Żuchniewicz et al. 2014). Summarising, it is not expected that CEE countries are going to lose significant number of projects for other BPO destinations, but shifts within regions are predicted.

The next significant challenge is a business process outsourcing for public institutions (compare: Żuchniewicz et al. 2014; Colliers International & A.T. Kearney 2010). Governments of developed countries such as USA and the Netherlands have been using BPO for a long time, but among CEE countries it is still not common (Cydejko and Krukowska 2010). Firstly, providers should convince governments and societies to business process outsourcing. Secondly, due a high complexity of outsourced projects (not only cost reduction and quality improvement, but also maximising capacity to deliver public services), providers should develop a more complex approach. Public institution BPO can close the gap that will result from automation.

The next challenge is freelance outsourcing. It means that "individuals offer their talents globally, primarily through freelance internet sites" (Lacity et al. 2008: 15)—e.g. elance.com; freelancer.com; upwork.com. In 2007, the freelance outsourcing market was worth $250 million and in 2015 it is expected to be $2 billion (Aggarwal 2007). It means that a lot of people, most often young professionals, have entered the BPO market. For instance, part of IT-related tasks are outsourced to freelance programmers, who very often work under a contract as well; freelance jobs are an additional income for them. Companies, not only from the CEE region, have to compete with new types of competitors that are not location-bound (no-location approach from A.T. Kearney), but can offer their services around the world almost without any limits. This situation is also common in different sectors. It seems that some business processes cannot be outsourced to freelancers, but this assumption cannot be upheld in view of innovative business models. It is hard to imagine that for example a call centre operation can be outsourced to an independent individual professional, but in fact it already happened. For instance, low-fare airlines called JetBlue outsourced their entire booking system to housewives in Utah, USA. Individuals, through the internet platform, served airlines' clients in their free time (see: Friedman 2007). To sum up, established companies have to learn how to compete with new entrants, or how to use these resources for their own benefits, but it requires implementation of innovative business models.

Conclusion

The outsourcing concept has been present for over 40 years at a global level and for over 10 years in Europe, and it continues to be treated as one of the most important management concepts. Business process outsourcing is a younger concept, but it is now becoming a well-established phenomenon, as well. BPO has significantly evolved over years. A client's geographical expansion and perceiving BPO as a strategic operation allowed for global BPO destinations as well as different forms of BPO to emerge.

Four major global BPO destinations have been identified: Asia Pacific, Central and Eastern Europe, Latin America and Middle East and North Africa. Indicated regions have different expansion area, besides CEE and Middle East and North Africa, which are focused on Western Europe. Each of regions has different core competencies, which allows them to gain different clients and develop different specialisations. However, one significant trend can be indicated, in that as countries become more mature, they turn to executing more advanced processes and start focusing on knowledge process outsourcing.

In this chapter, the Author concentrates on the bigger picture of business process outsourcing in Central and Eastern Europe and Author does not looks into details, which is a main limitation of the chapter. Therefore, further research should concentrate on companies, providers and clients, on macro- as well as micro level. Marco level researches should focus on clients' decisions about outsourcing direction and regions/countries' ways of attracting them. Micro-level analyses should concentrate on the clients' decisions about choosing particular providers, as well as the providers' methods of attracting them.

References

ABSL. (2010). *Sektor SSC/BPO w Polsce*. Accessed October 20, 2010, from http://www.absl.pl/c/document_library/get_file?uuid=657b9691-9a09-4684-bf89-006238f286dd&groupId=10155

Aggarwal, A. (2007). *Person-to-person offshoring. Offshoring of services reaches small business and homes*. Accessed June 10, 2015, from http://www.evalueserve.com/uploads/tx_arxdownload/Evalueserve_White_Paper_-_Person-to-Person_Offshoring_-_June_2007.pdf

Atesci, K., Bhagwatwar, A., Deo, T., Desouza, K. C., & Baloh, P. (2010). Business process outsourcing: A case study of Satyam Computers. *International Journal of Information Management, 30*, 277–282.

Blanaru, C. (2015). *30% of top 100 global outsourcing companies are in CEE*. Accessed June 10, 2015, from http://www.adhugger.net/2015/04/30/30-of-top-100-global-outsourcing-companies-are-in-cee/

Borman, M. (2006). Applying multiple perspective to the BPO decision: A case study of call centers in Australia. *Journal of Information Technology, 21*, 99–115.

Carmel, E. (2003). The new software exporting nations: Success factors. *Electronic Journal on Information Systems in Developing Countries, 13*(4), 1–12.

Carmel, E., & Tjia, P. (2007). *Offshoring information technology: Sourcing and outsourcing to a global workforce*. New York: Cambridge University Press.

Colliers International. (2014). *Outsourcing and offshoring in CEE: A rapidly changing landscape.* Accessed June 15, 2015, from http://www.colliers.com/-/media/Files/EMEA/Eastern Europeaninformation/2014EEResearch Page/Office/EE-2014-Outsourcing-and-Offshoring-Q2-2014

Colliers International & A.T. Kearny. (2010). *Improving through moving. BPO/SSC opportunities in Central and Eastern Europe.* Accessed October 20, 2010, from http://www.colliers.com/-/media/files/emea/easterneuropeaninformation/2014eeresearchpage/office/ee-2010-bpo-reportimproving-through-moving.pdf?la=en-gb

Corbett, M. F. (2004). *The outsourcing revolution. Why it makes sense and how to do it right.* New York: Kaplan Publishing.

Cushman & Wakefield. (2013). *Business process outsourcing location index.* Accessed June 10, 2015, from http://www.cushmanwakefield.com/~/media/global-reports/BPO%20Location%20Index%202013.pdf

Cushman & Wakefield. (2015). *Where is the world. Business process outsourcing and shared service location index.* Accessed June 10, 2015, from http://www.cushmanwakefield.com/~/media/global-reports/Where%20In%20The%20World_Business%20Process%20Outsourcing_low_2015.pdf

Cydejko, G., & Krukowska, M. (2010). *Funkcje państwa – wyprowadzić.* Accessed October 20, 2010, from http://www.forbes.pl/artykuly/sekcje/sekcja-dossier/funkcje-panstwa---wyprowadzic,3378,1

Duening, T. N., & Click, R. L. (2005). *Essentials of business process outsourcing.* Hoboken, NJ: Wiley.

Farrell, D. (2006). Smarter offshoring. *Harvard Business Review, June*, 84–92.

Friedman, T. (2007). *The world is flat. A brief history of the twenty-first century.* New York: Farrar, Straus and Giroux.

Gay, C. L., & Essinger, J. (2002). *Outsourcing strategiczny. Koncepcja, modele i wdrożenie.* Kraków: Oficyna Ekonomiczna.

Grudzewski, W. M., & Hejduk, I. K. (2004). *Metody projektowania systemów zarządzania.* Warszawa: Difin.

Halvey, J. K., & Melby, B. M. (2007). *Business process outsourcing. Process, strategies and contracts.* Hoboken, NJ: Wiley.

Jorek, N., Gott, J., & Battat, M. (2009). *The shifting geography of offshoring. A.T. Kearney Global Services Location Index™ 2009.* Accessed June 20, 2015, from https://www.atkearney.com/documents/10192/fda82529-b60a-4fae-8d92-22cfd69b95b3

Kubicka, J. (2010). *Rozwój gospodarczy Chin w dobie globalizacji – wybrane aspekty.* Katowice: Wydawnictwo Akademii Ekonomicznej w Katowicach.

Lacity, M. C., Khan, S. A., & Willcocks, L. P. (2009). A review of the IT outsourcing literature: Insights for practice. *Journal of Strategic Information Systems, 18*, 130–146.

Lacity, M. C., & Rottman, J. W. (2008). *Offshore outsourcing of IT work.* Basingstoke: Palgrave.

Lacity, M. C., Willcocks, L. P., & Rottman, J. W. (2008). Global outsourcing of back office services: Lessons, trends, and enduring challenges. *Strategic Outsourcing: An International Journal, 1*(1), 13–34.

Laudicina, P., Gott, J., & Peterson, E. (2014). *The 2014 A.T. Kearney Global Service Location Index. A wealth of choices: From anywhere on earth to no location at all.* Back-office services are now embarking on a third wave of arbitrage, as automation becomes simpler. Accessed June 12, 2015, from https://www.atkearney.de/documents/856314/5132494/BIP_A+Wealth+of+Choices.pdf/8fa1d356-f8cf-4aa3-934a-dc54790ba316

Majchrzak, M. (2012). *Konkurencyjność przedsiębiorstw podsektora usług biznesowych w Polsce. Perspektywa mikro-, mezo- i makroeknomiczna.* Warszawa: CeDeWu.PL.

Micek, G., Działek, J., & Górecki, J. (2009). *Centra usług w Krakowie i ich relacja z otoczeniem lokalnym.* Kraków: Wydawnictwo Uniwersytetu Jagiellońskiego.

Mucisko, D., & Lum, E. (2005, April). *Outsourcing falling from favor with world's largest organizations.* Deloitte Consulting LLP Report.

Oshri, I., Kotlarsky, J., & Willcocks, L. P. (2009). *The handbook of global outsourcing and offshoring*. Basingstoke: Palgrave Macmillan.
PARP. (2010). *Realizacja procesów B2B z wykorzystaniem technologii ICT*. Accessed May 12, 2011, from https://www.web.gov.pl/g2/big/2010_09/79ca4a2cb8c5af87b815fe48d0ced981.pdf
Phelps, T., & Fleischer, M. (2002). *Strategic outsourcing. Decision guidebook*. Accessed March 10, 2010, from http://down.cenet.org.cn/upfile/21/2008821211413109.pdf
Power, M. J., Desouza, K. C., & Bonifazi, C. (2008). *Outsourcing: podręcznik sprawdzonych praktyk*. Warszawa: MT Biznes.
Romanowska, M. (2009). *Planowanie strategiczne w przedsiębiorstwie* (2nd ed.). Warszawa: PWE.
Szukalski, S. M. (2007). Transgraniczny transfer usług biznesowych. Potencjał i szanse polskiej gospodarki. *Acta Universitatis Lodziensis Folia Oeconomica, 213*, 107–123.
Szukalski, S. M. (2008). Chiny i Indie na globalnym rynku usług. Stan i perspektywy. In K. Kłosiński (Ed.), *Chiny-Indie Ekonomiczne skutki rozwoju* (pp. 49–68). Lubin: Wydawnictwo KUL.
Trocki, M. (2001). *Outsourcing: metoda restrukturyzacji działalności gospodarczej*. Warszawa: PWE.
Von Rosing, M., Doucet, G., Jansson, G. O., Von Scheel, G., Stoffel, F., Bach, B., Kuil, H., & Waters, J. (2015). Business process outsourcing. In M. Von Rosing, A. W. Scheer, & H. Von Schee (Eds.), *The complete business process handbook. Body of knowledge from process modeling to BPM* (Vol. 1, pp. 657–670). Waltham, MA: Elsevier.
World Bank Group. (2014). *Doing Business 2015. Understanding regulations for small and medium-size enterprises*. Accessed June 10, 2015, from http://www.doingbusiness.org/~/media/GIAWB/Doing%20Business/Documents/Annual-Reports/English/DB14-Full-Report.pdf
World Bank Group. (2015). *Doing Business 2015. Going beyond efficiency*. Accessed June 10, 2015, from http://www.doingbusiness.org/~/media/GIAWB/Doing%20Business/Documents/Annual-Reports/English/DB15-Full-Report.pdf
Zarzycka, E., & Michalak, M. (2013). Centra usług wspólnych (SSC) jako forma organizacji procesów rachunkowości – wyzwania dla praktyki i badań naukowych. *Zeszyty Naukowe Studia i Prace Kolegium Zarządzania i Finansów, 130*, 182–207.
Żuchniewicz, M., Colquhoun, A., Wykrota, K., Przesmycka, B., Cihova, K., Boucek, V., et al. (2014). *Outsourcing sector in key CEE markets*. Accessed June 10, 2015, from http://www.outsourcingportal.pl/pl/userfiles/image/raporty/2014/12/17/Outsourcing_sector_in_key_CEE_markets.pdf

Part II
Firm-Level Developments

Contrasting Methods: An Explorative Investigation on Firm-Level Export Competitiveness Based on Qualitative and Quantitative Research Findings

Erzsébet Czakó, Péter Juhász, and László Reszegi

Abstract Exports and exporting firms have long been studied in the fields of both international business (IB) and competitiveness. While IB concentrates on the performance of firms and, within this scope of interest, on the processes from a company or managerial perspective, the competitiveness stream has primarily focused on country-level implications from the point of view of policy making. Qualitative studies are frequent in IB research, while quantitative methods have been more widespread in competitiveness research. The novelty of this work is to use both types of research in relation to the same population in order to compare findings. Based on the notion that the qualitative and quantitative research are complementary, this paper investigates how SME performance can be assessed based on financial performance patterns and what conclusions can be drawn for competitiveness at firm and national levels. An explorative qualitative research — where financial figures were also collected — was performed in the case of ten Hungarian small- and medium-sized enterprises (SMEs) to discover the processes and mechanisms of export excellence. A quantitative research was performed to explore the financial performance patterns of privately-owned companies in Hungary. Findings show that export intensive SMEs are amongst the financially high performing Hungarian firms. Based on qualitative research findings, we propose that outstanding management, continuous learning and innovation — also frequent in competitiveness narratives — may be the factors explaining the success of such firms.

Keywords Export • Financial Performance • Internationalisation • SMEs • Profitability • Domestic and foreign firms

---

E. Czakó (✉) • P. Juhász • L. Reszegi
Corvinus University of Budapest, Budapest, Hungary
e-mail: erzsebet.czako@uni-corvinus.hu; peter.juhasz@uni-corvinus.hu; laszlo.reszegi@businesskft.hu

Introduction

The year 2015 marked the 25th anniversary of the publication of Michael Porter's (1990) book, which has played a key role in advocating competitiveness research worldwide. While the book has sparked off academic and professional debates, it is indisputable fact that Porter put firms into the centre of competitiveness discourses and investigations, resulted in a seminal contribution to research on competitiveness. The observations of business reality and anecdotal evidence justify this approach in a more promising way than the mere theoretical advancements.

Competitiveness is interpreted in a number of ways — practically every international (e.g. EU Commission, World Economic Forum), national (e.g. government agencies), and academic organisation has elaborated their own specific definition (Chikán and Czakó 2010). Comparing these definitions it can be proposed that competitiveness is a multi-tier construct, whereby investigations focus on one or more units of economic performance, e.g. that of firms, industries, clusters, national economies, macro-regions, and global value chains in international comparison. There are also common research questions in competitiveness inquiries and investigations, for example: (1) what is the economic performance; (2) what is the potential for the future economic performance, and (3) what contextual factors may have an impact on the future economic performance. Investigations devoted to competitiveness are diverse and the selected performance and/or units of the analysis set the base and framework for academic and professional investigations.

Competitiveness research in Hungary relies on Chikán's (2008) definitions and concepts on firm and national competitiveness. His definition of national competitiveness corresponds with that of Scott (1985:14–15), which marked the 30th anniversary of its publication in 2015. Chikán claims that national competitiveness is "the capability of a national economy to operate ensuring an increasing welfare of its citizens with its factor productivity growing sustainably. This capability is realised through maintaining an environment for its companies and other institutions to create, utilize and sell goods and services that meet the requirements of global competitiveness and changing social norms" (Chikán 2008:25). For the purpose of our chapter we highlight the connections between national and firm level performance and select exports and exporting to match these. Chikán's definition of firm competitiveness is "the capability of a firm to sustainably fulfil its double purpose: meeting customer requirements at a profit. This capability is realised through offering goods and services at such a price that customers set a higher value on the given combination than those offered by competitors on the market. Achieving competitiveness requires a firm's continuous adaptation to changing social and economic norms and conditions". (Chikán 2008:24–25). In this chapter we focus on meeting customer requirements at a profit, which is quantifiable by financial performance measures (e.g. ROS). Capability is a common element in both definitions, and it is also a key term in competitiveness research in general, though it is the hardest element to measure. Matching qualitative and quantitative research findings is used to draw conclusions on internationalisation through export.

For the sake of the present chapter we consider exporting and export performance as proxies for competitiveness, whereby the units of analyses are the firms. Export competitiveness is a widely used proxy for competitiveness and is also a lens for investigating firm performance by quantitative and qualitative investigations, alike. A qualitative research was carried out to explore the processes and mechanisms in export intensive SMEs in Hungary and to conclude some critical success factors (Ábel and Czakó 2013). A quantitative research was conducted to describe performance patterns in internationalisation and reveal contributions to national competitiveness (Reszegi and Juhász 2014).

Based on the outcomes and findings, the present chapter investigates two questions: (1) how the exporting SMEs' financial performance can be evaluated based on the findings of quantitative research, and (2) what conclusions can be drawn from these results on competitiveness at firm and national levels. By using two different methodologies at the same time, we claim that quantitative and qualitative research are complementary by nature.

The paper is made up of four sections. The first two sections provide an overview of the core qualities of the two kinds of research that are in essence "lenses" through which we study the firms. The qualitative research lens section discusses the methodology, descriptive statistics and case study findings on ten export intensive Hungarian SMEs. In the paper, these firms will be referred to as export excellent firms (EEFs). At the end of this section, we present the propositions to be tested in the third section. Based on a far wider dataset, the second section provides a presentation of our quantitative research. The information presented was compiled from the publicly available financial reports of more than 4000 privately-owned enterprises in Hungary. This dataset will be referred to as the search of enterprise performance (SEP) sample. This section also provides an overview of the key findings of our analyses. In the third section the findings of the qualitative and quantitative research projects are matched and discussed, the key financial performance measures of the two research projects are compared. In practice, the financial measures of the EEFs will be plotted against SEP results. The aim of our study was to see and show how, based on SEP averages, EEFs can be positioned amongst the privately owned Hungarian enterprises. This section also relates to our first research question (1): whether EEFs can be categorised amongst the financially excellent firms. This section is descriptive and rich in financial measures, especially in ratios and may be of interest to academics and professionals working on financial performance. The last part entitled "Conclusions" interprets the obtained findings and formulates the limitations of the present study. It is also here that we assess our propositions and thus deal with our second research question (2).

The Qualitative Lens: In Search of Export Excellence — The EEF Sample and the Assessed Propositions

Two research projects were launched in parallel: a qualitative and a quantitative one to obtain insights into internationalisation and performance in 2012 (Ábel and Czakó 2013; Reszegi and Juhász 2014). The qualitative project included a review of the literature on internationalisation and was also based on ten EEF case studies. The key findings on internationalisation and its lessons for competitiveness were published by Czakó and Könczöl (2014). The internationalisation mechanisms were in focus of the interview-centric case studies and financial figures were also collected for further investigation. In this section we provide an overview of outcomes which serve as a basis for interpreting the findings of the plotting exercise.

All of the ten EEFs studied were owned by Hungarian investors, i.e. they were domestic or locally-owned firms, and they were founded in the market economy, i.e. after the 1989 regime transformation in Hungary. All of them were export-oriented with an export sales to sales revenue ratio higher than 25 %. They are headquartered in different parts of Hungary and they have diverse product scopes. Based on their number of employees (NoE), all are small and medium-sized enterprises. They represent five broadly defined industries (agriculture—A&P, machinery—B&G, car components—C&H, health care and pharmaceuticals—L, M,&S, and infocom services—E). Eight out of the ten were global from the beginning, or were international new ventures not only based on their export revenues figures, but also according to their founders' intentions. In 2011, the least experienced company (column 8) had 6 years', while the others had ≥ 10 years' exporting experience. Table 1 summarises the key facts on the ten EEFs.

Some of our originally formulated and tested propositions were based on the literature on internationalisation processes. The interview questions focused on the story of embarking on and being successful in internationalisation. Mind mapping technique was then used to distil common factors out of the ten case studies. With the mind mapping technique we explored critical success factors to apply these to the propositions and the managerial and policy implications. The findings of the ten EEF case studies supported the propositions on internationalisation (based on Johanson and Vahlne 1977, 2009), as well as the findings on the internationalisation of SMEs. The findings of Czakó and Könczöl (2014:73) useful from the point of view of this paper are as follows:

1. The role of the founder(s) and top level managers is the initiating and enabling factor of the internationalisation of SMEs.
2. Amongst the drivers of internationalisation, the supplier position is of the same importance as other national push factors (e.g. size of the market).
3. The strategic priorities of market development include the strategic partnership development with buyers.

Table 1 Key facts on the ten EEFs for year 2011

1	2	3	4	5	6	7	8	9	10	11
As referred to in the paper	Product scope	Year founded	NoE	SR (M HUF)	1st year of export	Export experience (years)	ER, (M HUF)	EI	VA/capita (M HUF)	Source
A	Feed premixes, concentrates, prestarter feeds for livestock	2001	118	15,496	2001	10	6939	62 %	17.689	Boda and Stocker (2013a)
B	Alumina-oxide industrial ceramic products	2000	135	1491	2000	11	1339	90 %	4.768	Kozma (2013)
C	High precision auto-motive parts with alumina die casting technology	1999	230	7897	1999	12	6030	76 %	5.202	Kiss (2013)
E	Designing, selling, installing and providing maintenance of CRM products	2000	38	649	2000	11	192	29 %	4.940	Tátrai (2013)
G	Grinding wheels and discs	2001	114	1566	2001	10	826	53 %	4.779	Juhász (2013)
H	Metal machined vehicle-industry components	2005	138	5822	2005	6	1910	33 %	9.900	Kazainé-Ónodi (2013a)
L	Pharmaceuticals for veterinary	1991	42	2880	1993	18	2010	70 %	20.200	Pecze (2013)
M	Human and preclinical imaging systems	1990	133	4736	1994	17	3041	64 %	11.900	Szántó (2013)
P	Oyster mushroom	1991	42	674	1991	20	513	76 %	2.029	Boda and Stocker (2013b)
S	Traumatologic, spine and dental implants	1996	218	2637	1996	15	1860	70 %	7.478	Szalay (2013)

Source: Czakó and Könczöl (2014:74) with re-edition and supplemented with facts from the ten EEF case studies. Further information is in Table 2.
NoE number of employees, *SR* sales revenues, *ER* export revenues, *EI* export intensity, *VA* value added

4. The geographical scope and foreign market entry modes are secondary in comparison with supplier position and strategic partnerships.

No proposition was formulated on learning, which is an inherent element of the internationalisation theory of Johanson and Vahlne (1977, 2009). We could identify learning as an inherent element of internationalisation in our research. The stories of all the ten EEF cases demonstrated conspicuously that learning is vital and embedded into the everyday operations in the internationalisation process. It was interesting to learn that searching for relevant knowledge, continuous learning and incremental innovation were dominant and integral elements in the attitude of both the founder(s), and the top-level managers in each case.

The collected financial figures and financial ratios calculated based on the former were presented in each of the case studies for two reasons. Firstly, in order to give orientation for readers on the size and performance of each company, and secondly to interpret them using the findings of the quantitative performance research project. From the outset, the sources of data and the calculation methods applied were identical for both the qualitative and the quantitative research. Table 2 provides the collected data and the figures calculated based on these data for both research projects.

The financial figures of the ten EEFs were also analysed within the qualitative research project. Its results did not provide any noteworthy pattern on financial performance of the given enterprises (Könczöl 2013). In Table 3 we summarise key figures and financial ratios (i.e. financial performance measures) of the EEFs for 2010 and 2011, respectively. These figures are inserted here to serve as a basis for interpreting the findings of the plotting exercise. The averages were calculated for the ten EEFs with the last two columns giving the minimum and maximum values. They are presented here to give an overview on the financial performance of

Table 2 Financial figures and ratios used for comparison

Abbreviation	Content	Measure	Source of data and/or their calculations
NoE	Number of employees	Persons	Financial reports by HAS[a]
SR	Sales revenues	M HUF[b]	Financial reports by HAS
ER	Export revenues	M HUF	Financial reports by HAS
EI	Export intensity	%	Calculated: ER/SR
PAT	Profit after taxes	M HUF	Financial reports by HAS
VA	Value added	M HUF	Calculated: EBITDA + wages and their contributions
ROS	Return on sales	%	Calculated: PAT/SR
VAOS	Value added content of the sales revenues	%	Calculated: VA/SR

[a]Publicly available complete financial reports compiled by the Hungarian Accounting Standards (HAS). The source was the www.e-beszamolo.hu government portal where all the Hungarian business entities publish their annual financial reports
[b]Values in HUF were used to compare and evaluate the order of magnitude. Based on data from the Hungarian National Bank, in 2011, the annual average exchange rate was HUF 279.21 for EUR, and HUF 200.94 for USD

Table 3 Key figures of the ten EEFs for comparison, 2010 and 2011

	2010	2011		2011	
	Average, N = 10		2011/2010	Min value	Max value
NoE—Number of employees	136.7	150.6	110 %	42	521
SR—Sales revenues, M HUF	3599.8	4385.0	122 %	649	7897
ER—Export revenues, M HUF	2310.8	2736.0	118 %	191	6029
EI—Export intensity (ER/SR), %	64 %	62 %	97 %	30 %	90 %
PAT—Profit after taxes, M HUF	448.9	419.4	93 %	3	870
PAT/capita, M HUF	3.3	2.8	85 %	0.1	20.7
VA—Value added, M HUF	1378.4	1354.5	98 %	175	2709
VA/capita—Value added per capita, M HUF	10.1	9.0	89 %	2.0	20.2
ROS—Return on Sales (PAT/SR), %	12 %	10 %	77 %	0.4 %	30 %
VAOS—VA/SR, %	38 %	31 %	81 %	13 %	62 %

Source: Czakó and Könczöl (2014:74), with re-edition and complemented figures from the ten EEF case studies

the ten EEFs, as well as to support the plotting exercise and the interpretation of its findings. Later on the data in Table 3 will be used and repeated by plotting them in the SEP performance landscape.

The plotting exercise is challenging for several reasons. There are ten EEFs to be assessed based on the results of a big dataset. For this reason, we decided to use propositions to facilitate the formulation of our conclusions. The International Business (IB) literature provides mixed results on the relationship between exporting and firm performance, and that of the foreign and domestic ownership and firm performance (Calof 1994; Dyker 2004; Hooly et al. 1996; Mayer and Ottaviano 2007; Singh 2009; Sullivan 1994). Based on international and the Hungarian research results (Kazainé Ónodi 2013b) and being aware of the figures in Table 3, we formulated the following propositions:

Proposition 1 (P1). The foreign-owned firms have better average financial performance measures than the domestic, locally-owned ones. The average financial performance of foreign-owned firms is better than that of the ten locally owned EEFs.

Proposition 2 (P2). Locally-owned exporting firms have better average financial performance measures than the non-exporting ones. The average financial performance measures of the ten export-intensive EEFs signal better performance than that of the non-exporting domestic firms.

The Quantitative Lens: In Search of Enterprise Performance — The SEP Dataset

Originally an explorative quantitative research on the financial performance of exporting firms was designed to compare and underpin the interpretations of qualitative research findings. The building up a proprietary dataset from the complete annual financial HAS reports of 2008–2011 made it possible to conduct an exhaustive analysis of Hungarian firms. The findings of this research project were published in a book by Reszegi and Juhász (2014). This section provides an overview of the key issues and outcomes which support the EEFs plotting exercise and the interpretation of the results.

The quantitative research focused on two key research questions. The first research question dealt with the relationship between financial performance measures and the internationalisation. The ER ratio and the foreign ownership served as key proxies for measuring internationalisation. Within the framework of this question it was proposed that higher internationalisation proxies are positively correlated with better financial performance measures.

The second research question focused on assessing the firm-level contributions to national level competitiveness. One possible proxy for national level competitiveness is GDP. It was proposed that there are several firm level contributions that can be evaluated by financial performance measures, and which in the end influence the GDP. Profits and profitability (e.g. higher profitability suggests higher contributions to the GDP), wages (e.g. higher wage level signals higher competitiveness and contribution to the GDP), and some efficiency and productivity ratios were analysed to gain insight.

The compilation of the dataset relied upon four criteria. (i) The quantitative research focused on for-profit business enterprises and excluded the firms of the financial, insurance and banking industries. (ii) The sample only included those firms with 20 or more employees. This criterion was to support a matured and transparent business-like operation. (iii) Much attention and effort were devoted to obtaining information on ownership structures. Only privately owned, for-profit business entities were included. Private ownership meant that owners were clearly identifiable and they were either foreign or domestic individuals, or for-profit business enterprises. This criterion excluded all state- and local government-owned firms, as well as those with non-transparent (e.g. tax heaven-registered) ownership. (iv) Only those companies are included in the sample which submitted complete, non-simplified financial reports to HAS for each and every year of the 2008–2011 period. Applying the above benchmarks, the SEP sample consists of 4641 enterprises which meet all four criteria. Subsets were also created out of the SEP sample for further analyses.

Table 4 compares the SEP sample to all the operating firms of their size in the Hungarian national economy. It is noteworthy that the SEP sample covers only 0.7 % of the firms operating in Hungary, but it covers almost two-thirds of the large enterprises, and half of the medium-sized ones. Other comparisons were also performed. When the SEP sample output was compared to the output of the manufacturing branch, the SEP sample covered 53 % of that. SEP firms provided jobs to 40 % of the total number of employees working in business enterprises and generated 71 % of the Hungarian merchandise exports. These comparative figures suggest that although the number of SEP firms appears to be low, they may, in fact, be the drivers of some national competitiveness contributions, such as exports and

Table 4 The SEP sample and the Hungarian operating firms as classified by size, 2011

NoE, persons (size classification)	Number of operating firms		SEP coverage of the NE
	In the national economy (NE)	In the SEP sample	
1–4 (Micro 1)	626,631	0	
5–9 (Micro 2)	37,857	0	
10–19 (Small 1)	18,067	0	
20–49 (Small 2)	8613	1889	21.9%
50–249 (Medium)	4640	2222	47.9%
250–(Big)	872	530	60.8%
Total	696,680	4641	0.7%

Source: The authors' calculations based on the SEP dataset

jobs. These figures also suggest that the size of the dataset should provide robustness for the findings at the national level of competitiveness.

The performance analyses focused on financial statement-based ratios for profitability, efficiencies and productivity, wages and employment, growth and added value. The 4-year time span, which started in 2008 (the year when the global crisis broke out), made it possible to examine growth trends. In their book, Reszegi and Juhász (2014) start with an overview on the descriptive statistics of the SEP dataset. One of its key analytical dimension is the shareholder value, where the return on invested capital (ROIC) ratios served as the basis for clustering. Cluster analyses were also done for the foreign and domestically owned firms. A total factor productivity (TFP) analysis was done to bridge the gap between the micro-, firm-level and the macro-, national economy-level analyses and their findings for a subsample of 1600 firms in the manufacturing industry. They investigated how each group of identified performance clusters contributed to the productivity of the Hungarian national economy. The multilayer and diverse analyses of the SEP sample resulted in some surprising findings. Of these findings, we refer to those which either support our propositions on EEFs or back our plotting exercises:

1. Within the same branches of industry, there were no significant regional performance differences;
2. In general, foreign majority-owned firms (FMOs) are neither more productive nor more profitable than the domestically-owned firms (DMOs). Two subgroups were identified within each group. It suggests that there is no single duality between the group of FMOs and DMOs (as usually assumed), instead, there are dualities within each group. Based on their ROIC performance, no significant differences were found between the FMOs and DMOs;
3. EI correlates with outstanding performance ratios (such as ROIC, VA), and exporting differentiates among DMOs.

After reviewing the most relevant characteristics of the SEP research we may raise the question how EEFs performance compares to those of the different clusters of identified firms.

The Plotting Exercise: The EEFs on the SEP Landscape

The key question in this section is how the financial performance measures of the ten EEFs can be assessed based on the results of the SEP sample. This section applies the EEFs figures presented in Tables 1–3. Data for the years of 2010 and 2011 are be compared. The plotting exercise focuses on profitability and value-adding performance measures. Three comparisons are made when the performance measures of the ten EEFs match with results of subsets of the SEP sample. First, we compare the ten EEFs to the subset of profitable SEP firms. Subsequently, we compare their figures with the SEP ownership clusters, and finally, we take the export-intensive DMO cluster as a basis for comparison.

Table 5 provides a comparison with a subset of the profitable SEP firms. This subset includes firms with positive financial results. They are described based on four average performance measures for the years of 2010 and 2011, respectively. This SEP subset suggests that the average performance measures of profitable SEP firms are better than that of the complete SEP sample. As the average ratios of the ten EEFs are above that of the profitable SEP firms, the ten EEFs belong to the most profitable firms in Hungary.

The average sales revenue (SR) figures show that EEFs had a much lower firm SR (51–60 % of the SEPs) than that of the profitable SEP subset. When we look at the average taxed profit (PAT) figures, we see that on average they are approximately the same in the two samples. Two ratios are compared: the return on sales (ROS) ratio of the EEFs is almost twice as high in both years studied as that of the SEP subset. Secondly, the VA/SR ratio was used to calculate a competitiveness contribution at firm level. For the profitable SEP subset this ratio is below 30 %, while the EEF figures are above that. This suggests that the ten EEFs studied contributed on average more significantly to competitiveness in this regard than the profitable SEP subsample. This plotting exercise proposes that although the EEFs are small in terms of their sales revenue, they are at the same time highly profitable: the ROS and VA/SR ratios of EEFs signal outstanding financial performance as compared to the profitable SEP subset.

Table 6 shows the SEP sample by ownership. Only those companies were selected and analysed which had positive owners' equity in 2010. The SEP

Table 5 EEFs and the subset of profitable SEP firms

	SEP		EEF	
	2010	2011	2010	2011
Profitable firms, N	3742	3632	10	10
Their share in the sample (4641), %	81 %	78 %		
Average SR by firm (HUF BN)	6.85	7.14	3.60	4.40
Average PAT by firm (HUF BN)	0.47	0.46	0.45	0.42
ROS (PAT/SR), %	6.8 %	6.4 %	12.0 %	10.0 %
VA/SR, %	28.6 %	29.1 %	38.0 %	31.0 %

Source: Reszegi and Juhász (2014:86) and the authors' calculations

Table 6 The performance of EEFs in comparison with ownership clusters, 2011

	Foreign—FMOs		Domestic—DMOs		EEFs	
	Median		Median			
	Low wage	High wage	Low wage	High wage	Below the lowest median	Above the highest median
EI, %	67.2	21.6	1.6	1.7	None	5 (B, C, L, P, S)
ROS, %	4.2	3.7	3.5	4.9	1 (P)	9 (A, B, C, E, G, H, L, M, S)
VA/SR, %	26.5	21.8	20.8	27.4	1 (A)	9 (B, C, E, G, H, L, M, P, S)
VA/capita, M HUF	4217	9729	3774	7173	1 (P)	4 (A, H, L, M)
N (4,261)	542	1076	1965	678		

Source: Authors' calculations

ownership subsample included 4261 firms (1618 FMOs and 2643 DMOs). The levels of wages divided the groups of FMOs and DMOs into two clusters. Average wages were compared to the nation-wide average in the sub-branch of the given company. Low wages show lower than average sub-branch wages, the high wages show higher than average sub-branch wages in the appropriate industry of the given firms. A detailed analysis on the performance of each cluster also uncovered some performance differences. Medians are used for comparison. There was no data on the wages of EEFs, which is why we took the lowest and highest medians as a benchmark in positioning EEFs amongst the ownership clusters.

When looking at the FMOs and DMOs, the EI ratios signal huge differences between the ownership clusters. The foreign owned firms (FMOs) export more intensively, while the majority of the DMOs hardly export, i.e. they sell predominantly within the national market. It was surprising that the low-wage FMOs have almost a three times higher EI than the high wage FMOs. When comparing the EIs of the ten EEFs, we see that all are close to the medians of the FMOs, and five of the EEFs have an EI that is higher than the highest EI figure in Table 6.

The medians of ROS and VA/SR ratios with FMOs and DMOs were much closer to each other than that of the EI. The ROS figures signal a narrow variance. This is the only measure where all the EEFs are above the median. When looking at the VA/SR figures, they are positioned between the 20.8 and 27.4 % in SEP ownership clusters. Of the ten EEFs two are below the lowest (20.8 %), and eight are above the highest median (27.4%) value. When looking at the VA/capita we found that medians were highest for the high wage companies and lowest for the low wage firms.

When the EEFs are plotted on this performance map, all ten have EI figures above the medians of the FMO clusters. Their ROS profitability ratios is outstanding, which is also true for the VA/SR ratios. These findings support the claim that although the ten EEFs are SMEs, their overall financial performance is amongst the outstanding ones. These results — shown in Table 6 — also suggest that EEFs are

Table 7 EEFs' profitability and value added based on intensive exporting DMO clusters, 2011

Clusters	N	PAT/capita, M HUF		VA/capita, M HUF	
		SEP subset	EEF	SEP subset	EEF
1	240	2.3		7.1	
2	71	2.7		8.1	
3	30	3.3	A, H, L, M	8.1	S, A, H, L, M
4	177	0.5	P, S, E, G, B, C	4.3	P, E, G, B, C
Total/average	518	1.8	2.8	6.3	9.0
EEF min			0.1		4.1
EEF max			20.7		20.0

Source: Authors' calculations

not only amongst the outstanding firms, but most of them are on par with the group of FMOs.

Table 7 shows the clustering results of the intensive exporting DMOs, which were selected out of the DMOs that in 2010 had an EI ratio higher than 25 %. Less than 20 % (518 firms) out of the 2646 DMOs fall into this category. Based on their profitability and value-added figure, there were four clusters. PAT/capita and VA/capita averages were calculated for each cluster and the results were compared to those of the EEFs. The average figures of the ten EEFs are in both cases higher than those of the averages of clusters of the intensive exporting DMOs. When looking at individual EEF figures, however, they signal a diverse pattern. Based on PET/capita, four EEFs belong to the group with the highest average (Cluster 3), and six ones to the group with the lowest average (Cluster 4). When studying the VA/capita figures, EEFs firms also fall into these two clusters equally (Cluster 3 with one of the highest values, and Cluster 4 with the lowest one).These results suggest that, based on their averages, EEFs belong to the most profitable export intensive DMOs, but individual cases show a rather mixed picture regarding efficiency.

Conclusions

The main novelty of our research pertains to the application of two generally used research methods, i.e. case studies (typical of international business studies) and quantitative analysis of financial statements (mainly used for analysing competitiveness) on the same population for the same timeframe. Our findings show that a better understanding of links and processes is available if the results obtained by using the two methodologies are contrasted against each other.

The authors matched the financial performance measures of ten experienced EEFs with those of 4641 privately owned SEP enterprises in Hungary. EEFs are domestically-owned firms and — based on their sales revenues and the number of their employees — belong to the small- and medium-sized enterprises. Their ROS and VA/SR ratios signalled outstanding performance by the SEP profitable subset averages. At first sight, this suggests positive contributions to both firm- and national-level competitiveness.

Two subsets of SEM sample were selected for comparison: the one related to ownership (FMOs and DMOs clusters), and the other one comprising export intensive DMOs. EEFs performance measures by their medians showed that they are amongst the outstanding firms and in parity with the FMOs. The results of the comparison with the intensive exporting DMO clusters provided a subtitle picture on the performance of the ten EEFs. Although the average figures for the PAT/capita and the VA/capita are higher for the ten EEFs, there is significant diversity behind these figures. A simplification of these results shows that half of the EEFs belong to the lower, and half to the higher performer intensive exporting DMOs.

The formulated proposition P1 should be modified in light of the results of SEP analysis and the plotting exercise as follows:

> Modified P1: The financial performance measures of high wage DMOs are on par with those of the high wage FMOs. At the same time, low wage FMOs do not have significantly better performance measures than low wage DMOs, while based on their performance measures, both fall behind the high wage companies.

The modification reflects that domestic and foreign ownership does not signal significant differences in financial performance measures in privately-owned firms that have at least 20 employees.

The results of the SEP sample suggest that both of the FMOs and DMOs groups should be further segmented. It proposes, that instead of duality of foreign and domestic ownership, raised by Dyker (2004), based on their comparable performance measures, several dualities may exist amongst privately owned companies. Export intensity and wage level were presented in this paper as reasons for the dualities. Export intensity and high wages correlated positively with higher or better financial measures. Our results also propose that foreign ownership in itself does not necessarily correlate to the expected competitiveness contribution (e.g. more jobs, higher wages and higher added value).

This P2 proposition was supported both by the SEP results and the plotting exercise of the ten EEFs, and is maintained:

> P2: Locally owned exporting firms have better average financial performance measures than the non-exporting ones. The average financial performance measures of the ten export-intensive EEFs signal better performance than those of the non-exporting domestic firms.

This proposition also suggests that a sustained, high export intensity is a better signal for positive outcomes of internationalisation (e.g. higher profitability) than foreign ownership. From the point of view of competitiveness, enhancing and supporting internationalisation of SMEs may be only a first step. The key challenge is how SMEs can achieve and sustain a high (over 20 %) export intensity ratio.

In other words, by contrasting the findings of the two research projects, it has been shown that exporting may go hand in hand with profitability (ROS, VA/Sales). However, describing the best practices of more export-focused firms with quantitative or qualitative measures is not equal to devising the key to outstanding performance. It is vital to see that above-average efficiency ratios (e.g. PAT/capita, VA/capita) were not strongly linked to higher profitability even among intensive exporters. We also showed that high profitability and efficiency were present amongst the companies with less intensive (i.e. IE $\leq 25\,\%$) export activity. This means that tracking back competitiveness is more complex than simply focusing on one or other characteristics of the firm. Different dimensions of competitiveness at firm-level (like growth opportunities offered by exporting, efficiency, profitability, and renewal) may not signal at the same time. A consequence of that for the national economic policy makers might be that it is not enough to promote exporting to boost competitiveness of the country. For that companies need to be efficient, and profitable and capable for learning at the same time. That is a combination that might require the proper strategy and its management at firm-level.

Based on the findings of the ten EEF case studies and the results of the plotting exercise, we can claim a firm conjuncture on the positive relationships amongst management and managerial capabilities, innovation, learning and financial performance. These factors are hard to measure with data from financial reports. The findings of qualitative research, especially those based on case studies, highlight their everyday role in outstanding exports and other dimensions of performance. Survey-based research findings, where data for financial performance are also available, may be rewarding in this respect.

Our findings have their own limitations. The ten EEFs represent only a handful of experienced export-intensive enterprises from a single country. Their financial figures may be applied only as possible signals. The financial performance measures, together with the insights of case studies and their propositions, suggest possible further investigations on the aforementioned factors which are hard to measure (e.g. management, innovation, and learning). A subtle approach is needed not only for academic and research purposes, but also to direct and facilitate the work of policy makers.

Take for example innovation. Innovation is most commonly measured by R&D spending and the number of patents at macro- (national-) and firm-levels. R&D spending and the number of patents are generally frequent in asset-intensive and product-related innovation. The national accounting standards also have a say in how R&D spending can be calculated at the firm-level. Case studies show that several types of processes and incremental innovations are needed at the firm-level to remain competitive in international arenas. These innovative solutions may neglect both the R&D spending in the book of accounts and registered patents especially with SMEs. They are, however, necessary from the point of view of continuous learning and incremental innovation practices, and were detected and described in each of the EEF case studies.

The size of the SEP sample with its 4641 firms in itself warrants the robustness of the findings. It is a noteworthy and generalisable implication, that a few firms are able to drive the key competitiveness measures of a national economy, such as its exports. However, there may be more "happy few" firms (Mayer and Ottaviano 2007) than the macro-level data would suggest.

While such research exercises are resource-intensive, small countries may have advantages in relying on and contrasting of both firm-level (micro) and national-level (macro) research findings. The SEP dataset is proprietary, which limits its access. Its data are from annually published and publicly available financial reports. The applied national standards, like HAS sets a limit on international comparison, however, it ensures a common understanding and interpretation of performance data for every company that complies with the same standards in a given country.

The financial reports also have their own limitations in measuring firm performance. Only the type of performance can be measured that can be calculated with data from financial reports. Besides, in order to minimise reporting work and optimise tax payment, SMEs often use tax regulation rules for financial reporting instead of providing a more realistic picture by considering all options offered by more flexible accounting standards, which might lead to a blurred financial picture. Moving beyond the financial analyses based only on financial reports in performance evaluation, and interpreting their findings in more depth, may signal fields for further investigations and development.

References

Ábel, I., & Czakó, E. (Eds.). (2013). *In search of export excellence*. Budapest: Alinea Kiadó (in Hungarian).

Boda, G., & Stocker, M. (2013a). Savers of unutilized knowledge capital: The case of Agrofeed. In I. Ábel & E. Czakó (Eds.), *In search of export excellence* (pp. 107–116). Budapest: Alinea Kiadó (in Hungarian).

Boda, G., & Stocker, M. (2013b). Champion of the once chance and the mushrooms. In I. Ábel & E. Czakó (Eds.), *In search of export excellence* (pp. 85–92). Budapest: Alinea Kiadó (in Hungarian).

Calof, J. L. (1994). The relationship between firm size and export behavior revisited. *Journal of International Business Studies, 25*(2), 367–387.

Chikán, A. (2008). National and firm competitiveness: A general research model. *Competitiveness Review, 18*(1 and 2), 20–28.

Chikán, A., & Czakó, E. (Eds.). (2010, November). *Theoretical and practical context and implications of competitiveness. Round-table discussion with Stephane Garelli*. Competitiveness Research Centre. Accessed June 20, 2015, from http://www.uni-corvinus.hu/fileadmin/user_upload/hu/kutatokozpontok/versenykepesseg/belso_linkek/Round_table_with_Profes sor_Garelli_vegleges.pdf

Czakó, E., & Könczöl, E. (2014). Critical success factors of export excellence and policy implications. The case of Hungarian small and medium-sized enterprises. Chapter 5. In: A. S. Gubik, & K. Wach (Eds.), International entrepreneurship and corporate growth in Visegrad countries. Miskolc: University of Miskolc, pp. 69–83. Accessed December 20, 2015, from http://www.visegrad.uek.krakow.pl/publications_miskolc.html

Dyker, D. A. (2004). Closing the productivity gap between Eastern and Western Europe: The role of foreign direct investment. *Science and Public Policy, 31*(3), 279–287.

Hooly, G., Cox, T., Shipley, D., Fahy, J., Beracs, J., & Kolos, K. (1996). Foreign direct investment in Hungary: Resource acquisition and domestic competitive advantage. *Journal of International Business Studies, 27*(4), 683–709.

Johanson, J., & Vahlne, J.-E. (1977). The internationalisation process of the firm. A model of knowledge development and increasing foreign market commitments. *Journal of International Business Studies, 1*, 23–32.

Johanson, J., & Vahlne, J.-E. (2009). The Uppsala internationalisation process model revisited. From liability of foreignness to liability of outsidership. *Journal of International Business Studies, 40*, 1411–1431.

Juhász, P. (2013). Granite: The exports grinded brightness. In I. Ábel & E. Czakó (Eds.), *In search of export excellence* (pp. 129–140). Budapest: Alinea Kiadó (in Hungarian).

Kazainé Ónodi, A. (2013a). From washing machines to silencer systems: Skills and capabilities. In I. Ábel & E. Czakó (Eds.), *In search of export excellence* (pp. 155–168). Budapest: Alinea Kiadó (in Hungarian).

Kazainé Ónodi, A. (2013b). National research findings on exporting enterprises. In I. Ábel & E. Czakó (Eds.), *In search of export excellence* (pp. 55–80). Budapest: Alinea Kiadó (in Hungarian).

Kiss, J. (2013). Csaba Metál: Exports success in the neighbourhood of the cornfields. In I. Ábel & E. Czakó (Eds.), *In search of export excellence* (pp. 169–176). Budapest: Alinea Kiadó (in Hungarian).

Könczöl, E. (2013). The critical success factors of exports. In I. Ábel & E. Czakó (Eds.), *In search of export excellence* (pp. 199–214). Budapest: Alinea Kiadó (in Hungarian).

Kozma, M. (2013). The Bakony ceramics: Success baked in a kiln. In I. Ábel & E. Czakó (Eds.), *In search of export excellence* (pp. 141–154). Budapest: Alinea Kiadó (in Hungarian).

Mayer, T., & Ottaviano, F. I. P. (2007). *The happy few: The internationalisation of European firms. New facts based on firm-level evidence*. Bruegel Blueprint Series, Brussels.

Pecze, K. (2013). Veterinary science at world class – the case of Lavet. In I. Ábel & E. Czakó (Eds.), *In search of export excellence* (pp. 177–186). Budapest: Alinea Kiadó (in Hungarian).

Porter, M. E. (1990). *Competitive advantage of nations*. New York: The Free Press.

Reszegi, L., & Juhász, P. (2014). *In search of enterprise performance*. Budapest: Alinea Kiadó (in Hungarian).

Scott, B. R. (1985). U.S. competitiveness: Concepts, performance, and implications. In B. R. Scott & G. C. Lodge (Eds.), *U.S. competitiveness in the world economy* (pp. 13–70). Boston: Harvard Business School Press.

Singh, D. A. (2009). Export performance of emerging market firms. *International Business Review, 18*, 321–330.

Sullivan, D. (1994). Measuring the degree of internationalisation of a firm. *Journal of International Business Studies, 25*(2), 325–342.

Szalay, Z. E. (2013). From international joint venture into Hungarian majority ownership – the case of Sanatmetal. In I. Ábel & E. Czakó (Eds.), *In search of export excellence* (pp. 93–106). Budapest: Alinea Kiadó (in Hungarian).

Szántó, R. (2013). MEDISO: They have got the nerve to grow. In I. Ábel & E. Czakó (Eds.), *In search of export excellence* (pp. 187–198). Budapest: Alinea Kiadó (in Hungarian).

Tátrai, T. (2013). Good luck and fantasy – engineers at the steering wheel. In I. Ábel & E. Czakó (Eds.), *In search of export excellence* (pp. 117–128). Budapest: Alinea Kiadó (in Hungarian).

Emerging CEE Multinationals in the Electronics Industry

Magdolna Sass

Abstract In spite of the quite recent start of outward foreign direct investment from the Central and East European region and the relative backwardness of the region in terms of the electronics industry, certain countries have become homes to multinational companies in this industry. The chapter makes the first attempt to identify and describe certain characteristics of these CEE electronics multinationals. Its methodology relies on a macro approach in terms of identifying the CEE countries with substantial electronics outward FDI and of a micro approach in terms of having a look at certain information about the companies identified. Given the limits of the comparable information available, the chapter concentrates on a few characteristics of these companies and compares them first with each other, and second, with other emerging electronics multinationals. Preliminary findings include the proof for the existence of CEE electronics multinationals, the presence of the efficiency-seeking and the innovation-seeking motive as well as calling attention to certain differences between the analysed CEE electronics multinationals.

Keywords Electronics multinationals • Central and Eastern Europe • Hungary • Poland • Slovenia

Introduction

While outward foreign direct investment (OFDI) has started relatively recently from the Central and Eastern European (CEE) region, there are already some indigenous emerging multinationals originating from this region. While services dominate in CEE-based OFDI, there are also manufacturing companies, whereof certain electronics companies which have established subsidiaries abroad. The present chapter analyses the internationalisation of CEE firms via FDI in this industry, which is considered to be highly competitive, as well as capital and R&D intensive. Thus, one would not expect substantial OFDI in it by CEE

M. Sass (✉)
Hungarian Academy of Sciences, Budapest, Hungary
e-mail: sass.magdolna@krtk.mta.hu

companies, whose level of international competitiveness is understandably far below that of their counterparts in developed Western economies, or of newly emerged Asian multinationals.

The present chapter represents the very first step of analysing indigenous CEE electronics multinational companies. It is mainly a descriptive one, trying to find out what the most important characteristics of these companies are, and to what extent they differ from each other and from emerging, non-developed country multinationals in the same industry. These are the main research questions, which are approached here first by relying on macro- and micro-level data on electronics OFDI and multinationals from the CEE region, as well as on other firm-level data available from the Emerging Markets Global Players project (see EMGP 2016).

The chapter is organised as follows. A brief theoretical overview and literature review is followed by a short note on the methodology used in the chapter. Subsequently, the most important features and developments in the CEE electronics industry are presented. The next section shows and analyses the macro-level data on OFDI from the electronics industry in the CEE countries. In a second step, firm-level data of CEE outward investors in the electronics industry are analysed and compared. Then a first, admittedly incomplete attempt is made to compare these firms with emerging or non-developed country electronics multinationals in those areas where comparable data are available. The final section concludes the chapter and formulates several indications for further research.

Theoretical Background and Literature Review

The analysis relies on four strands of literature. First of all, the motivations of CEE multinationals investing abroad are dealt with using the well-known categories of Dunning and the elements of his OLI-framework to show why these companies internationalise through FDI, to the level of details and extent that is possible given the available data (see e.g. Dunning 1993 or Dunning and Lundan 2008).

The second strand of literature connected closely to the OLI-framework concerns the so-called emerging multinational companies. While the eclectic paradigm can well explain the phenomenon of foreign investment by multinationals from developed countries, it is less appropriate in the case of non-developed country multinationals (see e.g. Mathews 2006 or Contessi and El-Ghazaly 2010), especially in the case of their horizontal investments (see e.g. Lall 1983 or Caves 1996). These companies are referred to with different terms in the literature: "third-world multinationals" or "latecomer firms", "unconventional multinationals" or "emerging multinationals". In this chapter, we shall use the notion of "emerging multinationals".

The main finding of the literature on emerging multinationals is that they are essentially different from developed country multinationals (Ramamurti 2012). Emerging multinational companies are very heterogeneous and do not seem to possess ownership advantages which would be identical to those of developed country multinationals, e.g. strong R&D and innovation or marketing activities, or strong global brands. Certain emerging multinationals invest abroad even with the explicit aim of obtaining ownership advantages (see e.g. Aulakh 2007 or Mathews 2006). Guillén and García-Canal (2009:31) collected different types of intangible assets of emerging multinationals from the literature. They show that technology adaptation, early adaptation of new technology, ethnic branding, efficient production and project execution, product innovation, institutional entrepreneurial ability, expertise in the management of acquisitions, networking skills and political know-how are among those intangible assets which may constitute the basis for ownership advantages of these multinational companies. This supports the statement of Ramamurti (2012) concerning the difference of ownership advantages of 'traditional' and emerging multinational companies. Other authors point out that while ownership advantages of emerging multinationals are different, over time they become more and more similar to those of developed-country ones (Lessard and Lucea 2009; Sass et al. 2014).

Referring to another element of the OLI-framework of Dunning, other studies underline that internalisation capabilities of emerging multinationals are weaker than in the case of developed country multinationals, and rely mainly on their home-country specific factors of production (Buckley et al. 2007). Location advantages, which help to exploit their ownership advantages, also seem to differ from those of developed-country multinationals. For instance, emerging multinationals are able to handle relatively disadvantageous local conditions in less developed countries that otherwise would scare off investors from advanced countries (Lall 1983). Overall, other differences between developed-country or 'traditional' multinationals on the one hand, and emerging multinationals on the other, are discussed among others in Guillén and García-Canal (2009). Their speed of internationalisation is accelerated as opposed to the gradual internationalisation of 'traditional' multinationals. Their competitive advantages are weaker, thus upgrading of resources is required, while their political capabilities are stronger due to the experience of dealing with unstable political environments. Their expansion paths are dual: they simultaneously enter developed and developing countries, while 'traditional' multinationals go from less to more distant countries. They opt more for entry modes offering external growth through alliances and acquisitions, while 'traditional' multinationals go for more integrated entry modes, such as wholly-owned subsidiaries. The organisational adaptability of emerging multinationals is higher, because of their limited international presence. Furthermore, their motivations are manifold, as documented in the literature (Guillén and García-Canal 2009:29).

A related strand of relatively scarce literature is analysing post-transition multinationals, as a 'special' case of emerging multinationals. While the literature on emerging multinational companies itself is large, it analyses mainly firms located in BRIC(S)[1] countries, while multinationals originating from CEE are studied much

---

[1]Brazil, Russia, India, China and South Africa.

less often (see e.g. Andreff (2003), Svetličič and Rojec (2003) or Kalotay (2004), who analyse post-transition multinationals). Svetličič and Jaklič (2006) underline the special characteristics of multinational companies originating from CEE countries. These '(post) transition country multinationals' fit neither the traditional theories of advanced MNCs (i.e. originating from developed countries), nor theories of emerging multinationals. According to Svetličič (2004), CEE multinationals are somewhere in between the developed and developing countries' multinational companies. He showed the differences between Third World' multinationals and Central European transition economies' multinationals in the following areas: their overall characteristics, their motivations and their advantages and strategies. Among others he showed that while both groups are very heterogeneous, everywhere large firms are the dominant foreign investors, and investments are concentrated within the larger geographical region of the investing country. As for the roots of or motivation for outward FDI, he emphasised the difference between the push factors of internationalisation, including socialism *per se* for certain CEE countries, and the not ideally functioning capitalist economy for Third World multinationals. The predominant motive was related to market seeking. Concerning ownership, it is mainly 100 % in the case of transition economies, while more diverse in the emerging multinationals' group. As for the sectors, in (post-) transition economies, manufacturing dominated, whilst trade followed later. Due to the low number and relatively short history of multinational companies originating from Central European transition economies', he emphasised the importance of further studies. However, the number and importance of post-transition multinationals is still relatively low. For example, Foster et al. (2011) found one of the explanations for the relatively low intra-Visegrad FDI in the lack of (potential) multinationals in the region. More recent studies delineated some further important features. Just to mention the findings of those which compare foreign investor companies from more than one CEE countries, Svetličič et al. (2007) found when analysing internationalising Central European small and medium-sized enterprises that the market-seeking motive was the most important one. Radlo and Sass (2012) showed on the basis of company cases that the dominant entry mode was privatisation-related acquisition and that horizontal type of FDI dominated intra-Visegrad[2] investments. Papers dealing with this issue are not numerous, the analysis and comparison of CEE MNCs is still in its nascent stage.

The third strand of the literature must also be mentioned. The distinction between direct and indirect outward FDI is analysed by a few studies (see among others UNCTAD 1998; Kalotay 2012). The importance of this distinction is underlined by the fact that both direct and indirect FDI is included in the outward FDI statistics of a given country. Both these categories are present in the electronics industry, which will be discussed later in the chapter. Indirect FDI is an investment abroad undertaken by an affiliate of a foreign multinational company that has been established in a different host country from that of the host country of the new

---

[2]Visegrad countries: Czech Republic, Hungary, Poland and Slovakia.

investment. Thus, in our case foreign investment projects undertaken both by indigenous CEE multinationals and by local subsidiaries of foreign (non-CEE) multinationals are included in the data. Furthermore, there is no separate statistical data available about direct and indirect outward FDI, though some estimation exists. For example, based on the studies prepared within the EMGP project concerning overall outward FDI, in the case of Slovenia (Jaklič and Svetličič 2009) and Poland (Kaliszuk and Wancio 2013), it is mainly indigenous firms that venture abroad with direct investments. In the case of Hungary (Sass and Kovács 2013), on the other hand, it is a handful of mainly foreign majority-owned, but at the same time Hungarian-controlled firms, which are responsible for the overwhelming majority of outward FDI. Rugraff (2010) also showed the importance of indigenous companies in the case of Polish and Slovenian outward FDI, while in the case of Hungary he found that majority foreign-owned multinationals dominate. This latter specialty induced Sass et al. (2012) to introduce the notion of "virtual indirect" investors, in the case of which foreign majority ownership does not correspond to foreign control, thus these investors are much closer in their characteristics to direct than to indirect investors.

The fourth strand of the literature used as a background in this short study is related to the internationalisation of companies and multinationals in the electronics industry from emerging economies. The literature on global value chains analyses in detail the fragmentation and the process of internationalisation of production in the industry (see e.g. Dicken 2011; Sturgeon and Kawakami 2010). More details from that literature will be presented in the section on the industry background. Furthermore, among emerging electronics multinationals, it is mainly the Korean Samsung, for which case studies are available (see e.g. KABCLTD 2012 or Jung 2014).

Methodology

Due to data availability, electronics is defined in this chapter as covering categories C26 (manufacture of computer, electronic and optical products) and C27 (manufacture of electrical equipment) in accordance with NACE rev. 2 (2008). Data availability is, however, very problematic in various areas. It is mainly C27 for which data are missing: presumably for confidentiality reasons, Eurostat and certain national banks do not provide certain data on this industry (for more details see: Sass 2015). However, based on available information, this subindustry is of minor importance in CEE-based OFDI as compared to C26.

In the analysis, two data sources are used. Firstly, the most important CEE home countries of electronics outward FDI are identified on the basis of the Eurostat data on outward FDI at the industry level. The problems of FDI stock and flow data for measuring the size of foreign-owned activity (Lipsey 2006) are dealt with here through concentrating on the company level in the analysis. Thus, secondly, firm-level data are used first, so as to double-check whether the investing firms are incumbent/indigenous (locally controlled, though not necessarily locally majority-owned) companies in order to differentiate between direct and indirect outward FDI, which is not yet done so in the macro data. Third, company level analysis is conducted on the basis of the information available from the Emerging Markets Global Players project of the Columbia Center on Sustainable Investment (EMGP 2016). Originally, we concentrated our analysis on the Visegrad countries (Czech Republic, Hungary, Poland and Slovakia) plus Estonia and Slovenia, as these countries have significant electronics capacities in the region (Chan 2013) and significant outward FDI. However, company information in EMGP is available only for the following CEE economies: Hungary, Poland and Slovenia. Fortunately enough, as we will see, these are the most important countries from the point of view of the analysis, as only these have significant outward FDI in electronics.[3] Apart from information from the EMGP project, other sources (company websites, balance sheets, case studies, articles in specialised journals) are also used in the analysis. One disadvantage of the EMGP database should be mentioned: it contains the list of the top outward investor companies, thus data on smaller sized electronics multinational firms is missing from it. Furthermore, for certain countries only relatively outdated reports are available.

Fourth, a more detailed case study is presented for the Hungarian Videoton, one of the largest indigenous CEE electronics foreign investor companies. This choice may be justified first, on the basis of historical reasons, as Videoton was among the first indigenous electronics investor companies in the CEE region. Second, data and literature availability is also relatively high for that company. The case of Videoton, supplemented by company cases from the other two countries (Poland and Slovenia) may provide later a good basis for a more thorough analysis of the problem.

Industry Background[4]

The global importance of the electronics industry is obvious. It has been one of the main drivers of globalisation, as well as one of the most integrated industries in global terms and one of the most fragmented ones, at the same time. At the country level, the industry has similar features: it can influence economic development through its impact on other industries to a much larger extent than other industries. Thus, its importance is evident, particularly for countries at a lower level of development or those still in the catch-up phase, such as CEE countries. The industry manufactures a large number of widely heterogeneous products, in terms of factor and R&D intensity, level of fragmentation, availability of economies of scale etc. (OECD 2004; UNCTAD 2004).

---

[3]Obviously, there could be smaller-sized emerging electronics multinationals in other CEE countries, as well in smaller segments.

[4]This section is based on the main findings of the research published in Sass (2015).

The analysed CEE countries emerged as new locations for the global electronics industry after they started their transition process from the planned to the market economy in 1989–1990. Beforehand, their electronics industries lagged significantly behind those of developed countries and were to a large extent dependent on foreign technology (Radosevic 2005). All countries participated in the CMEA[5] division of labour in electronics, thus they had substantial capacities. Production was concentrated in large conglomerates and had strong ties with the military sector. Of these large conglomerates, the only one to survive was the Hungarian Videoton, on the basis of an innovative strategy and alliances with large multinationals (Radosevic and Yoruk 2001), a company which later became one of the most substantial CEE electronics multinationals. The others were mostly cut up into smaller units and privatised or liquidated (Szanyi 2006). However, the industry's relatively well-developed human capital and expertise remained in place, which provided a good background for its further development. This started at the mid-1990s based mainly on the establishment of new production facilities by foreign multinational companies.

This FDI-based revival began at different times in the countries analysed (Linden 1998; Radosevic 2005; Szanyi 2006; Sass and Szanyi 2012). Hungary was the first to open up its economy to FDI, including electronics investments. The special regulation of industrial free trade zones was especially attractive for large, greenfield projects assembling mainly imported inputs for export, using relatively cheap local unskilled or semi-skilled labour—thus attracting certain segments of the electronics manufacturing industry to the country (see e.g. Antalóczy and Sass 2001). The Czech Republic offered substantial incentives to (among others) electronics projects starting in around 1998, while Poland and Slovakia caught up later. Overall, incentives for FDI projects in the electronics industry have been considerable in CEE countries (Drahokoupil 2009) and could influence location choices of multinationals as locations and locational advantages were similar to each other in the CEE region. As a result of these developments, by 2003 the highly export-oriented production of Hungary, the Czech Republic and Poland exceeded that of Mexico, though it still remained considerably lower than that of the East Asian economies and lower than that of Ireland. The exports of the CEE countries were not diversified in terms of the industry's sub-segments, consisting mainly of computers, parts and components and consumer electronics, and indicative of the persisting technological backwardness of the analysed countries (Radosevic 2005).

This FDI-based development went together with the creation of new capacities, as well as substantial relocations from mainly Western Europe targeting the CEE region (Hunya and Sass 2005). A few substantial relocations during that period had already highlighted the industry's high concentration and low locational loyalty and its vulnerability to changes in the demand structure and relative wages (UNCTAD 2003). Connected to that, the parallel emergence of competitive foreign locations

---

[5]The abbreviation CMEA stood for the Council for Mutual Economic Assistance, an economic organisation for the socialist countries, dissolved in 1991.

offering enormous amounts of cheap labour, especially in Asia, but also at the Eastern borders of the EU, has also been shaping European developments to a much greater extent than in other industries, as electronics is relatively more rootless (Dicken 2011).

In all four Visegrad countries, subsidiaries of foreign multinationals (with the exception of a few, usually smaller-sized locally-owned companies) dominated the industry; with a high integration in global value chains (Kaminsky and Ng 2001; Sass and Szalavetz 2013). There have also been signs of upgrading in the operating structures of foreign-owned electronics companies and increasing local value added in the Visegrad countries (Szalavetz 2004; Sass and Szalavetz 2013). The FDI-based integration in global value chains (GVCs) went hand-in-hand with considerable technology transfer, one indication of which is the changes in the (revealed) comparative advantages of the analysed countries (IMF 2013; Rahman and Zhao 2013). This development came together with a one-sided specialisation of the analysed countries (Galgóczi 2009) through efficiency-seeking FDI, making them vulnerable to external shocks, an indication of which was the considerable fall in production levels during the recent crisis. Partly due to its strong links with other industries and sectors, and partly due to the high level and geographic spread of fragmentation, electronics is very sensitive to business cycles, thus it was one of the industries that were hit by the crisis the most hard. This resulted in a large decline in the CEE countries in production and exports, especially in 2008–2009 and in a restructuring process featuring increased merger and acquisition (M&A) and relocation activities in the multinational companies affected, present in the CEE region as well as the indigenous companies operating in the industry. After the crisis, electronics output climbed back close to pre-crisis levels and in a few countries (Estonia, Poland and Slovakia) even surpassed that slightly (Sass 2015).

CEE Outward FDI in the Electronics Industry

As already indicated, the electronics industry in the CEE region is usually dominated by subsidiaries of large foreign multinational companies, with only a few indigenous firms being able to gain relatively substantial market shares (Sass 2015). We could thus expect relatively low outward FDI by indigenous firms (i.e. direct outward FDI) due to their relative weakness, while indirect outward FDI by foreign multinationals using their subsidiaries located in CEE as parents for FDI realised in third countries could be more substantial. According to the data, the outward FDI stock in the period 2008–2013,[6] which contains data of both types (i.e. direct and indirect outward FDI), has been negligible in the electronics industry from those CEE countries that have substantial capacities in the industry, with the exception of Poland, Hungary and Slovenia (Table 1). Even these countries represent only a

---

[6]Data from Eurostat are available only for this period.

Table 1 Direct investment position abroad in C26 (products), selected countries, 2008–2013, million euros

	2008	2009	2010	2011	2012	2013
EU-27	194,369	191,009	207,472	421,791	n.a.	n.a.
Czech Republic	1	2	3	2	n.a.	n.a.
Estonia	2	−1	2	1	5	n.a.
Hungary	388	473	502	563	909[a]	n.a.
Poland	n.a.	n.a.	847	836	n.a.	n.a.
Slovakia	2	1	1	0	n.a.	n.a.
Slovenia	27	30	35	30	30	32

Source: Eurostat, EU direct investment positions, breakdown by country and economic activity NACE Rev. 2
[a]Data of the Hungarian National Bank
n.a. data not available

negligible share of total EU27 investment abroad in the electronics industry: their combined share was 0.3 % in 2011. However, it is important to note that Eurostat publishes data only for the C26 (products) subsector, while data for C27 (equipment) are basically missing.

Outward FDI in C27 (equipment) may be non-negligible: the National Bank of Hungary publishes data for C27 outward stock, and according to that in the case of Hungary, between 2008 and 2012 Hungarian companies invested around 20 million euros abroad in that subindustry. Still, outward FDI in C27 (electronics equipment) seems to be much smaller than in C26 (electronics products). Further data from Eurostat reveal that the most important host countries in the case of Hungarian electronics outward FDI are Slovakia and Brazil with smaller projects in the Netherlands, and in the case of Poland various developed European countries (France, Germany, Netherlands, UK) and developed countries outside of Europe (in North America, and in Asia, notably Singapore). For Slovenia, apart from smaller projects in South-East Europe, in Russia and in China. With this information, now we shall attempt to descend to the level of firms in the three countries, in which there is substantial outward FDI in the electronics industry: Hungary, Poland and Slovenia.

CEE Multinationals in the Electronics Industry

The fact that the majority of CEE multinationals are in their nascent stage is underlined by the fact that there are very few publications analysing foreign investing companies originating from that group of countries. A valuable source is the EMGP project of the Columbia Center on Sustainable Investment, in which three countries of the region: Hungary, Poland and Slovenia are covered for different time periods. These are the countries at the forefront of CEE outward FDI: Poland is first in terms of the total stock of outward FDI, Slovenia in outward

FDI per capita, and Hungary is second behind them in both areas. As we could see, these are the most important home countries for CEE electronics outward FDI, as well.

In order to identify the most important indigenous electronics investor companies, we use the database provided by the country reports prepared in the framework of the EMGP project. The identification of companies helps us to separate direct (i.e. realised by locally controlled and/or owned firms) and indirect (i.e. realised by foreign-controlled firms, in most of the cases local subsidiaries of foreign multinationals) outward FDI.

In the case of Hungary, in 2012, there was a relatively substantial outward FDI stock in the extent of almost 1 billion euros in C26, the "product-part" of electronics, and a minor one (only 20 million euros, as we were able to see), in C27, the "equipment-part" of electronics. The EMGP report for Hungary covering the years 2012 and 2013 (Sass and Kovács 2015) contains two electronics companies among the top investors: Videoton, which had foreign assets of USD 277 million (around 200 million euros) with investments in Bulgaria and the Ukraine and Mediso with USD 43 million (around 31 million euros) with investments in Poland and in Germany. These two Hungarian-owned companies thus represent around one-fourth of the total outward FDI stock in the industry. In order to find further substantial investors, we assume that these must be local subsidiaries of electronics multinationals. While analysing the list of the largest investors and checking their balance sheets for foreign assets, we found that the Hungarian subsidiary of the Korean electronics firm, Samsung, is the parent company of a Slovakian and a Czech subsidiary and of one Romanian branch. The electronics outward FDI of Hungary in Brazil can be attributed to a Hungarian Foxconn subsidiary, FIH Europe. The other Foxconn (a Taiwanese electronics multinational) subsidiary in Hungary, PCE Paragon Solutions has four foreign subsidiaries: in Brazil, in Poland, in Ireland and in the Netherlands. The value of foreign assets of the Hungarian Samsung subsidiary is 22 million euros (2012), while in the case of Foxconn, the first subsidiary covered the losses of its Brazilian subsidiary in the value of 116 million euros and for a Danish subsidiary of 3 million euros and the second subsidiary had foreign assets with the value of 70 million euros. These five companies (two Hungarian, the Samsung subsidiary and the two Foxconn subsidiaries) are thus 'responsible' for around half of the Hungarian outward FDI stock in electronics. Apart from them, the Hungarian subsidiaries of the US multinational GE (operating in a holding structure) may be important foreign investors, with subsidiaries in: the Netherlands, United Arab Emirates, and partly-owned subsidiaries in Romania, Lithuania, Czech Republic, Slovenia, Slovakia, Latvia and Estonia. However, in the case of GE, information is missing about the values of foreign assets. The presented information shows that indigenous firms are in the minority among foreign investors, though some of them, especially Videoton, have substantial foreign assets.

In the case of Poland, the list of the top 30 non-financial foreign investor companies in the EMGP report contains six electronics companies: Polimex-Mostostal, with USD 169 million foreign assets, AB SA with USD 101 million,

TelForceOne with USD 41 million, Apator with USD 10 million, Relpol and Aplisens, with 4 million euros each (Kaliszuk and Wancio 2013). It is important to note that in the case of Polimex-Mostostal, there is a wide range of activities carried out in Poland and abroad, only a small part of which may be classified as electronics. Similarly, AB SA is an IT services provider and hardware, software and consumer electronics distributor. A clearer case is that of Apator, which manufactures switchgear, switchboards and equipment for the energy and mining sectors. TelForceOne is the largest Polish importer, distributor and producer of mobile devices and accessories, with foreign subsidiaries in the Czech Republic, Slovakia, Romania and Ukraine. Relpol manufactures electromagnetic relays and relay sockets, widely used in electric circuit control of various machines and equipment, vehicles, domestic appliances and electronics, with two production plants abroad (Lithuania and Ukraine) and distribution offices in other European countries. Aplisens has design, production and distribution affiliates in several European countries. The overall outward FDI of these six companies amounted to 240 million euros, thus covering also about one-fourth of the total outward FDI stock in the industry. It is thus most probable that, again, the other three-fourths of outward FDI may be carried out by local subsidiaries of foreign multinationals, and thus it is indirect outward FDI.

In Slovenia, the list of the top indigenous outward investor firms is led by Gorenje (the well-known white goods producing firm), which cannot be counted as an electronics firm in a strict sense and its foreign investment highly exceeds that of Slovenia in electronics. Kolektor Group seems to be a good candidate for an electronics company, as its foreign assets amounted to USD 42 million in 2008 and it is partly operating in electronics. Hidria, a producer of among other climate technologies may be another one, with USD 30 million foreign assets. The third company which contributes to Slovenian FDI in electronics is Iskra, for which the value of foreign assets is available only for 2006, and that year it amounted to USD 80 million (Jaklič and Svetličič 2009). Thus, in the case of Slovenia one can conclude that it may be most probably only indigenous companies that invest abroad in electronics, while indirect outward FDI may actually be negligible there.

The most important characteristics of the Hungarian, Polish and Slovenian electronics companies analysed in the EMGP project can be found in Table 2.

On the basis of the information provided by Table 2, a few important common and distinguishing characteristics of CEE electronics multinationals can be listed.

A *common feature* is that—partly because of the nature of the EMGP project, which tries to list the largest foreign investor companies, all firms are large with the exception of one Hungarian company. The presence of the medium-sized Hungarian Mediso draws attention to the fact that there may be numerous smaller-sized, recently established companies, a few of them qualifying as 'born globals' in CEE electronics, which internationalised successfully within a short period of time. Their presence is expected not only in the three analysed countries, but in other CEE countries as well.

Ownership advantages of the investing firms interact with the location advantages of host countries. On the basis of specificities of location advantages of the

Table 2 Top indigenous electronics multinationals from Hungary, Poland and Slovenia

Name	Country	Listed?	Year of establishment	Year of first OFDI	No. of employees	Foreign assets (million USD)	Foreign empl./total (%)	Foreign sales/total (%)	TNI	No. of affiliates	No. of host countries	Regions present	Main region
Videoton	HU	No	1938 (private: 1992)	1999	7,474	277	9.5	4.8	21	3	2	Eastern Europe and East Central Europe	East Central Europe
Mediso	HU	No	1990	1996	208	43	76.0	78.0	81	2	2	East Central Europe and Western Europe	Equal
Polimex-Mostostal	PL	Yes 1997	1945	2008	14,290	169	n.d.	27.8	20	8	6	East Central Europe and Eastern Europe	East Central Europe
AB SA	PL	Yes 2006	1993	2007	704	101	52.6	39.7	41	6	2	East Central Europe	East Central Europe
Apator	PL	Yes	1949 (private: 1992, EBO)	1999	1,923	10	12.5	13.4	11	5	4	East Central Europe and Eastern Europe	Eastern Europe

Relpol	PL	Yes 1996	1958 (transform.: 1991)	1993	729	4	35.2	33.3	27	7	6	East Central Europe and Eastern Europe	Eastern Europe
Aplisens	PL	Yes	1992	2001	291	4	11.7	30.0	18	7	6	East Central Europe and Eastern Europe	Eastern Europe
Kolektor Group	SI	No	1963	2002	2,395	42	26.9	64.3	37	12	11	Western Europe, South Europe, Central and South America, Asia	Europe
Hidria	SI	No	1960	n.d.	2,511	30	11.3	78.1	34	20	11	Europe, CIS, Americas, Asia, Australia	Europe
Iskra	SI	No	1945	n.d.	1,910	n.d. (80)	2.1	52.5	18	7	7	Europe, CIS, North America	Europe

Source: Author's compilation based on the country reports available in the EMGP project: http://ccsi.columbia.edu/publications/emgp/
Note: Latest available data (for Hungary: 2013, for Poland: 2011, Slovenia: 2008, due to their availability in the EMGP project); TNI is calculated by averaging the following three ratios: foreign assets to total assets, foreign sales to total sales, and foreign employees to total employees and is expressed as a percentage, meaning the higher the TNI the more internationalised the company is

host countries, we can assume that companies in Table 2 have multiple motivations. While the market-seeking motive dominates in the case of CEE multinationals, as we could see in the literature review (see e.g. Svetličič et al. 2007 or Radlo and Sass 2012), in at least two cases discussed here we can identify the efficiency-seeking motive. There are signs that parallel to the growth of local wages, resident firms, including a few indigenous local firms, are attempting to enhance their productivity and competitiveness through relocating the most labour-intensive activities to neighbouring or geographically close countries with lower wages, i.e. realising efficiency-seeking investments. There are at least two firms with efficiency-seeking investments. As the Slovenian EMGP report formulated it (Jaklič and Svetličič 2009): in the case of Kolektor, cost considerations also have motivated the relocation of production to Bosnia and Herzegovina. For the Hungarian Videoton, cost considerations connected to wage differences were important when they moved production to foreign affiliates in Bulgaria and Ukraine (see more details in the short company case study of Videoton at the end of this section). In the case of the other companies with investments in Eastern European countries with considerably lower wage costs (four Polish firms and two other Slovenian ones), the efficiency-seeking motive may also be present. Thus this may be an industry specific feature. However, the market-seeking motive clearly dominates in the case of Polimex-Mostostal, which is present abroad through an international sales network (agencies or locally registered branch offices) and manufacturing plants (Kaliszuk and Wancio 2013:41), whereby the latter also sell products in their local markets.

On the other hand, the strategy of certain indigenous and highly competitive companies includes outward FDI to developed countries, where they are acquiring existing brands, patents, technologies etc. or simply establish a subsidiary in order to be much closer either to the innovative centres of the given segment of the industry (thus investing with a strategic asset-seeking motive) or to their (potential) customers (market-seeking motive) or both. That may be the case for the smaller Hungarian investor, Mediso with its investment in Germany, and assumedly for other Polish and Slovenian firms as well, which are present in Western Europe and in North America with investment projects.

It is obvious, that the year of the first FDI project is quite recent, which is understandable on the basis of the specificities of the transition process that these countries underwent. The earliest outward FDI project was executed by a Polish firm in 1993, followed by a Hungarian one in 1996. For the Slovenian companies it is difficult to identify the start of outward expansion, as it was initially carried out into other Yugoslav Republics, which was not counted as foreign at that time. Nonetheless, the survival of these contacts after the break-up of the former Yugoslavia turned these projects into outward FDI. Thus, the Slovenian electronics companies may be considered as clear pioneers among the analysed firms.

An already underlined important *difference* is, that in Slovenia, locally-owned companies are responsible for all outward FDI in electronics, while in the case of Poland and especially Hungary we can assume that a large part of electronics outward FDI is carried out by local subsidiaries of foreign multinationals for various reasons (e.g. tax optimisation, organisation structure of the company, better knowledge of the foreign location by the management of the Hungarian subsidiary, see e.g. Kalotay 2012).

The geographic orientation of the firms seem to differ, especially for the Slovenian companies, for which Europe (and more distant continents, as well) play an important role, as opposed to a more East Central and Eastern European orientation of the Hungarian and Polish firms. This wider outreach of Slovenian firms may be attributed to their earlier start, as it is obvious that they have a more 'global', or at least European presence as compared to Hungarian or Polish ones. For example, the Slovenian Kolektor is producing commutators in a number of major markets: Germany, USA, China (one greenfield project, one joint venture), the Republic of Korea, Brazil, and Iran (Jaklič and Svetličič 2009).

In terms of the number of foreign affiliates, the Slovenian companies show by far the highest values. That may be attributed to their earlier start and wider global presence as compared to the Polish and Hungarian companies. Hungarian firms, on the other hand, have the lowest number of affiliates, though they are on average larger than in the case of the other two countries. A similar situation exists with regard to the number of host countries. Thus, the starting date of internationalisation and country size may both have an impact on this feature of internationalisation.

The size of the foreign assets of the companies is very diverse, stretching from USD 4 million (two Polish firms) to USD 277 million (the Hungarian Videoton). Overall, the foreign assets of the companies are moderate, with the exception of the Hungarian Videoton. Similarly, the share of foreign employees in total is moderate, with the exception of the two recently established and quickly internationalising companies, the Hungarian Mediso and the Polish AB SA. For these two latter, more than half of the employees are hired in subsidiaries abroad. The foreign/total sales indicator is the highest for the Hungarian Mediso: 78 %, followed by the Slovenian Hidria (78 %), the Kolektor Group (64 %) and Iskra (53 %). For these companies, more than half of the sales revenues come from abroad. At the other extreme, the Hungarian Videoton sells only less than 5 % abroad—the reason for that is that the firm's most important partners are Hungarian subsidiaries of large multinational companies.

As a result, the companies in Table 2 differ considerably in terms of their TNI,[7] but this is mainly due to the Hungarian Mediso, one of the youngest companies with a very high TNI, which draws attention to the fact that the firm had an accelerated internationalisation process which makes it similar to international new ventures or born global firms. Mediso's TNI is 81 %, by far the highest, followed by the also relatively recently established AB SA from Poland with 41 % and by the Slovenian Kolektor Group (37 %) and Hidria (34 %). All other companies on the list have a relatively modest TNI of below 30 %.

---

[7]TNI = transnationality index, a composite index measuring the level of internationalisation of a multinational firm. It is an arithmetic mean of the ratio of foreign assets to total assets, foreign sales to total sales and foreign employment to total employment.

An interesting difference referring to a home country factor is that all Polish companies are listed on the Warsaw Stock Exchange, while neither the Hungarian, nor the Slovenian firms' shares are traded on relevant stock exchanges. This refers to differences in local financing and financial institutions and thus raises the issue of the importance of home country factors in explaining the development of ownership advantages.

Videoton

It may be interesting to have a closer look at the largest investor in terms of foreign assets, Videoton. Videoton is a large Hungarian-owned electronic manufacturing services (EMS) provider, which now belongs to the largest regional players supplying European, US and Japanese electronics and automotive companies. It supplies, among others, Robert Bosch, Continental, Delphi, Luk, Suzuki and Visteon in the automotive sector and ABB, Braun, Electrolux, Legrand, Panasonic, Philips, Siemens, Stadler, Schneider Electric in electronics mainly through their Hungarian subsidiaries. It is the fourth largest European EMS. Based on its own traditional technologies and competencies and close cooperation with its partners, the company manufactures parts, sub-assemblies and modules in electronics, plastics and machinery. Videoton provides a wide range of products for the automotive, consumer electronics, household appliances, IT, office equipment and telecommunication industries (Radosevic and Yoruk 2001; Videoton 2015).

Its predecessor was established back in 1938. It was nationalised after the Second World War and became a major state-owned company in the 1980s, employing 18,000 people. After the collapse of its regional markets it was acquired by three Hungarian individuals in the framework of privatisation in 1992. The company group currently employs almost 7500 employees, out of which more than 700 work in foreign subsidiaries. Its revenues amounted to more than 300 million euros in 2011. With regard to its production operations, apart from producing electronics and automotive products, the company also produces related metal and plastic products. It also provides various services to its customers, such as engineering, supply chain management, back-end technologies, logistics etc. The company's headquarters are located in Székesfehérvár (a town located about 60 km from Budapest, connected with the capital city by a highway), though it has 11 locations in and outside Hungary. It is a group of at least 20 companies linked to each other through various direct and indirect equity holdings (Sass and Kovács 2013).

As for its foreign subsidiaries, Videoton acquired 98 % of the shares of a Bulgarian firm in Stara Zagora in 1999. It established a joint venture with a Ukrainian company, Tochpribor, in Mukachevo in 2009. Moreover, it owns a Bulgarian holding company located in the capital, Sofia. Wages in both countries were and still are substantially lower than in Hungary. As a response to pressure to increase wages in Hungary, the company transferred its most labour-intensive activities to these foreign subsidiaries, explaining why it is considered as one of the few examples of efficiency-seeking outward investors in Hungary (Sass and Kovács 2013).

CEE and Emerging Electronics Multinationals

After having a look at the group of CEE indigenous electronics multinationals, we can use the information provided by the EMGP project to compare at least some features of them with those of other emerging electronics multinationals. The table in the Appendix is compiled from the data of the electronics multinationals of the countries, which take part in the EMGP project: Argentina, Brazil, China, Chile, India, Israel, Korea, Mexico, Russia, Taiwan and Turkey.

When comparing CEE electronics multinationals with other emerging electronics multinationals, the most obvious difference is the significantly larger size of the latter in terms of employment or foreign assets. However, it is important to note, that this is the result of home country size differences on one hand: electronics multinationals from "smaller-sized" countries (e.g. Israel and to some extent Argentina) are of a comparable size in terms of their foreign assets to those from CEE in Table 2. On the other hand, these differences may be due to the earlier start of the internationalisation process of the emerging electronics. Together with their overall larger size, emerging electronics multinationals have a larger share of foreign sales in total sales, though the share of foreign employment in total employment is not necessarily larger compared to the ten CEE electronics multinationals. Mainly due to the large foreign assets and large foreign sales per total revenues and less to foreign/total employment, the TNIs of emerging electronics multinationals are usually and on average higher than those of the CEE ones. From the 28 companies, 15 have a higher than 50 % TNI and not necessarily those from smaller countries. We can attribute that partly to their earlier start compared to the CEE firms analysed here.

Another important distinguishing feature is, that while similarly to CEE electronics multinationals, the companies in the Appendix have the strongest presence in their home regions, almost all of them have at the same time a strong global presence, with affiliates in the majority of the continents, including faraway ones. According to the available information, that can be attributed in many cases simply to the fact that these are more "mature" multinationals, which were established and started their foreign expansion much earlier compared to the CEE ones, as it is obvious at least in the case of Korean and Taiwanese electronics multinationals, for which relevant data are available. Another possible conclusion from the geographical 'coverage' of the subsidiaries of these multinationals is that they went through the gradual way of foreign expansion starting in neighbouring or geographically close countries and then entering more faraway countries. CEE multinationals, especially the latecomer Polish and Hungarian ones seem to be in an earlier phase of internationalisation, as their subsidiaries are more concentrated in geographically close countries—although with certain exceptions.

Almost all companies in the Appendix are listed on the respective stock exchanges: in that respect, Polish electronics multinationals have the same features from the CEE companies analysed here as opposed to Hungarian and Slovenian ones.

Overall, there are only few areas where these two groups of electronics multinationals can be compared, mainly due to the lack of data. On the basis of these, it can be assumed that the earlier start of emerging multinationals and larger sized home countries may be important factors explaining their divergent characteristics. Obviously, further research is required in that area.

Conclusion and Further Research

This chapter constitutes the first step in analysing electronics multinationals in the CEE. The first important fact is that there are indigenous electronics multinational companies originating from the CEE region, while outward investments by local subsidiaries of foreign multinationals (indirect outward FDI) seem to dominate outward FDI in the industry analysed with the exception of Slovenia. Larger CEE electronics multinationals are concentrated in a few countries: Hungary, Poland and Slovenia. There may be further smaller-sized players in the industry in other CEE countries (and in the three analysed countries, as well). In the sample there are at least two very quickly internationalising, medium-and large-sized companies with high TNIs, which fact presumably indicates the presence of 'born globals' apart from gradually internationalising large companies in the industry in the CEE region. All these foreign investor companies obviously have the ownership advantages which enable them to invest abroad successfully. Further research is required in order to analyse the actual elements and content of these ownership advantages, which may be specific to the post-transition context.

Based on the locational advantages of their host countries, in addition to the dominant market-seeking, efficiency-seeking motivations may also be important for at least two larger companies, which transfer labour-intensive production to countries with lower wages (or lower total costs). On the other hand, for quickly internationalising highly innovative companies, we assume that the strategic asset seeking or innovation seeking motive may also be present when they invest in highly developed Western European and/or North American countries. The presence of these motivations may be connected to the specificities of the industry, as according to the literature the overwhelmingly dominant motive of foreign investment by indigenous CEE companies is market seeking.

Slovenian electronics multinationals have a wider geographic outreach: they are more global or at least more European than their Hungarian and Polish counterparts. They also have the highest number of foreign affiliates and host countries. That may be partly due to their earlier start and partly to their historic heritage of having been part of a larger country, Yugoslavia which had been dissolved afterwards and with that domestic economic ties became foreign.

The Hungarian Videoton is by far the largest foreign investor company in the industry; otherwise the foreign assets of the companies are moderate. This is especially so compared to other emerging electronics multinationals. In size, CEE multinationals are similar only to one Argentinian and three Israeli firms, while Indian, Chinese, Korean, Taiwanese and Turkish electronics multinationals (some of them holding companies with a number of different activities) are much larger. In these cases, even the home countries are considerably larger than in the case of the CEE, which partly explains their larger size. TNIs are also bigger on average for emerging firms, mainly due to larger relative foreign assets and sales (but not employment). Thus these latter companies have a much more global presence, though—similarly to the CEE firms—their main region is still their home region.

As for future research, one should again emphasise that the present chapter contains only very preliminary results concerning the analysis of CEE electronics multinationals. More detailed company case studies would make the analysis more valid, more topical and more nuanced. Other areas, which are completely left out here in relation to the internationalisation strategies of the companies in question could also be researched through these case studies. These topics include, for example, entry modes, the ownership advantages of the companies, confluence of motivations, especially market-seeking, efficiency seeking and strategic asset seeking; history and timing of internationalisation etc. These would also give more food for thought when comparing CEE electronics multinationals with their emerging and developed country counterparts. Another possible direction may be the collection of statistical data for the indigenous outward investing electronics firms in the region for statistical analysis, which at present seems to be less relevant, as the number of significant foreign investor CEE electronics companies is still minor—but with their growth in future that type of analysis could lead to significant results.

Acknowledgment This research was supported by the Hungarian research fund (OTKA no. 109294).

Appendix

Characteristics of emerging electronics multinationals

Name	Country	Listed?	No. of employees	Foreign assets (million USD)	Foreign empl./total (%)	Foreign sales/total (%)	TNI	No. of affiliates	No. of host countries	Regions present	Main region
Weg	BR	Y	18,670	509	15.5	34.0	21	n.a.	n.a.	n.a.	n.a.
Itautec	BR	Y	6,218	131	6.4	22.8	16	n.a.	n.a.	n.a.	n.a.
OMZ	RU	Y	16,000	478	11.9	65.4	38	8	4	Eastern Europe and Central Asia; Other Europe; Latin America	Other Europe
Videocon	IN	(2015)	10,000	1,626	n.a.	59.2	65	16	11	Europe, Middle East, Africa, Americas, Asia	Latin America
ZTE	CN	Y	61,350	3,143	31.0	60.6	44	n.a.	n.a.	n.a.	n.a.
Lenovo	CN	Y	22,511	2,732	23.1	56.8	41	n.a.	n.a.	n.a.	n.a.
BGH SA	AR	N	1,892	2	27.2	31.1	20	5	4	Latin America	Latin America
Elbit	IL	Y	n.a.	405	75.0	75.0	41	21	10	West Europe, East Europe and Central Asia, Americas, Asia	North America
Tower	IL	Y	n.a.	248	62.0	98.0	70	2	2	North America, East Asia and the Pacific	Equal
Lumenis	IL	Y	n.a.	42	68.0	81.0	73	16	13	West Europe, Americas, Asia	East Asia and the Pacific
Gilat Satellite Networks	IL	Y	n.a.	27	85.0	85.0	59	9	6	West Europe, Americas	Americas
Samsung	KR	Y	286,284	18,449	66.5	89.0	56	135	n.d.	Asia, Europe, Americas, Middle-East and Africa	Asia

Emerging CEE Multinationals in the Electronics Industry

LG Electronics	KR	Y	24,683	3,456	16.0	71.2	34	124	n.a.	Asia, Europe, Americas, Middle-East and Africa	Asia
Hon Hai	TW	Y	611,000	10,699	84.0	99.0	72	314	27	Asia, Europe, Americas	East Asia and the Pacific
Asustek	TW	Y	113,324	6,416	61.0	96.0	71	142	36	Asia, Africa, Europe, Americas, Australia	East Asia and the Pacific
Quanta	TW	Y	64,719	5,524	33.0	93.0	58	50	12	Asia, Europe, Americas, Australia	East Asia and the Pacific
ACER	TW	Y	6,624	4,897	84.0	97.0	78	139	52	Asia, Europe, Americas	Western Europe
AU Optronics	TW	Y	51,378	4,874	75.0	98.0	66	26	13	Asia, Australia, Europe, Americas	East Asia and the Pacific
Wistron	TW	Y	39,239	4,667	56.0	81.0	73	43	13	Asia, Europe, Americas	East Asia and the Pacific
Taiwan Semiconductor	TW	Y	26,390	3,661	9.0	55.0	28	24	11	Asia, Western Europe, Americas	Latin-America
Compal	TW	Y	58,025	3,458	58.0	99.0	63	56	15	Asia, Europe, Americas	East Asia and the Pacific
Delta	TW	Y	58,000	3,212	77.0	92.0	82	37	11	Asia, Western Europe, Americas	East Asia and the Pacific

(continued)

Name	Country	Listed?	No. of employees	Foreign assets (million USD)	Foreign empl./total (%)	Foreign sales/total (%)	TNI	No. of affiliates	No. of host countries	Regions present	Main region
United Microelectronics	TW	Y	13,051	2,591	44.0	62.0	46	18	11	Asia, Western Europe, Americas	East Asia and the Pacific
Inventec	TW	Y	29,646	2,399	95.0	80.0	76	21	10	Asia, Eastern Europe, Americas	East Asia and the Pacific
Synnex	TW	Y	5,192	1,708	77.0	82.0	78	24	10	Asia, Africa, Australia, Americas	East Asia and the Pacific
Qisda	TW	Y	41,942	1,323	49.0	43.0	43	64	26	Asia, Africa, Europe, Americas	East Asia and the Pacific
Andalou	TR	n.a.	27,500	4,443	50.0	42.5	44	20	17	West Europe, Other Europe, Asia, Africa	Europe
Koc	TR	n.a.	82,158	3,333	10.1	3.9	7	41	24	West Europe, Other Europe, Asia, Africa	Europe

Source: Country reports prepared in the framework of the EMGP project: http://ccsi.columbia.edu/publications/emgp/
Notes: Brazil: 2009; Russia: 2009; India: 2006; China: 2008; Argentina: 2009; Chile: 2011—no electronics among the top 20; Israel: 2011; Korea: 2013 (note: both companies are present with more than one parent); Mexico: 2013—no electronics; Taiwan: 2009; Turkey: 2012, both Andalou and Koc conglomerates, only part of their businesses is in electronics
n.a. data not available

References

Andreff, W. (2003). The newly emerging TNCs from economies in transition: A comparison with Third World outward FDI. *Transnational Corporations, 12*(2), 73–118.

Antalóczy, K., & Sass, M. (2001). Greenfield investments in Hungary: Are they different from privatization FDI? *Transnational Corporations, 10*(3), 39–60.

Aulakh, P. S. (2007). Emerging multinationals from developing economies: Motivations, paths and performance. *Journal of International Management, 13*, 235–240.

Buckley, P., Clegg, J., Cross, A., Liu, X., Voss, H., & Zheng, P. (2007). The determinants of Chinese outward foreign direct investment. *Journal of International Business Studies, 38*(4), 499–518.

Caves, R. E. (1996). *Multinational enterprise and economic analysis*. Cambridge: Cambridge University Press.

Chan, L. (2013, November 15). *ICT Hungary: Eastern Europe's emerging electronics hub*. HKTDC. Accessed January 15, 2016, from http://economists-pick-research.hktdc.com/business-news/article/Research-Articles/ICT-Hungary-Eastern-Europe-s-emerging-electronics-hub/rp/en/1/1X000000/1X09V8VH.htm

Contessi, S., & El-Ghazaly, H. (2010). Multinationals from emerging economies. Growing but little understood. *The Regional Economist, July*, 6–18.

Dicken, P. (2011). *Global shift. Mapping the changing contours of the world economy* (6th ed.). Thousand Oaks, CA: SAGE.

Drahokoupil, J. (2009). The investment-promotion machines: The politics of foreign direct investment promotion in Central and Eastern Europe. *Europe-Asia Studies, 60*(2), 197–225.

Dunning, J. H. (1993). *Multinational enterprises and the global economy*. Reading, MA: Addison-Wesley.

Dunning, J. H., & Lundan, S. M. (2008). *Multinational enterprises and the global economy* (2nd ed.). Cheltenham: Edward Elgar.

EMGP. (2016). *Emerging market global players*. Accessed February 23, 2016, from http://ccsi.columbia.edu/publications/emgp/

Foster, N., Hunya, G., Pindyuk, O., & Richter, S. (2011). *Revival of the Visegrad countries' mutual trade after their EU accession: A search for explanation*. WIIW Research Reports 372. Vienna: The Vienna Institute for International Economic Studies.

Galgóczi, B. (2009). Boom and bust in Central and Eastern Europe: Lessons on the sustainability of an externally financed growth model. *Journal of Contemporary European Research, 5*(4), 614–625.

Guillén, M. F., & García-Canal, E. (2009). The American model of the multinational firm and the "new" multinationals from emerging economies. *Academy of Management Perspectives, 23*(2), 23–35.

Hunya, G., & Sass, M. (2005). *Coming and going: Gains and losses from relocations affecting Hungary*. WIIW Research Reports 323. Vienna: The Vienna Institute for International Economic Studies.

IMF. (2013, August). *IMF multi-country report. German-Central European supply chain – cluster report*. IMF Country Report No. 13/263. Washington, DC: IMF.

Jaklič, A., & Svetličič, M. (2009). *Survey ranking Slovenian multinationals finds them small and vulnerable, but flexible and increasingly international*. Accessed January 15, 2016, from http://ccsi.columbia.edu/files/2013/11/Slovenia_2009.pdf

Jung, S. C. (2014). The analysis of strategic management of samsung electronics company through the generic value chain model. *International Journal of Software Engineering and Its Applications, 8*(12), 133–142.

KABCLTD. (2012, February). Global value chain analysis on Samsung electronics. Accessed January 15, 2016, from http://albertacanada.com/korea/images/GlobalValueChainAnalysisSamsungElectronics.pdf

Kaliszuk, E., & Wancio, A. (2013). *Polish multinationals: Expanding and seeking innovation abroad*. Accessed January 15, 2016, from http://ccsi.columbia.edu/files/2013/10/Poland_2013.pdf

Kalotay, K. (2004). The European flying geese. New FDI patterns for the old continent? *Research in International Business and Finance, 18*(2004), 27–49.

Kalotay, K. (2012). Indirect FDI. *The Journal of World Investment & Trade, 13*(4), 542–555.

Kaminsky, B., & Ng, F. (2001). *Trade and production fragmentation*. Central European Economies in European Union Networks of Production and Marketing, World Bank Policy Research Working Paper, 2611. Washington, DC: The World Bank.

Lall, S. (1983). *The new multinationals*. New York: Wiley.

Lessard, D., & Lucea, R. (2009). Mexican multinationals: Insights from CEMEX. In R. Singh (Ed.), *Emerging multinationals in emerging markets* (pp. 280–311). Cambridge: Cambridge University Press.

Linden, G. (1998). *Building production networks in Central Europe: The case of the electronics industry*. BRIE, Working Paper 126. Accessed January 15, 2016, from http://brie.berkeley.edu/publications/WP126.pdf

Lipsey, R. E. (2006). *Measuring the impacts of FDI in Central and Eastern Europe*. NBER Working Paper 12808. Accessed January 15, 2016, from http://www.nber.org/papers/w12808

Mathews, J. A. (2006). Dragon multinationals: New players in 21. century globalisation. *Asia Pacific Journal of Management, 23*(1), 5–27.

OECD. (2004). *Information technology outlook*. Paris: OECD.

Radlo, M.-J., & Sass, M. (2012). Outward foreign direct investments and emerging multinational companies from Central and Eastern Europe: The case of Visegrád countries. *Eastern European Economics, 50*(2), 5–21.

Radosevic, S. (2005). The electronics industry in Central and Eastern Europe: A new global production location. *Papeles del Este, 10*, 1–15.

Radosevic, S., & Yoruk, D. E. (2001). *Videoton: The growth of enterprise through entrepreneurship and network alignment*. Accessed January 15, 2016, from http://eprints.ucl.ac.uk/17578/1/17578.pdf

Rahman, J., & Zhao, T. (2013). *Export performance in Europe: What do we know from supply links?* IMF Working Paper 13/62. Washington, DC: IMF.

Ramamurti, R. (2012). What is really different about emerging market multinationals? *Global Strategy Journal, 2*(1), 41–47.

Rugraff, E. (2010). Strengths and weaknesses of the outward FDI paths of the Central European countries. *Post-Communist Economies, 22*(1), 1–17.

Sass, M. (2015). FDI trends and patterns in electronics. In B. Galgóczi, J. Drahokoupil, & M. Bernaciak (Eds.), *Foreign investment in eastern and southern Europe after 2008: Still a lever of growth?* (pp. 257–295). Brussels: ETUI.

Sass, M., Antalóczy, K., & Éltető, A. (2012). Emerging multinationals and the role of virtual indirect investors: The case of Hungary. *Eastern European Economics, 50*(2), 41–58.

Sass, M., Antalóczy, K., & Éltető, A. (2014). Outward FDI from Hungary: The emergence of Hungarian multinationals. *Entrepreneurial Business and Economics Review, 2*(3), 47–62.

Sass, M., & Kovács, O. (2013). *A snapshot of the leading Hungarian multinationals 2011*. Accessed January 15, 2016, from http://ccsi.columbia.edu/files/2013/10/Hungary_2013.pdf

Sass, M., & Kovács, O. (2015). *Hungarian multinationals in 2013 – a slow recovery after the crisis?* Accessed January 15, 2016, from http://ccsi.columbia.edu/files/2015/04/EMGP-Hungary-Report-2015-covering-2013-FINAL.pdf

Sass, M., & Szalavetz, A. (2013). Crisis and upgrading: The case of the Hungarian automotive and electronics sectors. *Europe-Asia Studies, 65*(3), 489–507.

Sass, M., & Szanyi, M. (2012). *Two essays on Hungarian relocations*. Discussion Papers; MT-DP 2012/23. Budapest: Institute of Economics, Centre for Economic and Regional Studies, Hungarian Academy of Sciences, 55 p.

Sturgeon, T. J., & Kawakami, M. (2010). Global value chains in the electronics industry: Was the crisis a window of opportunity for developing countries? In O. Cattaneo, G. Gereffi, & C. Staritz (Eds.), *Global value chains in a post-crisis world* (pp. 245–302). Washington, DC: World Bank.

Svetličič, M. (2004). Transition economies' multinationals – are they different from third world multinationals? In C. Chakraborty (Ed.), Proceedings of the 8th International conference on Global Business and Economic Development, Guadalajara, Mexico, January 7–10, 2004. Montclair: Montclair State University.

Svetličič, M., & Jaklič, A. (2006). *Outward FDI from new European Union Member States*. Accessed January 15, 2016, from https://www.oenb.at/dam/jcr:d5ca2613-63f2-4915-8a18-fbd9472e18ac/07_ceei_2006_paper_svetlicic_jaklic.pdf

Svetličič, M., Jaklič, A., & Burger, A. (2007). Internationalisation of small and medium sized enterprises from selected Central European countries. *Eastern European Economics, 45*(4), 36–65.

Svetličič, M., & Rojec, M. (2003). *Facilitating transition by internationalization: Outward direct investment from Central European economies in transition*. Famham: Ashgate.

Szalavetz, A. (2004). *Az információtechnológiai forradalom és a felzárkózó gazdaságok. (The information technology revolution and the emerging economies)*. Budapest: Kossuth.

Szanyi, M. (2006, January). *Competitiveness and industrial renewal via production relocation by global multinational networks. Post 1990s development in Hungary's electrical industry*. IWE Working Paper No. 166. Budapest: IWE.

UNCTAD. (1998). *World Investment Report 1998: Trends and determinants*. New York: United Nations.

UNCTAD. (2003). *World Investment Report. FDI policies for development: National and international perspectives*. New York: United Nations.

UNCTAD. (2004). *World Investment Report. The shift towards services*. New York: United Nations.

Videoton. (2015). *One company – infinite possibilities*. Accessed January 15, 2016, from http://www.videoton.hu/downloads/videoton_general_eng.pdf

Human Capital and HRM as a Source of Competitive Advantage and Effectiveness: Evidence from Poland

Anna Jawor-Joniewicz and Łukasz Sienkiewicz

Abstract The present chapter focuses on the interrelations between organisational human capital and human resources management of a company and their influence on the competitive advantage and company effectiveness. At the outset, we analyse three concepts related to Human Resources Management: High Performance Work System, Competency-Based HRM, and Diversity Management. We present the main benefits, as evidenced by findings from international surveys, which firms can draw from the implementation of such concepts. In the paper, we pay particular attention to the most recent Polish analyses related to each of the aforementioned concepts. They show that, taking into account the state of advancement of HR solutions, Polish organisations lag quite far behind European and American ones. This distance can be reduced, e.g. by the popularisation of tools for measuring human resources in Polish enterprises. One such recent tool is presented in this chapter. This tool could prove instrumental in making Polish employers appreciate the importance of investing in human capital; furthermore, it could increase their knowledge of the effect that HRM practices have on the performance of their enterprises and their competitive position.

Keywords Human capital • Human Resources Management • Organisational effectiveness

Introduction

In the available literature of the subject, organisational results are predominantly measured *via* two distinct, but interrelated concepts—organisational effectiveness and competitive advantage (Flamholtz and Hua 2003). According to the resource-

---

A. Jawor-Joniewicz
Institute for Labour and Social Affairs, Warsaw, Poland
e-mail: a.jawor@ipiss.com.pl

Ł. Sienkiewicz (✉)
SGH Warsaw School of Economics, Warsaw, Poland
e-mail: lukasz.sienkiewicz@sgh.waw.pl

based view of firms (Barney 1991), competitive advantage can be achieved through the absorption and effective utilisation of resources that are valuable, rare, inimitable and organised. This perspective can also be applied to human capital (HC), as people can be conceptualised as organisational assets that meet the aforementioned criteria. Moreover, as postulated by Prahalad et al. (1990), competitive advantage can be gained through company-specific "core competences" that relate to the unique capabilities of the firm, often embedded in organisational processes. These processes can, *inter alia*, include human resources management systems and practices. Therefore, not only can human capital as an asset be a source of competitive advantage, but Human Resources Management (HRM) practices, or the specific architecture of these practices (Lepak and Snell 2002), can also lead companies to comparably better results and a competitive edge over others.

In line with the concept of human resources accounting (Flamholtz et al. 2002), organisational human capital can be attributed a specific value, because it has the ability to generate future benefits for the company, calculated as the difference between revenues and the costs of investment in human capital. The opportunity to demonstrate such dependences, however, is conditioned by the ability of the organisation to generate evidence base on correlations and—even more importantly—causal relationships between human capital and human resources management and organisational performance. A number of complex approaches aimed at establishing a clear link between HRM practices and firms' effectiveness exist, including the world renowned Scandia Navigator (Edvinsson 1997), Balanced Scorecard (Kaplan and Norton 2005) and its HR equivalent—HR Scorecard (Becker et al. 2001), and Intangible Assets Monitor (Sveiby 1997). However, the measurement of such relationships is always problematic due to the complicated nature of causal dependency paths from ambiguity to performance (Powell et al. 2006).

Human capital serves as a primary source of value in the knowledge economy. Theodore Schultz, a Nobel Prize winner in 1971, concluded that human capital consists of the acquired qualitative characteristics of a population that are of value and can be enriched *via* appropriate investment. Human capital is, therefore, a set of individual characteristics such as knowledge, skills, health, and values that are impossible to separate from the individual. It is also an economic factor that can develop over time through appropriate investment. The use of human capital generates value—both at the level of a single organisation, and on a macroeconomic scale—for the society and the state. From the point of view of generating value through human capital, it is not only the individual features of employees (their potential) that are important, but also all the environmental factors (macroeconomic) that determine its correct utilisation.

It is therefore vital to understand both the underlying concepts behind the influence of human factors on the effectiveness of companies, and also the empirical evidence related to such relationships. The aim of this chapter is to analyse the state of the art of contemporary concepts of Human Resources Management in Poland, namely: High Performance Work System, Competency-Based HRM, Diversity Management and Measurement of Human Capital. For all of those concepts, we analyse their potential in supporting the effectiveness and competitive advantage of companies, as well as provide empirical evidence on their utilisation in Poland based on existing current research.

High Performance Work Systems

An attempt to learn about how selected HRM practices are related to company performance was at the origin of the concept of High Performance Work System (HPWS). Some theoretical and empirical studies which have focused on this topic have presented the view that the practices with the strongest effect on both the results of work and the acceleration of innovation in organisations are practices that foster the building of employees' involvement—High Involvement Work Practices (HIWP) (Benson et al. 2006). Results of surveys devoted to HPWSs and HIWP allow us to determine the combinations of HRM practices which, if introduced in a company, can bring about a visible improvement in its performance and a strengthening of its competitive position. And so, according to Benson, Young and Lawler (2006), the key solutions include:

- increasing employee participation in companies (both as regards decision-making and financial participation),
- use of performance-related pay (both in relation to individuals and teams),
- ensuring continuous development opportunities for employees,
- paying attention to good communication within the company.

Whether or not the above-mentioned practices are effective depends also on how interconnected they are. The point is that they should support and complement each other.

Analyses conducted over the last 20 years with respect to the benefits of HPWS implementation in enterprises indicate that the use of such an approach in a company contributes, *inter alia*, to:

- an increase in market value (Becker and Huselid 1998; Huselid 1995),
- increased profits (Becker and Huselid 1998; Huselid 1995; Guest et al. 2003),
- increased Return on Equity (ROE) (Benson et al. 2006),
- increased revenues (Benson et al. 2006),
- increased sales value per employee (Becker and Huselid 1998; Huselid 1995; Ericksen 2007),
- reduced staff turnover (Becker and Huselid 1998; Huselid 1995; Guest et al. 2003).

Polish analyses have focused mainly on the effect that HPWSs and HIWP can have on making an enterprise more innovative, and thus on strengthening its competitive position.

In a survey carried out by the Institute of Labour and Social Affairs (*Instytut Pracy i Spraw Socjalnych*) in 2008–2009 using a sample of 83 companies listed on the Warsaw Stock Exchange, 50 innovative businesses and their 2070 employees, three models of Human Resources Management were tested, especially their correlation with innovation (Borkowska 2010). The M1 model, the general one, was created from a majority of the HRM practices covered by the survey, such a majority taking into account nearly all areas of Human Resources Management. The M2 model was drawn up using an HPWS index designed on the basis of a set of four practices (in accordance with Becker and Huselid's approach): recruitment and selection, managerial staff development, performance-based pay, and involvement in the company. The M3 model, on the other hand, created from an HIWP index, took into account combinations of four practices which shape employees' involvement. These were: employees' training and development, performance-based pay, information and communication, as well as employee participation [in accordance with the approach by Benson et al. (2006)].

The results of the Polish surveys show that there is a strong correlation between HRM and the level and growth rate of innovation (the correlation being stronger in the case of the level than in the case of the growth rate), as well as the organisation's market value. These are definitely influenced to the largest extent by the involvement-based model (M3). Such an approach to HRM is a driver of innovation, contributing positively to companies' efficiency and competitiveness. Moreover, the model in question helps to create employee attitudes which are of key importance for the development of innovation: involvement and openness to innovation. On the other hand, the model with the least significant effect on the level of innovation is the HPWS model (M2), while the general HRM model (M1) has the least significant effect on market value. It has also been shown that the homogeneousness of HRM practices has a positive effect on enterprises' performance and the level of their innovativeness. Another factor ensuring a higher level and growth rate of innovation is achievement of cohesion in a company between its HRM strategy and its general strategy.

Analyses of the four sets of practices that are particularly brought into prominence in the M3 model (which is of key importance from the point of view of innovation enhancement) have shown that both companies quoted on the stock exchange and innovative businesses willingly use performance-based pay. This practice turns out to be highly correlated with innovation. In companies with a pro-innovation strategy, the results of team work are rewarded more often than in those quoted on the stock exchange. It seems, however, that management bodies of enterprises that operate in Poland underestimate non-financial motivation instruments that are significant from the viewpoint of building employees' involvement. In addition, employees of Polish companies are seldom offered solutions in the field of financial participation, and rewarding creativeness or innovativeness (e.g. suggesting improvements) occurs in just a small number of enterprises.

Easy access to information and good communication within a company are recognised by the managerial staff of the surveyed enterprises as a significant factor contributing to firm innovativeness. Nevertheless, in the organisations included in the analysis this practice did not have the features of a system and it was not used in Human Resources Management to a sufficient degree. For example, employees were not provided with information about the results of opinion or satisfaction surveys, and they were not told about the extent to which such surveys were used in corrective actions or improvements undertaken by management.

Similarly, solutions in the field of employee participation are not used frequently enough in firms operating in Poland. The managerial staff of the organisations surveyed seems to display a certain lack of trust when it comes to making employees co-responsible for a company's well-being. This can have a negative effect on the involvement of those employed, their innovativeness and results of their work.

According to the surveys under discussion, investment in employees' development, which is one of the pillars of the HIWP concept, has an unquestionably positive effect on companies' innovativeness and on fostering employee attitudes that facilitate it. However, for development programmes geared towards increasing the creativity of employees to be more effective, the following activities must become more widespread: use of group and individual coaching, providing broad access to training events to all employees, conducting training sessions about innovation and independent problem-solving, use of rotation and learning-by-doing as part of various teams, providing employees with ambitious, challenging tasks, promotion of knowledge-sharing, and ensuring clear career paths.

For those enterprises which strive to achieve a sustainable competitive advantage, the setting up of a comprehensive system for career development that will allow for working out and keeping unique competency resources in the company is becoming one of the key challenges.

Competency-Based Human Resources Management

The view that competency resources are of vital importance for the current and future health of enterprises was the basis for the concept of Competency-Based HRM. According to international surveys, the use of a competency-based approach in HRM brings tangible benefits to companies (Cook and Bernthal 1998). The broader the implementation scope of the competency-based perspective, the greater those benefits. Introducing the competency approach strengthens the HRM system and has a positive effect on the results HRM obtains through its work. Moreover, most of the companies which took part in the aforementioned surveys (67 %) reported improvement in the enterprise's performance after the competency-based approach was introduced to many HRM areas. Among the organisations which implement that concept in six areas of HRM, as many as 91 % declared a marked improvement in the results of their work. As for the group of enterprises which used the competency-based approach in one area only, on the other hand, only 30 % noticed a positive change in the company's performance. The HRM areas that European companies are the most eager to restructure using a competency-based approach include: assessment, recruitment and selection, staff development, planning and creation of career paths, as well as pay systems and promotion (Rostkowski 2004).

The use of the competency-based approach in relation to the whole HRM system not only improves performance, as mentioned above, but also contributes to boosting a company's productivity and increasing its flexibility and adaptability to volatile market conditions. Moreover, it has a strong impact on its employees, providing them with continuing development opportunities and increasing their involvement, work satisfaction and creativity (Levenson et al. 2006). Other advantages of introducing a competency-based HRM system listed by Salter (2002) include: increasing employees' flexibility and facilitating their career planning; rapid adjustment to changes in the technologies used; greater employee involvement in problem-solving; ability to reduce staff numbers through including specialised tasks among skills required at group level; reducing the need to use third-party experts.

The main factor that motivates companies to implement Competency-Based HRM is the hope for a definite improvement of work outcomes (Miller et al. 2001; Lans et al. 2008). Less frequently, enterprises' management bodies hope that the training programmes that they offer can be adjusted to employees' individual needs better, so that such adjustments lead to employees' improved competencies and greater involvement.

Introduction of Competency-Based HRM, as is the case with every strategic change, brings the best results only after some time. A marked improvement in firm performance was recorded by 86 % of the companies which used that approach for over 10 years, by 75 %—for at least 2 years, and only by 50 % of the organisations which used it for a year (Cook and Bernthal 1998). The benefits of using of a competency-based model have been the decisive factor in making this approach vastly popular in the USA and in EU countries. According to data gathered by Cook and Bernthal (1998), in the 1990s Competency-Based HRM was implemented by 75 % of American companies. In Poland, on the other hand, this model of HRM is still not popular enough, although in recent years it has enjoyed steady growth in popularity. Surveys carried out in 2011–2012 by the Educational Research Institute (*Instytut Badań Edukacyjnych*—IBE) as well as by Deloitte and the Polish Human Resources Management Association (*Polskie Stowarzyszenie Zarządzania Kadrami*—PSZK) show that the competency-based approach is more frequently used by large companies than medium-sized ones (Sienkiewicz et al. 2014; Jończak and Woźny 2011). Analyses by IBE indicate that a comprehensive Competency-Based HRM was put in place by 27.7 % of the surveyed enterprises, and another 15.6 % were in the process of its implementation or designing while the survey was being carried out. Similar results were obtained in the survey by Deloitte and PSZK; according to them, in Poland competency-based models have been implemented by 42 % of organisations. Unfortunately, as the authors of the report "*Trendy HRM w Polsce*" ("HRM trends in Poland") have noted, Competency-Based HRM in enterprises often does not constitute a coherent system, and the potential of the models that have been designed is not fully exploited. The continued relatively low popularity of the competency-based approach in Poland is surprising in view of the fact that Polish entrepreneurs are aware of the effect the lack of specific competencies has on the competitive position of firms. As many as two-thirds of those surveyed by IBE defined this effect as "significant".

The most frequent factor motivating Polish entrepreneurs to restructure HRM so that it is competency-based is related to an attempt to increase employees' productivity and efficiency; correlating of employees' behaviour with the values and strategy of the organisation; and building clear career paths for employees (Sienkiewicz 2004). Other quoted reasons include the development of competencies in directions forced out by the market; easier introduction of organisational changes through increasing employees' flexibility; integration of different systems of managing human resources, as well as a corporate policy imposed from the top—the latter reason providing some tangible evidence that some entrepreneurs are not sold on the idea of Competency-Based HRM.

The competency-based models implemented in firms operating in Poland usually do not include all areas of HRM, only selected ones, which can make them less effective. Therefore, it is difficult to say that a comprehensive competency-based HRM strategy is operative in such cases. And so, according to Sienkiewicz et al. (2014), the competency-based approach is applied most often in: recruitment and selection (69.6 % of the surveyed companies); creating job descriptions and their evaluation (63.2 %); training and development (58.2 %); remuneration systems (56.1 %), and assessment (47.9 %).

The discussed surveys show that the enterprises which decided to implement a competency-based model more often than not recorded such benefits as an improvement in work results of staff and an increase in their flexibility. Moreover, the use of the competency-based approach allowed companies to expand the previous knowledge, skills and experience of their employees by adding new competencies.

Diversity Management

The issue of the effects that skilful human resources management has on improving the competitive position of the firm is reflected in the concept of diversity management (DM), which has been gaining increasing popularity in the USA and the EU since the late twentieth century. It is based on the assumption that personnel's diversity, understood as all aspects in respect to which people differ from or are similar to one another, constitutes one of the key resources of organisations. In certain conditions, it can become a source of business benefits (Kirton and Greene 2005). The list of factors which can create conditions for the occurrence of the above-mentioned differences and similarities between employees seems to be endless; e.g. gender, age, disability, ethnic origin, nationality, sexual orientation, family status, education, political beliefs, trade union membership, religion, employment for a definite or indefinite period of time, on a full- or part-time basis, under a contract of employment or civil law contract, professional experience, and even attitude towards life or learning style. Nevertheless, the majority of analyses related to diversity management tackle the aspect of employees' gender. They have shown that creating teams that are diversified in terms of gender and including women on a wide basis as members of managerial staff results e.g. in improved profitability (Adler 2001). International surveys provide ample evidence that implementation of a diversity management strategy (that includes not just gender, but also many other qualities which are shared by employees or make them different) brings tangible benefits to enterprises. Such benefits include, *inter alia*: higher profits, profitability and productivity at the company, reductions in costs, more creativity and innovation, increased employee involvement, a positive effect on employer branding, increased of adaptation capabilities, better adjustment to customer needs, more effective talent management, and a reduced risk of unwanted phenomena in the company, such as discrimination (Allen et al. 2008; Kochan et al. 2003; Mor Barak 2014).

The advantages of introducing diversity management should constitute an important argument for enterprises to reach out for solutions in the area of DM. Indeed, European enterprises do seem to notice the benefits of DM. According to surveys carried out in 2005 among organisations from 25 EU member states, 42 % of the companies surveyed (members of the European Business Test Panel—EBTP) had managed diversity for over 5 years, and another 27 % had put the relevant management place in the 5 years preceding the survey. As regards how widespread the use of DM is, Polish enterprises are trailing far behind other European ones. Analyses by the Responsible Business Forum (*Forum Odpowiedzialnego Biznesu*) and periodic surveys by the Polish Confederation *Lewiatan* (Diversity Barometer) indicate that in Poland this approach is used by approx. 20 % of companies (Lisowska and Sznajder 2013, 2014), while an official strategy of diversity management is employed by only about 2 % of companies (Gryszko 2009). The results of surveys carried out in January 2015 by the Institute of Labour and Social Studies (ILSS)[1] are even more depressing. Among 104 enterprises covered by the analyses, only in 3 had a DM strategy been created and implemented in business reality. In addition, most of the surveyed heads of HRM units (60 %) had never heard about the concept of diversity management, and those who were not unfamiliar with the term usually confused it with a strategy of equal opportunities and counteracting workplace discrimination. More often than not, the DM-oriented restructuring of HRM is pursued by large firms, especially the Polish branches of international corporations, in which this strategy has been standard for quite a while now.

---

[1]The survey was carried out in 104 medium and large enterprises operating in Poland from knowledge-intensive industries (on the sample of 2045 employees and 104 heads of HRM units) as part of the project "Creating engagement in the context of diversity management", financed from the funds of the National Centre for Science (*Narodowe Centrum Nauki*) pursuant to agreement No. UMO-2012/07/B/HS4/03008.

It seems that Polish entrepreneurs are still at the beginning of the road when it comes to unleashing the full potential of human capital, and they do not completely notice the benefits of diversifying management methods when dealing with varied groups of employees. Even though the managerial staff of the organisations surveyed do not manage diversity, and oftentimes do not even see a need to do so, slightly more than half of the employees (52 % of women and 53 % of men) believe that the diverse needs and expectations of those employed in their companies are noticed. The percentage of people who claim that those diverse needs and expectations are not only noticed by the employer, but also taken account of in the management process, is slightly smaller—the differences between women (48 %) and men (45 %) are insignificant here, too. Similarly, a little less than half of the women (48 %) and men (47 %) employed in the companies surveyed believe that all employees have equal chance of promotion, and that it only depends on their competencies. Easy access to development programmes and training events in their enterprises was declared by respondents a little more often (by 62 % of women and 59 % of men).

Interesting conclusions can be drawn from an analysis of the issues discussed above if one takes employees' age into account. Those expressing the most positive opinions about their companies are the youngest employees, below 35 years of age, whereas those most sceptical are the oldest employees, aged over 56 years. While 63 % of young women and men claim that the fact employees have different needs and expectations is taken note of in their companies—and half of them believe that such needs and expectations are taken account of in the management process, among the oldest employees the relevant percentages stand at 43 % and 35 %, respectively. Similarly, over 60 % of 20- and 30-year-olds (64 %) consider access to training events and development programmes in their organisations to be easy, whereas in the group over 56 years of age such an opinion is expressed by slightly more than half of those surveyed (52 %). Equal—competency-related promotion opportunities are identified more often than not by employees with considerable professional experience, from the 46 to 55 years age bracket. Such an opinion was expressed by over half (54 %) of the surveyed workers from that age group, while in the older group—the figure was 43 %, and in the youngest one—49 %. Interestingly, the youngest people (up to 35 years of age) are close—with respect to their views—to employees from the group of 46 to 55 year-olds, whereas representatives of the so-called Generation X (aged 35–45 years)—are more similar to the oldest group, those above 56 years of age.

In Polish surveys, scientific investigations have also been devoted to the relationship between diversity management and the following two factors: building an attitude of involvement (which is particularly desirable from the viewpoint of the performance of any enterprise and its competitive position) and providing motivation. The researchers' interests focused first of all on such aspects of diversity as gender and age. According to surveys by Wziątek-Staśko (2012), carried out on a sample of 287 people from 28 countries around the world, including from Poland (the biggest representation—178 respondents), women and men from different age groups vary in their assessment of the effects of selected motivational instruments.

In addition, certain similarities were shown in the involvement-building instruments preferred by women and men of a similar age. Similar conclusions were reached by researchers from ILSS in their analyses conducted as part of the previously mentioned surveys. The results they obtained indicate that there are a number of differences in the assessment of instruments for providing motivation between representatives of medium-sized and large companies and between women and men belonging to different age groups. Polish employees working for medium-sized organizations, born between 1946 and 1964, especially value non-financial incentives, expecting greater appreciation of their work from their superiors (*via* words of recognition etc.) and also wishing that more attention be paid to good relations at work. For employees over 35 years of age, especially women, additional benefits are increasingly important, e.g. medical care which also includes family members, or reimbursement of the costs of commuting to work. They also appreciate additional payments awarded to employees who have children, as well as opportunities to obtain loans at no interest. The youngest staff (up to 35 years of age) of medium-sized companies point to the importance of instruments that provide non-financial motivation. The way they see it, such instruments include not only appreciation of their work, but also attention paid to ergonomics and ensuring good conditions at the workplace. Nevertheless, when it comes to employees from the youngest generation, the fundamental factor in building their involvement is increasingly often the level of pay and a clearly defined career path. In the opinion of those surveyed, the remuneration they receive should allow them to live in comfort and make plans that are not connected with their job. This can be facilitated by other instruments of motivation that they particularly appreciate, i.e. additional benefits, e.g. packages for sports and leisure services, or subsidies to attend cultural events.

The presented outcomes of the surveys show beyond doubt that the implementation of diversity management in companies can support the managerial staff in the effective building of employees' involvement, which usually translates into better work result. It should be noted that this particular motivation for implementing the strategy in question—an increase in efficiency was declared in the ILSS surveys by a majority of employers. Why, then, in spite of the proven advantages of the use of DM, does this approach still remain not particularly popular in Poland? According to the analyses by Gryszko (2009), the three most important barriers to implementing this concept in real life are: prevalent stereotypes and prejudices, a lack of well-developed anti-discrimination and anti-bullying policies in enterprises, and a lack of knowledge and access to good practices.

The barriers mentioned above can be regarded in the broader context of HRM in Poland as a whole. It can be assumed that inadequate knowledge amongst managerial staff is the main factor limiting investment in human capital (such as referring to competency-based HRM, diversity management or building commitment among employees). In Poland, there is still quite a large group of entrepreneurs who see their employees primarily in terms of the costs they generate. Thinking of them as valuable resource is not common. The lack of knowledge and awareness that HRM, when used skilfully, can contribute to the improvement of company performance, and having a team with unique competence increases the likelihood of developing innovative solutions and gaining a competitive advantage, leads to serious omissions with regard to the development of human capital.

Measurement of Human Capital

The study conducted as part of the project *Human capital as a company value component*[2] confirms that entrepreneurs have a low awareness of the effect of human capital and Human Resources Management on the performance and effectiveness of companies. This lack of awareness amongst Polish entrepreneurs induced those running the project to conduct an in-depth study of this issue. With a sample of 600 enterprises interviewed, it showed that human capital measurements often result from a desire to reduce personnel costs (39 % answered "definitely yes" to whether this was the reason, and 42 % "probably yes"). An important reason for measuring human capital, especially for large enterprises, is a top-down decision from their Management Board, on which an HR Department's employees (or others involved in measurements) have no impact (33 % gave this as a reason, and 29 % said it "probably" was). But, it is worth noting that the largest group of companies indicated, as the main objective of the measurements, the fact that owing to the analysis of human capital they could make more informed personnel decisions (e.g. on promotion, training, etc.). This motivation to introduce the measurement was indicated by 80 % of the companies (44 % said "definitely yes", 36 % "probably yes").[3]

The perceived benefits of measuring human capital, however, vary according to the size of the enterprise (see Table 1). It is clear that the factors indicating (HRM-related) management awareness of the measurement benefits, are often indicated by large and medium-sized enterprises. This applies to issues such as facilitating planning and making decisions on staff development; preventing the best employees from leaving a company; providing information on management areas that require improvement; and an impact on the increased importance and functioning of the HR Department. Interestingly, the difference between entities of different sizes is not that big in the case of factors related to cost-efficiency

---

[2]The *"Human capital as a company value component"* project (No. POKL.02.01.03-00-036/11) is a system innovative project implemented by the Polish Agency for Enterprise Development (Project Leader) and the Warsaw School of Economics (Partner), co-financed from the funds of the European Social Fund as part of the Human Capital Operational Programme—Priority II Development of human resources and adaptation potential of enterprises and improvement in the health conditions of working persons, Submeasure 2.1.3 *"System support* for *increasing* adaptability of *employees* and enterprises".

[3]Based on the responses to the survey of 600 companies conducted under the project "Human capital as a company value component".

Table 1 Benefits from measuring human capital according to the enterprise size [in %]

		Enterprise size			
		Micro (n = 114)	Small (n = 197)	Medium (n = 138)	Large (n = 48)
Facilitates planning and making employee development decisions	Yes	42.1	71.1	81.9	83.3
	No	57.9	28.9	18.1	16.7
Prevents the best employees from leaving a company	Yes	32.5	29.4	45.7	64.6
	No	67.5	70.6	54.3	35.4
Allows a company to better control personnel costs	Yes	68.4	67.0	71.0	81.3
	No	31.6	33.0	29.0	18.8
Provides information on management areas requiring improvements	Yes	31.6	54.8	57.2	64.6
	No	68.4	45.2	42.8	35.4
Allows a company to use human resources more effectively	Yes	39.5	45.2	54.3	52.1
	No	60.5	54.8	45.7	47.9
Affects the increased importance of HR Department/function in a company	Yes	18.4	22.3	32.6	47.9
	No	81.6	77.7	67.4	52.1
Facilitates the functioning of the HR Department itself	Yes	24.6	24.9	31.2	45.8
	No	75.4	75.1	68.8	54.2

Source: Authors' elaboration based on the survey conducted under the project "Human capital as a company value component". *What are (may be), in your opinion, the benefits of measuring human capital? Base: n = 497 (Enterprises confirming the existence of benefits to measuring human capital)*

measurement aspects, such as better control of personnel costs and more efficient use of the company's human resources.

This observation is confirmed by an analysis of the scope of human capital metrics and indicators used in the interviewed enterprises according to their size (see Table 2). While absolute differences between smaller enterprises (micro and especially small ones) and larger (medium and large ones) with respect to indicators such as payroll costs, training costs and absence from work are low, there is a vast gap between these enterprises in terms of the use of more advanced, HR-related metrics. This applies to both simple indicators (staff turnover costs, fluctuation and replacement time, the percentage of trained employees and training time) and more advanced metrics (average profit per employee). No lack of human capital measurement can therefore be accounted for only by a lack of advanced human capital measurement tools (because it also applies to simple metrics), but first and foremost, all of it is due to the low awareness of how such measurement is important.

The primary cause of attitudes associated with a low tendency to invest in human capital is the lack of awareness of the direct relevance of human capital development to the company, and consequently all development expenditures are considered as a cost rather than as an investment. This also results from difficulties in measuring human capital itself which, as an intangible asset, can be quantified only to a small extent. At the same time, steps taken to develop systems for measuring human capital and its impact on the effectiveness of an organisation are necessary to understand and identify future sources of company value.

Table 2 Use of indicators and metrics for human capital measurements in interviewed firm according to firm size [in %]

	Enterprise size			
	Micro (n = 178)	Small (n = 222)	Medium (n = 150)	Large (n = 50)
Employee turnover costs	19.1	32.4	37.3	64.0
Payroll costs	67.4	80.6	84.7	88.0
Employee training costs	30.9	56.3	63.3	78.0
Staff fluctuation and employee replacement time	28.7	36.0	46.7	62.0
Absence from work	50.0	68.5	62.7	76.0
Percentage of employees trained	10.7	33.3	36.7	62.0
Training time	12.4	33.8	32.0	52.0
Average profit per employee	16.9	19.4	32.7	40.0
Return on human capital investment	5.6	16.2	22.7	36.0
Economic value added of human capital	5.6	11.7	16.0	30.0
Competence matching of employees	11.8	18.5	25.3	42.0
Employee attitudes	10.7	16.2	22.7	38.0
Employee experience	20.2	25.7	31.3	52.0
None of the above	25.3	15.3	12.7	6.0

Source: Authors' elaboration based on the survey conducted under the project "Human capital as a company value component". *Are the following indicators/metrics calculated and used for human capital in your organisation? The Table shows the companies that answered "yes". Base: n = 600 (all enterprises)*

Unfortunately, the intellectual and human capital measurement tools developed in recent years have not been widely used in enterprise practice due to their complexity, the need for very complicated financial reporting systems, and the expertise which is required to use such tools. Therefore, the main objective of the "Human capital as an enterprise value component" project is to change awareness amongst entrepreneurs with respect to the benefits derived from investing in a firm's human capital by creating a tool to measure human capital value (in short, the Human Capital Tool (HCT)), adjusted to firm size, taking into account the specificity of Polish enterprises and presenting information on enterprises based on quantitative and qualitative data.

The HCT uses a number of indicators to measure human capital in an organisation. The indicators in the business system include:

- cost ratios,
- quantity ratios,
- structural ratios,
- quality ratios,
- efficiency and profitability ratios.

Table 3 Human capital metrics and indicators used in the HCT tool

Metric	Metric description
Human capital profitability	This ratio shows what amount of added value (income less costs, excluding labour costs) accounts for 1 zloty[a] of labour costs.
Human capital productivity	This ratio represents the average value of the enterprise's income generated per 1 zloty of labour costs.
Average net profit (loss) per employee	This ratio represents the average net profit (loss) per employee.
Average income per employee	This ratio represents the average net income per employee.
Labour cost profitability	This ratio represents residual profit, calculated in terms of money as EBITDA less the Weighted Average Cost of Capital, per 1 zloty of labour costs.
Company market value per employee	This ratio represents the average market value of the company per employee.
Residual profit (loss) per employee	This ratio represents residual profit (loss) (EBITDA less the Weighted Average Cost of Capital in terms of money) per employee.
Added value per employee	This ratio represents average added value (surplus operating income over non-labour costs) per employee.
Economic Value Added (EVA) per unit labour costs	This ratio represents the Economic Value Added per 1 zloty of labour costs.
Economic Value Added (EVA) per employee	The ratio represents the Economic Value Added per employee.

Source: Authors' elaboration based on the project "Human capital as a company value component"
[a]Zloty is the name of the Polish currency

From the point of view of the subject of analysis, the most important is the last group—efficiency and profitability ratios. As part of this group, ten indicators that enable the analysis of the economic effects of human capital on a company (see Table 3) have been distinguished.

As shown by the analyses, there are a number of relations between the components of the tool, both between individual indicators and between the indicators and the results of surveys carried out with employees at the interviewed companies. Most correlations include the indicators related to the Economic Value Added (EVA). The Economic Value Added (EVA) is an indicator of the value created in the excess of the amount expected by investors (net profit less the cost of capital). The economic value added is calculated in the HCT tool according to the following formula:

$$NOPAT - WACC \times IC,$$

where:

NOPAT is the Net Operating Profit After Tax;
WACC × *IC* is the Weighted Average Cost of Capital (*WACC*) x Invested Capital (*IC*).

According to the interpretations adopted for the HCT, this indicator is at a low level when its value is less than zero. A negative value indicates that the operating profit does not come up to investors' expectations. There is a risk that the investors may withdraw, consequently resulting in a lowering of the company's value or liquidation. A value close to 0 means that the operating profit allows the company to cover just the cost of capital (to meet the expectations of investors). In this case, the company should be expected to attain financial stability but with no prospects for significant growth. It is recommended that innovative action be taken in the operational area. The index level is high when it has positive values. A positive EVA value means that the company's operating profit exceeds the expectations of investors. This proves the potential to build value. The accurate determination of threshold values obviously depends on the economic situation of a specific company.

With respect to human capital, particular relations were observed for two detailed metrics:

- Economic Value Added (EVA) per unit labour costs,
- Economic Value Added (EVA) per employee.

The first metric (Economic Value Added per unit labour costs) represents the economic value added per 1 zloty of labour costs. A low level means that the metric has negative values, an average level occurs in the case of low positive values, and a high level means that the metric has a value significantly greater than zero. In any case, the metric level should be considered in two cases—(1) when the share of investment components in labour costs is very small and (2) when the share of human capital expenditures in labour costs is very high. In the first case, the company cannot expect any improvement in the economic situation due to investments in human capital, because they are at a very low level, or the situation can deteriorate over a long period of time. In the second case, the company can expect to maintain its good economic situation in the long term or that any improvement in the situation may result from their investment in human capital.

The second metric (Economic Value Added per employee) represents the economic value added per employee. A low level of the metric (negative values) occurs when the operating result after tax is negative or its positive value is insufficient to cover the capital acquisition cost. The exact interpretation of the metric requires an analysis of the operating cost structure and the factors determining the income generated. However, this level of the metric points to the low efficiency of the human capital employed, and its persistence in subsequent accounting periods can result in profound restructuring changes in the company. This metric has values greater than zero when the company's operating profit after taxation is higher than the capital acquisition cost and reflects potential opportunities in the area of human capital that, if properly used, can have a positive impact on the economic situation of the company and, consequently, on the metric under consideration.

In the testing phase of the tool, in-depth research was carried out on 20 companies from Poland. These companies represented different areas of activity, predominantly in the services sector. In addition, they differed in terms of employment.

Five of the surveyed companies were micro-enterprises (below 9 employees), four companies were small enterprises (10–49 employees), seven were medium-sized (50–249 employees) and four were large enterprises (over 250 employees). Field research was conducted over the period of April–June 2014. The research was carried out by trained teams of experts, possessing full knowledge of the tool. In the 20 analysed companies a total of 560 employees were surveyed.

Statistical analysis of data from the research surveys and data collected as part of HCT implementation in the 20 companies included:

1. analysis of data from statistical surveys and the preparation of their results for individual companies;
2. analysis of relationships between HCT indicators;
3. statistical analysis of the survey data and development of summary reports for micro, small, medium-sized and large enterprises;
4. analysis of the impact of demographic factors (gender, age, education, work experience, occupational group), and the category of enterprise for the development of the qualitative dimensions of human capital.

The analysis of relationships between the HCT indicators included:

1. the selection of NKL indicators collected in 20 companies for correlation analysis: for this purpose only those indices were classified for which at least 10 companies provided data. Out of 107 indices in NKL, 81 were selected for further analysis;
2. the calculation of correlation coefficients between all indicators and between NKL indicators and average responses to questions from six questionnaires (a total of 204 questions);
3. the analysis of correlation coefficients calculated in the framework described above based on selection coefficients with values in the following ranges: 0.70–0.79; 0.80–0.89 and 0.90–1.00;
4. the selection of correlation coefficients were analysed in terms of substantive information coming from the existence of a strong relationship and correlation analysis for the validity of the relationship between the correlated variables to eliminate accidental compounds;
5. the grouping of strongly related variables (at least 0.7 of correlation coefficient) into a group correlated with similar information content.

According to the results of the conducted analyses, both metrics, i.e. Economic Value Added per unit labour costs and per employee, correlate positively with the voluntary departure ratio (at levels of 0.8102 and 0.8523, respectively). The voluntary departure ratio shows a relationship between the number of people who voluntarily leave a company and the total number of personnel employed under an employment contract. Both metrics are also correlated with:

- Capital Efficiency Ratio—this ratio represents a percentage relationship between the Economic Value Added (EVA) and equity, i.e. the amount of

Economic Value Added (EVA) per 1 zloty of equity (at levels of 0.8941 and 0.9416 for EVA per unit labour costs and EVA per employee, respectively);
- Return on Equity (ROE)—this ratio represents the ratio of net profit (loss) to the owner's capital, i.e. the amount of net profit (loss) per 1 zloty of equity (at levels of 0.8306 for EVA per unit labour costs and 0.8499 for EVA per employee);
- Return on Invested Capital (ROIC)—(at levels of 0.8482 for EVA per unit labour costs and 0.8499 for EVA per employee).

The Economic Value Added (EVA) metrics per unit labour costs and per employee are also strongly correlated with the results of surveys of employees from 20 enterprises involved in the tool testing process. The study included five surveys:

- Competence matching,
- Competence—according to the methodology used in the Study of Human Capital by the Polish Agency for Enterprise Development (PARP),
- Organisational culture,
- Satisfaction and commitment,
- Interpersonal relations.

A number of strong (above 0.7) correlations between both metrics and the items in the above questionnaires were observed. Some values of the line correlation coefficient were higher than 0.8 (see Table 4).

The use of the NKL tool allows companies to:

1. diagnose the situation regarding human capital in the company, and to show ways to fully exploit its potential as a driver of competitive advantage;
2. provide information about the level of accumulated human capital, the policy of investment in human capital (through acquisition, development and wages) and its impact on the functioning of the company, and thus facilitate personnel decision-making processes in the company in relation to the key areas of human capital management;
3. enrichment of the HR department with regard to strategic planning competences to provide human capital development in conjunction with the short- and long-term objectives of the company;
4. assist in a more effective control of staff costs and targeting investments in human capital development given the limited resources;
5. analyse quantitative information (cost, efficiency and profitability, financial) in combination with qualitative information;
6. present the strengths, weaknesses, opportunities and threats in the area of human capital in the form of reports intended for the owners/managers (internal report) and shareholders and potential investors (external report);
7. obtain the views of staff in key areas affecting the results (satisfaction and commitment, organisational culture, skills, interpersonal relations, and the sharing of knowledge) through the use of proprietary tools for employee surveys (questionnaires);

Table 4 Correlations between EVA measures and questionnaire items

Questionnaire	Questionnaire items	Line correlation coefficient values
Competence matching	I have much more autonomy compared to when I began working in the current company.	−0.8537 (for EVA per unit labour costs)
		−0.8013 (for EVA per employee)
	When I took up my current position, my level of competence was higher than required.	−0.8499 (for EVA per unit labour costs)
		−0.8302 (for EVA per employee)
	There is a possibility of performing various tasks at my present job.	−0.8221 (for EVA per employee)
Competence (according to the Study of Human Capital)	Making simple calculations	−0.8019 (for EVA per unit labour costs)
	Contact with people, both with associates and customers	−0.8724 (for EVA per unit labour costs)
	Availability	−0.8541 (for EVA per employee)
Satisfaction and commitment	I feel exploited and undervalued at work.	0.8036 (for EVA per unit labour costs)
		0.8522 (for EVA per employee)
Interpersonal relations	Employees are involved in setting individual and team goals.	−0.8124 (for EVA per unit labour costs)
		−0.8002 (for EVA per employee)
	I know and understand the rules and norms for contacting my superiors.	−0.8570 (for EVA per unit labour costs)
		−0.9148 (for EVA per employee)
	I think that difficulties and problems in communicating have an adverse impact on performing tasks and achieving the goals of our company in an effective and timely manner.	0.9398 (for EVA per unit labour costs)
		0.8621 (for EVA per employee)
	In our company, communication between employees takes place in an atmosphere of rivalry.	0.8041 (for EVA per unit labour costs)
		0.8726 (for EVA per employee)

(continued)

Table 4 (continued)

Questionnaire	Questionnaire items	Line correlation coefficient values
	There is purely task-oriented communication between employees and superiors in our company.	0.8130 (for EVA per unit labour costs)
		0.9036 (for EVA per employee)
	There is purely task-oriented communication between employees in our company.	0.8795 (for EVA per unit labour costs)
		0.8966 (for EVA per employee)
	I contact my superiors often and spontaneously.	−0.8609 (for EVA per unit labour costs)
		−0.9054 (for EVA per employee)
	I think that there are interpersonal problems at work.	0.8682 (for EVA per unit labour costs)
		0.8612 (for EVA per employee)
	I think that interpersonal problems at work have an impact on task performance efficiency.	0.8743 (for EVA per unit labour costs)
	I think that interpersonal problems reduce job satisfaction.	0.8750 (for EVA per unit labour costs)

Source: Authors' elaboration based on the survey conducted under the project "Human capital as a company value component"
The data for the 'Organisational culture' questionnaire is not included it the table, as no line correlation coefficient values higher than 0.8 were observed in the study

8. compare the strengths and weaknesses of the company to the competition (a benchmark of companies of similar size and characteristics) due to human capital measurement standards developed under the NKL.

Conclusions

The concept of human capital and HRM measurement methods and their impact on the effectiveness of a company have always been characterised by complexity. The concept should be based on a thorough analysis and make use of the results of various approaches, methods and measurement tools used in contemporary business. Only in this way can a tool with a wide range of applications in a diverse group of companies be developed. In particular, it is necessary to take into account the methods of analysing return on investment in human capital. The definition of human capital ROI resembles a classic definition of return on investment—with the exception that it only takes into account investments in human capital (Fitz-enz 2009).

This concept is based on the assumption that the most important element of the value creation cycle is people, and therefore investment in human capital is an important factor in determining company's value. Due to the comprehensive approach, measures applied in practice should include both financial and non-financial, but measurable, indicators of human capital. Financial ratios may include return on investment in human capital, human capital profitability or economic added value of human capital. Indicators for human capital may include: absenteeism rates, voluntary resignations, or indicators of investment in employees' development.

The key condition for using the measurement results in an enterprise and in the area of management is their credibility. First of all, the measures should be the result of a broad consensus, which is the result of multilateral agreements, rather than judgmental decisions made by a group of experts. In this way the measurements can be seen as credible both by decision-makers and the employees of each organisation. A clear definition of the measurements, so as to facilitate their broad understanding, and a unified interpretation of results also affects the reliability of the outcome. Good measurements should ensure a balance between the effort put into data collection and the utility of the findings. While observing some approaches to measuring human capital one often gets the impression that this golden rule is not observed, and large financial investments are lost in building methodologically advanced tools that are of little practical use.

Finally, while the measurement of human capital and HRM is indeed going to become a useful tool in the hands of management, allowing for the exploration of company-specific potential of human resources to generate return on investment, or influence results, it is necessary to unify these concepts. The most significant challenge remains to integrate various measurement concepts in a way that will allow companies to obtain the greatest possible synergistic effect. As a result, human resources management professionals will gain powerful support in their roles as strategic business partners in the creation of corporate value. For this reason, it is necessary to design a measurement process that will allow for the inclusion of firm-specific issues in a comprehensive manner, while allowing for comparability across different organisations.

References

Adler, R. D. (2001). Women in the executive suite correlate to high profits. *Harvard Business Review, 79*(3), 131–137.
Allen, R., Dawson, G., Wheatley, K., & White, C. (2008). Perceived diversity and organizational performance. *Employee Relations, 30*(1), 20–33.

Barney, J. (1991). Firm resources and sustained competitive advantage. *Journal of Management, 17*(1), 99–120.
Becker, B. E., & Huselid, M. A. (1998). High performance work systems and firm performance: A synthesis of research and managerial implications. *Research in Personnel and Human Resource Management, 16*, 53–101.
Becker, B. E., Huselid, M. A., & Ulrich, D. (2001). *The HR scorecard: Linking people, strategy, and performance*. Boston: Harvard Business School Press.
Benson, G. S., Young, S. M., & Lawler, E. E. I I I. (2006). High-involvement work practices and analysts' forecasts of corporate earnings. *Human Resource Management, 45*(4), 519–537.
Borkowska, S. (Ed.). (2010). *Creating innovation in the organization: The role of human resource management*. Warsaw: Instytut Pracy i Spraw Socjalnych.
Cook, K. W., & Bernthal, P. (1998). *Job/role competency practices survey report*. Bridgeville: Development Dimensions International.
Edvinsson, L. (1997). Developing intellectual capital at Skandia understanding knowledge management. *Long Range Planning, 30*(3), 366–373.
Ericksen, J. (2007). High-performance work systems, dynamic workforce alignment, and firm performance. In *Academy of Management 2007 Annual Meeting: Doing Well by Doing Good*. Academy of Management, New York.
Fitz-enz, J. (2009). *The ROI of human capital: Measuring the economic value of employee performance*. New York: Amacom.
Flamholtz, E. G., Bullen, M. L., & Wei, H. (2002). Human resource accounting: A historical perspective and future implications. *Management Decision, 40*(10), 947.
Flamholtz, E., & Hua, W. (2003). Searching for competitive advantage in the black box. *European Management Journal, 21*(2), 222–236.
Gryszko, M. (2009). Raport zarządzanie różnorodnością w Polsce. Forum Odpowiedzialnego Biznesu. Available via Forum Odpowiedzialnego Biznesu. Accessed June 30, 2015, from http://odpowiedzialnybiznes.pl/wp-content/uploads/2014/01/Zarzadzanieroznorodnosciaw Polsce_FOB.pdf
Guest, D. E., Michie, J., Conway, N., & Sheehan, M. (2003). Human resource management and corporate performance in the UK. *British Journal of Industrial Relations, 41*, 291–314.
Huselid, M. (1995). The impact of human resource management practices on turnover, productivity, and corporate financial performance. *Academy of Management Journal, 38*(3), 635–672.
Jończak, M., & Woźny, A. (2011). *Trendy HRM w Polsce*. Warsaw: Deloitte, Polskie Stowarzyszenie Zarządzania Kadrami.
Kaplan, R. S., & Norton, D. P. (2005). The balanced scorecard: Measures that drive performance. *Harvard Business Review, 83*(7–8), 172–180.
Kirton, G., & Greene, A. (2005). *The dynamics of managing diversity*. Oxford: Elsevier Butterworth-Heinemann.
Kochan, T., Bezrukowa, K., Ely, R., Jackson, S., & Joshi, A. (2003). The effects of diversity on business performance: Report of diversity research network. *Human Resource Management, 42*(1), 3–21.
Lans, T., Hulsink, W., Baert, H., & Muller, M. (2008). *Entrepreneurship education and training in a small business context: Insights from the competence-based approach*. ERIM Report Series Research in Management. Available via Erasmus University in Rotterdam. Accessed June 30, 2015, from http://repub.eur.nl/pub/12466/ERS-2008-028-ORG.pdf
Lepak, D. P., & Snell, S. A. (2002). Examining the human resource architecture: The relationships among human capital, employment, and human resource configurations. *Journal of Management, 28*(4), 517–543.
Levenson, A. R., Van der Stede, W. A., & Cohen, S. G. (2006). Measuring the relationship between managerial competencies and performance. *Journal of Management, 32*(3), 360–380.
Lisowska, E., & Sznajder, A. (2013). *Zarządzanie różnorodnością w miejscu pracy. Raport z I edycji Barometru Różnorodności*. Warsaw: Konfederacja Lewiatan.

Lisowska, E., & Sznajder, A. (2014). *Zarządzanie różnorodnością w miejscu pracy. Raport z II edycji Barometru Różnorodności*. Warsaw: Konfederacja Lewiatan.
Miller, L., Rankin, N., & Neathey, F. (2001). *Competency frameworks in UK organizations*. London: CIPD.
Mor Barak, M. E. (2014). *Managing diversity. Toward a globally inclusive workplace*. Thousand Oaks, CA: Sage.
Powell, T. C., Lovallo, D., & Caringal, C. (2006). Causal ambiguity, management perception, and firm performance. *Academy of Management Review, 31*(1), 175–196.
Prahalad, C. K., Hamel, G., & June, M. A. Y. (1990). The core competence of the corporation. *Harvard Business Review, 68*(3), 79–91.
Rostkowski, T. (2004). Zarządzanie kompetencjami w UE. In M. Juchnowicz (Ed.), *Standardy europejskie w zarządzaniu zasobami ludzkimi*. Warsaw: Poltext.
Salter, J. E. (2002). *Skill-based pay. Case analysis*. San Rafael, CA: Dominican University of California.
Sienkiewicz, Ł. (2004). Zarządzanie kompetencjami pracowników w Polsce w świetle badań. *Zarządzanie Zasobami Ludzkimi, 2*, 97–106.
Sienkiewicz, Ł. (ed.), Jawor-Joniewicz, A., Sajkiewicz, B., Trawińska-Konador, K., & Podwójcic, K. (2014). *Competency-based human resources management. The lifelong learning perspective*. Warsaw: Instytut Badań Edukacyjnych.
Sveiby, K. E. (1997). The intangible assets monitor. *Journal of Human Resource Costing & Accounting, 2*(1), 73–97.
Wziątek-Staśko, A. (2012). *Diversity management. Narzędzie skutecznego motywowania pracowników*. Warsaw: Difin.

Examination of Central and Eastern European Professional Football Clubs' Sport Success, Financial Position and Business Strategy in International Environment

Krisztina András and Zsolt Havran

Abstract The aim of this chapter is to examine the competitiveness of professional football clubs in the Central and Eastern European (CEE) region. We compare the sport-related and financial competitiveness of the CEE region to that of German and Russian professional leagues. We introduce the related literature of internationalisation of business and sport management. We define export in field of professional football and show the business trends of global football. We collect and describe the sport management articles that are prepared in the CEE region. We use data of international organisations and related case studies to show the empirical results of our research. Our main findings are that the football clubs of the CEE region have a weak sport-related and financial competitiveness in European Football, but in the market for football players they have a good opportunity to realise huge profits. In the last 4 years, the realised revenues from the transfer market decreased, which indicates that the competitiveness of the region in terms of youth players transfers is getting weaker.

Keywords Global sport • Professional football • Competitiveness • Export • Central and Eastern European region

Introduction

The aim of this chapter is to interpret and examine the sport and financial efficiency of the Central and Eastern European (CEE) region professional men's football clubs in the international football market. We examined nine countries from Central and Eastern Europe: Bulgaria, Croatia, the Czech Republic, Hungary, Poland, Romania, Serbia, Slovakia and Slovenia. Their common characteristics are the following: post-socialist history (similar tradition, economy, culture, external environment) and European Union membership or candidate members of the EU (Serbia).

K. András (✉) • Z. Havran (✉)
Corvinus University of Budapest, Budapest, Hungary
e-mail: krisztina.andras@uni-corvinus.hu; zsolt.havran@uni-corvinus.hu

Professional football players in the Top Leagues (England, Spain, Germany, France, Italy) or in Western Europe are a commonly discussed topic in relevant literature, but there are only very few articles about football in Eastern Europe. However, many players from CEE countries play in Top Leagues, or in Western Europe, and talented players of Serbia won the FIFA (Fédération Internationale de Football Association) U20 World Championship in June 2015.

Even back in the 1980s, the sport results of the clubs from the CEE region were relatively good. For instance, the Romanian Steaua Bucarest won the European Cup in 1986; in 1989 this team played in the finals and in 1991 the Croatian Crvena Zvezda won the European Cup. After the start of the Champions League (CL) in 1992, the results of the clubs in the region started to decline significantly.[1] The reason of this should be searched in the context of the negative consequences of the transition period in the socialist block (e.g. remarkable decrease of subsidies), but also in light of the external changes which have been supported by the evolution of television that facilitated access to the international customer base. The well-known football clubs from Western Europe have a significant advantage in reaching international customers.

The increase of the international (not local) incomes (international sponsors, customers, foreign TV-incomes) is related to the second reason, as well as the liberalisation of the players' market and the facilitation of the certification process. Clubs in the CEE region were able to compete with increasing difficulties for the favour of both the qualified players and international customers. Therefore, they have been breaking away more and more from the clubs of the West European championships, which could realise higher income due to their larger capital base, more solvent customers and better management knowledge than companies working under market conditions a longer time. In recent years, UEFA (Union of European Football Associations) has brought about many changes in the Champions League, such as increasing the number of participating teams, having separated qualifying rounds for the champions, introduction of regional qualifying rounds, due to which CEE-clubs got an opportunity to close up. The important question, however, is how they can reduce the existing competitiveness gap.

In the past few years clubs in the region have become more successful; they are participating more often in international tournaments and, as a result, the export of players has increased, as well. Naturally, there is a mutual connection between the two phenomena, since the better a club performs internationally, the more visibility can the players get, and the more players it can export, the higher are its revenues. In the same way higher revenues provide the opportunity to build better teams and improve youth training systems, which again enables the clubs to develop further.

Our main goal is to measure the sport-related and financial performance of football clubs. We collected data on the international achievements of the CEE leagues from the past 5–10 years and we attempted to quantify their financial

---

[1]On the UEFA-ranking of European football leagues the examined CEE-leagues are located between 14 and 31. *Source*: UEFA (2015).

performance. Central and Eastern Europe is our research area; hence, we were evaluating the whole region and the differences among countries at the level of both clubs and leagues. It is a peculiarity of the region that a lot of publicly available financial data cannot be accepted unconditionally, since the operations of firms and sport organisations are not completely transparent. Either the reported revenues connected to football are close to zero, or they lack credibility. Our research question is how competitive are the football clubs of the CEE region in European football. Our aim is to show the main competitive advantage of the clubs and describe successful business strategy for clubs of this region. In the previous study (András and Havran 2014) the aim was to present and examine the CEE-based football companies' export skills on the players' market. In this study, we undertake an international comparison and provide more depth to our analysis and the interpretation of its findings.

Literature Review

The definition of efficiency in professional football is highly complex. Firstly, we can talk about the efficiency of sport companies and national teams, but also about professional sports and financial efficiency. From the viewpoint of a national association, the aim is to be a successful national team that can be based on talented football players playing in strong championships. From the viewpoint of a sport company, in order to reach professional sports goals there is a need for qualified players and due to their achievement these sport companies can start in international championships and they can reach higher incomes in the field of sport markets. The main business revenues of the football companies are the following: ticket and season-ticket revenues (consumer market), revenues on player transfers (players' market), revenues generated from broadcasting rights (broadcasting rights market), and revenues from commercial rights: sponsorship revenues (sponsorship market) and merchandising revenues (merchandising market) (András 2003). Besides borrowing players, they can realise further incomes from their sale. The football companies' huge question is when to sell these talented players. In the CEE region (in the lower level championships) both the associations and the sport companies are interested in selling players to stronger championships, in means the exportation of the player. With the help of this on the one hand, a player's own career could develop further, on the other hand, the sport company which is selling the player could realise an additional source of revenue. Thirdly, this player with his better knowledge could mean more substantial help to the team. Therefore, there could be a common interest of the private sector and of the state to invest in the youth training system.

The foundations of our study are, first if all, the sections dealing with human resource management in the international business economy (Chikán 2008; Czakó 2010), and also the literature of sport companies internationalisation inside a sport economy (András et al. 2012).

To facilitate the understanding of the specialities of sport business, we have devised a summary about the markets of professional football and the characteristics of the players' market. Due to media capability and international competitions, professional football has clearly become a global sport. The players' market is a special labour market, where a personal right with special value of property is the subject of the agreement: the control over the playing licence for a given period which is maximum 5 years in the EU (András 2003). This right with the value of property is very closely linked to the person of the player and includes all his abilities, both physical and mental, related to his sporting activities. Therefore, it is not transferable or vendible, but like a license agreement, the control over the playing licence is transferable. During the term of contract, a football company can transfer the right of disposition to another football company in exchange for compensation (called a transfer fee). The transfer of a player is a double transaction from the point of view of the buying club: it means labour force recruitment, and also an investment in a value of property which is an intangible asset (András 2003; András and Havran 2014).

The added value of our study is related to the literature review, whereby we collected, classified by themes and summarised the articles in English arising from the CEE region and dealing with professional football. These can be divided into two large groups: literature in the first group is about the socialist transition period in the mentioned country and literature in the second group is about the actual business case related to professional football in the mentioned countries. Almost in every country one can find an English publication, case study or thesis which facilitates the understanding of similar situations and problems of the different countries in the region.

The authors in different countries report similarly about the economic transition: the regime change was a difficult process and the organisations operating professional football clubs in many countries were started to be regulated only in the mid-1990s. After 1989, state funds declined, therefore the clubs experienced significant financial difficulties. Local governments started to enter clubs as owners to strengthen the urban identity. Apart from losing state support, another serious problem was the increasing wrangling of hooligans. Scholars including Lenartowicz and Karwacki (2005) in the context of Poland, Girginov and Sandanski (2008) analysing the Bulgarian case, McDonald (2014) studying the situation of Romania, Hodges and Stubbs (2013) writing about Croatia, and András (2003) and Vincze et al. (2008) focusing on Hungary have raised almost the same problems. In Table 1, we summarised the actual articles in English about professional football in Central and Eastern Europe.

A former study about CEE-football (András and Havran 2014) shows the specialty of the region which is that many publicly available financial data cannot be accepted unconditionally, since the operations of companies and sport organisations are not completely transparent. In the related papers of the examined countries, we found further support for this lack of transparency.

Mihaylov (2012) discussed and set the goals of the hypothetical league, which are promotion of football as the most popular sport in the region, increasing the

Table 1 Relevant studies about professional football of Central and Eastern Europe

Country/topic	Financial activity of clubs	Transition
Slovakia	Nemec and Nemec (2009)	
Czech Republic	Procházka (2012)	
Romania	Roşca (2012)	McDonald (2014)
	McDonald (2014)	
	Mihaylov (2012)	
	Roşca (2014)	
Bulgaria	Mihaylov (2012)	Girginov (2008)
Hungary	András (2004)	András (2003)
	András-Kozma (2014)	Vincze et al. (2008)
Serbia	Mihaylov (2012)	
	Mladenović and Marjanović (2011)	
Poland	Bednarz (2014)	Lenartowicz and Karwacki (2005)
Croatia		Hodges and Stubbs (2013)

Note: Authors' elaboration

quality and the competitive balance in football, organisation of a regional championship, which gives the opportunity for the big regional clubs to compete and perform internationally. The paper states that a Balkan league could be the solution to overcome the crisis in the region and stop talented players from running away from regional clubs and choosing Western leagues. In 2011, six Bulgarian clubs, Dinamo Bucarest from Romania and Red Star from Serbia started negotiations related to the creation of a Balkan football league, but UEFA uttered its clear position against such regional league. According to Mihaylov (2012) the big problem of the overspending competitions (Champions League—CL and European League—EL) has led to a low interest in the national championships in the CEE region. The conclusion of the paper is that the necessity for a product such as the Balkan League cannot be supported because of the low number of interested solvent consumers. In spite of this in other sports, we could find some good examples for regional competitions: Erste Ice Hockey League (Erste Bank Liga 2016), Seha Handball League (Seha Liga 2016), ABA Basketball Leagues (ABA Liga 2016).

Roşca (2014) examined the nature of Romanian football club websites from a customer (supporter) relationship management perspective. The results show that while clubs use their websites as informational platforms, several issues have to be addressed regarding the use of websites as bonding factors between clubs and supporters. The research reveals that Romanian clubs have failed to implement business solutions to help supporters buy online merchandise products, which would also increase the revenues of football clubs. We describe the further main points of these papers in the results and discussion section.

Methodology

In order to find the answer to our research question, we took the following review steps:

1. Regional comparison of nine countries of the CEE region with German and Russian league;
2. Collection and summary of the sport results of clubs in the CEE region;
3. Overview of case studies of youth players' academies and investigation of transfer results of the CEE region in two different intervals of 4 years each to show the trends in the transfer market;
4. Summary of the financial results and trends of Central and Eastern European Football.

We describe the relevant topics and case studies based on published studies about sport success and financial results of leagues and clubs of the examined region. Our review uses data from reliable statistical sources such as transfermarkt.de, while we have tracked the realised transfers on uefa.com. One limitation of the research is that transfermarkt.de only provides estimations, because almost every transfer is a business secret. Nonetheless, there is no other reliable and public database and transfermarkt.de uses consistent methods, thus the data are comparable.

Results and Discussion

Regional Comparison

Roşca (2012) examined the financial contribution of international footballers trading to the Romanian economy. The analysis takes into account five consecutive seasons, starting with 2006–2007 and ending with 2010–2011. At the macroeconomic level, it can be argued that footballer exports influence the financial structure of Romanian football. Therefore, they also affect the entire Romanian economy, as well, since professional football is an integral element of this economy.

In the beginning of our research, we examined the economic results at the macro level. We compared nine countries from the region to a Western and an Eastern country, which are similar in population size to the nine countries examined altogether.

It can be seen in Table 2 that in nine countries from the CEE region, the economic development is similar to Russia, but significantly weaker than in Germany. The transfer-related income is more than 60% of the German first class' income, although the costs are also significantly higher there, which leads to the situation in which the clubs in Bundesliga had almost half a billion euros losses due to certifications in the past 6 years, whereas the nine CEE championships' clubs

Table 2 Comparison of CEE Region' transfer results with German and Russian Leagues

	CEE Region	Germany	Russia	Source
GDP/capita	US$11,997	US$45,028	US$14,174	IMF (2014)
Value of players (2015)	1172 M euros	2400 M euros	1040 M euros	Transfermarkt (2015)
Profit/loss from transfers (2009–2014)	475.30 M euros	−453.55 M euros	−405.47 M euros	Transfermarkt (2015)
Revenue of transfers (2009–2014)	700 M euros	1130 M euros	711 M euros	Transfermarkt (2015)

Note: Authors' elaboration

realised almost the same value of profits. The incomes of Russian players' market compound the incomes in the region, but due to expensive certifications it has the same negative balance as the German championship. Accordingly, in international clubs' football, Germany and Russia are clear purchasers and the CEE region has a strong transfer role. It is also important to analyse this result at an aggregate level within the region. According to other research (András and Havran 2014), 27 % of the profits acquired in the transfer market are realised at the Serbian, 21 % at the Croatian and 16 % at the Romanian championships, and they are spread specifically across a few clubs. As the results of this research indicate, there are significant differences within the region and, more specifically, within certain championships.

Sport Results of CEE Region's Clubs

We looked at the sport success of Central and Eastern European clubs in international championships. In the past few years clubs in the region have become more successful; they are participating more often in international tournaments, but the opportunities to move forward are very limited. The number of clubs from the CEE region (9 countries) between 2010 and 2014 in the Group Stage (best 32 teams) of the Champions League was 12, and in the Group Stage of Champion League it was 43. However, only 8 teams from the CEE region played matches in the eighth finals (best 16 teams) in this period (András and Havran 2014: 8).

The secondary role of CEE-based clubs in European Championships is well represented by the UEFA-ranking of European football clubs: in the first 200 teams, there are 31 clubs from the CEE region (or 15.5 %), but only 5 clubs can be found in the first 100 teams (András and Havran 2014: 8).

Efficiency of Youth Players' Academies and Investigation of the Transfer Markets in CEE

Mladenović and Marjanović (2011) examined the differences in sport motivation of young football players from Russia, Serbia and Montenegro. The research included 178 young football players aged 12–15 and significant differences were found between young football players from these countries regarding intrinsic and extrinsic motivation. Young football players from Serbia and Montenegro were found to be considerably more motivated than their Russian peers by the intrinsic desire to achieve their sports competence. Additionally, all aspects of extrinsic motivation were present in young football players from Serbia and Montenegro in a much higher degree than in young athletes from Russia. The 12-year-old football players were also significantly more motivated than their peers aged 13, 14 and 15.

From ECA (2012) survey along with two German clubs, we enhanced the surrounding countries' examples. The number of young players and trainers are the same, but the German clubs have many times as large budget than their CEE competitors. The German clubs generate losses in the transfer market because they are able to buy the best adult players and these clubs' direct goal is not to fill out the full team from their own youth academies.

In Table 3 we could notice that the Croatian Dinamo Zagreb runs their academy within a budget of approximately 400 million HUF a year and its adult club (mainly designed to sale the club's own trained players) has reached more than 60 million euros profit in the players' market in the past 6 years. The Czech Teplice, temporarily with a much lower budget, could not generate profit. In the study, there was no focus on Hungarian clubs, but according to the information published by the academies, approximately ten academies were functioning from that size of budget as the Zagreb academy and during the last 6 years together they reached just a fraction of the transfer gain of Zagreb. Consequently, from this perspective their function is not effective.

Table 3 Comparison of youth academies of related clubs

Country	Club	Number of players	Number of coaches	Cost per year (euros)	Transfer profit last 6 years (euros)
Germany	FC Bayern München	185	26	3,000,000	−190,750,000
Croatia	NK Dinamo Zagreb	200	21	1,300,000	60,300,000
Czech Republic	FK Teplice	284	26	<500,000	−240,000
Germany	FC Schalke 04	190	34	>3,000,000	−18,530,000
Hungary	All league	n.a.	n.a.	700,000–1,000,000 per club	10,740,000

Source of data: ECA (2012), authors' elaboration
Note: n.a. - data not available

In order to demonstrate temporal changes, we have compared the periodic results of the transfer market in 2011–2014 and 2007–2010 in the CEE region (in Table 4 the incomes, the costs are realised by all clubs of the first division in a given country). For this purpose, we have used data from transfermarkt.de.

Considering the average level of the region, we can see a decline, as the income from selling players only reached 60 % as compared to the previous 4 years and the purchases have decreased to an even larger extent. Overall, the transfer profit has declined by 30 %, as well. It is interesting to note that in spite of the strong decline of incomes, the balance of Romanian championship became visibly positive from its previously negative value, in which the bankruptcies of some clubs there have contributed definitely. The transfer incomes have grown only in Poland and Bulgaria (although Bulgaria had only a very low starting point), whilst in all other countries they have decreased sharply. As compared to the data of Germany and Russia, the data of the CEE region reveal a remarkable difference. Both in the case of Germany and in the case of Russia the traffic has grown, therefore the revenues and costs have changed by 20–30 %, which also means an increase of losses in the transfer market. Accordingly, for the last period in the large purchaser championships, the number and value of certifications have grown further, but the import has begun to turn from the CEE region into other areas. The geographic patterns of this apparent shift should be a question for another research, but from the perspective of the CEE region it is undoubtedly not a favourable development.

Summary of the Financial Results and Trends of Central and Eastern European Football

In the previous paper (András and Havran 2014: 9), we collected the revenues of CEE-clubs. According to UEFA estimations, the internationally active clubs of different championships can be categorised based on their revenues.

Only 3 clubs have revenues higher than 10 million euros and 29 clubs have revenues between 1 and 10 million euros in the entire CEE region. The majority of income of CEE clubs is derived from the sales of players and (undercover) government subsidies. In a previous study (András and Havran 2014), by virtue of investments into youth players and due to the size of economy, it was identified that Serbian and Croatian championships are mostly capable of exports. The former accounts for 27 % and the latter for 21 % of players' sales of the whole region. After the analysis of the UEFA Report, we collected information about the financial position of CEE football clubs in selected literature.

Procházka (2012) focuses on the specificity of Czech professional football clubs. The research sample consists of 36 football clubs, which played in the first and second football league from 2005 to 2010. The number of 180 sets of financial statements should be available, but the sample comprises 97 sets only because a significant proportion of the clubs do not fulfil their information duty. The annual

Table 4 Transfer results of examined countries from 2007 to 2014 (data in million euros)

	2011–2014			2007–2010			% changes of revenues	% changes of costs	% changes of P/L
	Revenue	Cost	Profit/loss	Revenue	Cost	Profit/loss			
Hungary	13.62	3.67	9.95	23.18	8.95	14.23	58.76	41.01	69.92
Czech Republic	39.47	12.98	26.49	100.66	25.75	74.91	39.21	50.41	35.36
Slovakia	5.81	1.43	4.38	18.84	3.3	15.54	30.84	43.33	28.19
Slovenia	8.26	0.87	7.39	24.37	2.19	22.18	33.89	39.73	33.32
Croatia	94.22	27.03	67.19	140.57	28.72	111.85	67.03	94.12	60.07
Poland	64.24	21.36	42.88	58.6	42.53	16.07	109.62	50.22	266.83
Romania	87.09	34.56	52.53	140.76	145.81	−5.05	61.87	23.70	1040.20
Serbia	87.36	10.34	77.02	115.38	22.74	92.64	75.72	45.47	83.14
Bulgaria	38.4	15.02	23.38	32.64	9.43	23.21	117.65	159.28	100.73
Total CEE	438.47	127.26	311.21	655	289.42	365.58	66.94	43.97	85.13
Germany	789.42	1180	−390.58	618.55	909.46	−290.91	127.62	129.75	134.26
Russia	457.77	727.58	−269.81	380.86	595.16	−214.3	120.19	122.25	125.90

Source: Transfermarkt (2015), authors' elaboration

EBIT (earning before tax) of an average club reached amount of −4952 thousand CZK over the analysed 5-year period. In several years, the average equity is lower than the subscribed capital. Fundamental data retrieved from financial statements imply that a long-term stability of Czech football clubs is threatened. In 61 % of cases, clubs reported a negative value of earnings before interests and taxation, which supports the previous conclusion about an overall poor financial performance. All mentioned factors lead to a situation where the Czech football scene represents a very risky environment for all parties, which do not have any other access to financial information than to those contained in financial statements.

Nemec and Nemec (2009) show that all Slovak first league football clubs operated as companies in 2008. Their annual turnover was between 40 and 100 million Sk. Revenues are predominantly derived from commercial activities. The assumption that clubs in popular sports with large turnovers and a prevalence of "business type" revenues will decide to function as private companies, is clearly reflected in this sample.

According to Roşca (2012), Romanian football clubs need to diversify their revenue sources, one of them being footballer exports (i.e. selling football players from Romanian clubs to foreign clubs). At a microeconomic level, such operations bring revenues to the clubs. Research has shown that the gross exports of the entire top division Romanian football amounted to an average of 18.1 million euros per year between 2006 and 2011, and the realised profit for the same 5 years amounted to 4.5 million euros. McDonald (2014) examined oligarch football club investments in Central and Eastern Europe. One case raised in the paper was the Steaua Bucarest from Romania during last decade. The owner of Steaua Bucarest is Gigi Becali, currently in prison. Many people in Romania know Becali as a politician because of his team ownership. Acquiring a historically popular team gave Becali a great opportunity to achieve political capital through visibility to the Romanian public. With complete control of FC Steaua, Becali utilises the media and publicity to promote his platform through the team. Meanwhile, a significant proportion of the revenues of Steaua Bucarest is not considered as business incomes.

Bednarz (2014) examines the case of Polish football and he finds more signs of business activities there. In 2011, sponsorship and advertising in Poland were the most important source of club incomes, accounting for about 35 % of their budgets. Starting from 2011/2012, one game of each round is broadcast live on Eurosport2, where it is shown in more than 20 countries in Europe. Each two clubs whose game is broadcast earn 100,000 PLN. In the case study of the Lech Poznan club, Bednarz (2014) shows that decent international performance has a strong effect on business revenues. Lech Poznan was able to play matches against Manchester City or Juventus Turin, hence the revenues of club increased from 50 to 85 million PLN.

Conclusions

As it was demonstrated, the CEE region was relatively weak in professional sports compared to Western Europe and in the last few years, the income of the transfer market declined. Probably in the future, the clubs are going to reach similar results in professional sports as in recent years (some clubs in the CL and EL group stage). The clubs' incomes are mostly derived from players' sale, but due to selling players, also the clubs with the best academies cannot step forward. A vital question is also where the gains received from sales transactions are allocated.

The national youth players teams perform well (mainly in Serbia), but at the adults level it is questionable which results the national teams in the region can achieve and why they cannot repeat the European-Championship and World-Championship gold medals, as they were able to in their youthful years.

With recent rule set and international business circles, the CEE clubs cannot compete with larger clubs. For example, in many countries of the region, the fans do not consistently identify their favourite club from their own country. In Romania, the Steaua Bucarest, in Bulgaria the Levski Sofia, in Serbia the Crvena Zvezda and in Czech the Sparta Praha are the most popular teams in the circle of paying consumers, but in Slovakia, Poland and Hungary Barcelona is the favourite one (UEFA 2012: 41). The football markets have become international today; therefore, the clubs from the CEE region have to cope with Barcelona not only in the soccer field, but also through the entertainment activities built around football, which sounds more than hard.

According to Roşca (2012), the gap between the CEE-leagues and the Western European football is growing. Sporting performance can be improved, but the CEE clubs need professionalised strategic management in order to understand the importance of diversifying revenue streams, and then to choose one on which to build the development of the club. In other words, CEE football clubs need to adopt a strategy aimed at the realisation of surpluses from footballer trading, which would be invested in the further development and expansion of the clubs.

References

András, K. (2003). *Business elements in sports, through example of football*. Unpublished doctoral dissertation, Budapest University of Economics Sciences and Public Administration, Budapest. Retrieved December 9, 2013.

András, K. (2004). *A hivatásos sport piacai, Vezetéstudomány XXXV*. pp. 40–57. (In English: The markets of professional football.)

András, K., & Havran, Z. (2014). Regional export efficiency in the market of football players. *Theory Methodology Practice (TMP), 10*, 3–15.

András, K., Havran, Zs., & Jandó, Z. (2012). *Üzleti globalizáció és a hivatásos sport: sportvállalatok nemzetközi szerepvállalása*. Corvinus University of Budapest (In English: Business globalization and the professional sport: international activity of sport companies).

Bednarz, B. (2014). Case study of a Polish Football Club – KKS Lech Poznan, Year 2009–2013. In A. Jaki & B. Mikula (Eds.), *Knowledge, economy, society. Managing organizations: Concepts and their applications* (pp. 53–60). Crakow: Foundation of the Cracow University of Economics.

Chikán, A. (2008). *Vállalatgazdaságtan* (4th ed.). Budapest: AULA Kiadó (In English: Business economics).

Czakó, E. (2010). A nemzetközi stratégia területei. In C. Erzsébet & R. László (Eds.), *Nemzetközi vállalatgazdaságtan* (p. 179). Budapest: Alinea Kiadó (In English: The fields of international strategy).

ECA. (2012). *Report on youth academies in Europe.* Accessed November 15, 2014, from http://www.ecaeurope.com/news/eca-publishes-report-on-youth-academies/

Girginov, V., & Sandanski, I. (2008). Understanding the changing nature of sports organisations in transforming societies. *Sport Management Review, 11*(1), 21–50.

Hodges, A., & Stubbs, P. (2013). *The paradoxes of politicisation: Football supporters in Croatia.* Accessed November 9, 2014, from http://free-project.eu/documents-free/Working%20Papers/The%20Paradoxes%20of%20Politicisation%20football%20supporters%20in%20Croatia%20%28A%20Hodges%20P%20Stubbs%29.pdf

Kozma, M., & András, K. (2014). Winning in Europe: International strategies for Hungarian professional sports clubs. *Entrepreneurial Business and Economics Review, 2*(4), 31–49.

Lenartowicz, M., & Karwacki, A. (2005). An overview of social conflicts in the history of polish club football. *European Journal for Sport and Society, 2*(2), 97–107.

McDonald, M. (2014). *How regimes dictate oligarchs & their football clubs: Case studies comparison of Oligarch Football Club ownership in Dagestan, Romania, & Transnistria from 1990–2014.* Diss., The University of North Carolina at Chapel Hill.

Mihaylov, M. (2012). *A conjoint analysis regarding influencing factors of attendance demand for the Balkan Football League.* Accessed July 26, 2015, from www.academia.edu/download/30964444/Mihaylov_MasterThesis15.09.2012_A_Conjoint_analysis_regarding_influencing_factors_of_attendance_demand_for_the_Balkan_League.pdf

Mladenović, M., & Marjanović, A. (2011). Some differences in sports motivation of young football players from Russia, Serbia and Montenegro. *SportLogia, 7*(2), 145–153. doi:10.5550/sgia.110702.en.145M. ISSN 1986-6089.

Nemec, J., & Nemec, M. (2009). Public challenges for sports management in Slovakia: How to select the optimum legal. *Economic Studies and Analyses, 3.* Accessed January 17, 2015, from http://www.vsfs.cz/periodika/acta-2009-02.pdf

Procházka, D. (2012). Financial conditions and transparency of the Czech Professional Football Clubs. *Prague Economic Papers, 21*(4), 504–521. Accessed January 13, 2015, from http://ssrn.com/abstract=2234175.

Roşca, V. (2012). The financial contribution of international footballer trading to the Romanian football league and to the national economy. *Theoretical and Applied Economics, XIX*(4), 145–166.

Roşca, V. (2014). Web interfaces for e-CRM in sports: Evidence from Romanian football, management and marketing. *Challenges for the Knowledge Society, 9*(1), 27–46.

UEFA. (2012). *Club licensing benchmarking report financial year 2012.* Accessed July 15, 2014, from http://www.uefa.org/MultimediaFiles/Download/Tech/uefaorg/General/02/09/18/26/2091826_DOWNLOAD.pdf

Vincze, G., Fügedi, B., Dancs, H., & Bognár, J. (2008). The effect of the 1989–1990 political transition in Hungary on the development and training of football talent. *Kinesiology, 40*(1), 50–60.

Internet Resources of the Collected Dataset

ABA Liga. (2016). Accessed January 15, 2016, from http://www.abaliga.com
Erste Bank Liga. (2016). Accessed January 15, 2016, from http://www.erstebankliga.at
IMF. (2014). Accessed November 15, 2014, from www.imf.org
SEHA Liga. (2016). Accessed January 15, 2016, from http://www.seha-liga.com
Transfermarkt. (2015). Accessed July 15, 2015, from www.transfermarkt.de
UEFA. (2015). Accessed July 15, 2015, from http://www.uefa.com/memberassociations/uefarankings/country/index.html

Local Heroes in Hungary

Miklós Stocker

Abstract There is an intensive debate in literature pertaining to the analysis of successful companies. The present chapter applies the definition of Local Heroes by Schuh to the Hungarian context. The Hungarian Corporate Tax Database was used to analyse the whole population of Hungarian companies in the period 2009–2013. The database consists of 385,723 companies in 2009 and 425,739 companies in 2013. Local Heroes were selected out of them (183–240 companies met the criteria) and analysed according to their business performance level with emphasis on export and value added. Hungarian Local Heroes are a very well-defined group of companies consisting of around 200 companies. Although the number of companies is just slightly increasing, their revenue and added value are increasing to a significant extent (with 32 % CAGR and 24 % CAGR from 2009 to 2013, respectively). Hungarian Local Heroes are locally-owned, medium-sized or large, very successful, but very underleveraged, mostly manufacturing companies with around 64 % Export Intensity. The business performance of Hungarian Local Heroes is mostly based on their own company characteristics (resources and capabilities) and not on industry factors. Those companies that employ more employees are creating even more added value per employee. Hungarian LHs are very profitable companies with around 20 % return on equity on average.

Keywords Hungarian firms • Local Heroes • Business performance • Export intensity

Introduction

The debate in literature as to factors affecting corporate success has taken place for several decades. In this chapter, the Local Heroes definition of Schuh (2014) was used in the Hungarian context. The Hungarian Corporate Tax Database was used, the whole population of Hungarian companies in years 2009, 2010, 2011, 2012 and

M. Stocker, PhD (✉)
Corvinus University of Budapest, Budapest, Hungary
e-mail: miklos.stocker@uni-corvinus.hu

2013 was analysed. The database consists 385,723 companies in 2009 and 425,739 companies in 2013. Among them, Local Heroes were selected (183–240 companies met the criteria) and analysed according to their business performance with emphasis on export and value added. The aim of this chapter is to show the business characteristics of Hungarian Local Heroes, which is a small group of export intensive companies that jointly account for about 3.5 % of the country's GDP.

Literature Review

Corporate success can be measured in several ways, however some authors coined terms which referred to groups of successful companies sharing similar characteristics. Moreover, extensive research was done on this topic. For instance, Simon defined Hidden Champions in the 1990s and published his seminal work in the topic in 1996 and 2009. Hidden champions are companies which fulfil the following criteria:

> "number one, two or three in the global market or number one on its continent, revenue below $4 billion, and low level of public awareness" (Simon 2009:15).

Based on research on the Hidden Champions of the twenty-first century, McKiernan and Purg (2013) noted in their edited volume devoted to research on Hidden Champions in CEE and Turkey that:

> "Hungarian HCs are typically medium-sized enterprises according to their average number of employees" (Stocker and Szlávik 2013:205).

These companies are highly innovative and characterised by a strong leadership, but established in historically strong industries or scientific areas (Stocker and Szlávik 2013).

Schuh's definition of Local Heroes is somewhat more lenient, but in most dimensions even stricter than that of Hidden Champions:

> "Local heroes are well-run companies that have a strong position in their relevant market segments at home and a considerable foreign business, grow fast and often are among the technology/innovation leaders in their segments" (Schuh 2014, p. 5).

Local Heroes can be described along the following characteristics according to Schuh: their foundation and management base is located in the CEE, the share of local ownership exceeds 50 %, while the share of state-ownership remains below 25 %. These firms do not belong to financial services, energy and commodity businesses, they employ more than 100 employees and realise a minimum of 25 % of sales abroad. Finally, they should have been profitable in the last 3 years (Schuh 2014:5). Schuh found that Local Heroes mostly belong to IT, pharma, industrial, consumer goods and retail sectors.

Reszegi and Juhász (2014) have analysed those Hungarian companies which employ more than 20 people, have local ownership and do not feature state or local governmental ownership, provide complete financial statements and fulfil these criteria in the period of 2008–2011 (Reszegi and Juhász 2014). Although these criteria are very similar to Schuh's criteria, Local Heroes have a significantly stricter criteria related to the number of employees, export intensity and profitability.

Békés and Muraközi (2011, cited by Kazainé Ónodi 2013) found that manufacturing companies export intensity was 36 % for medium-sized enterprises and 56.6 % for large enterprises in 2005. Czakó found that all Hungarian medium-sized enterprises recorded export intensity of 17.9 %, while all Hungarian large enterprises were at the level of 41.9 % (Czakó 2009). Therefore, Hungarian manufacturing companies are much more export-oriented than their peers in other industries.

Materials and Methods

This chapter reports an explorative study about the Hungarian Local Heroes, their characteristics, business performance and export intensity. The full Hungarian Tax Database from the Hungarian Tax Authority for 5 years (2009–2013) was used, where data from basic financial statements and some additional tax data are included for all companies following the double-entry bookkeeping system. Basically, these companies formed the whole private sector. Companies that met the criteria designed by Schuh (2014) for Local Heroes were selected from this database and formed our Local Heroes database. The period taken for analysis is 5 years (2009–2013).

The selection criteria are the following:

- local ownership has to be higher than 50 % (this criterion is precisely met in the selection);
- no State-ownership or Local Government ownership (Schuh allows 25 % state-ownership, however in Hungary 0 % state or local government ownership is a better measure, therefore this criterion is stricter than that of Schuh's);
- export intensity has to be at least 25 % (export intensity was calculated as export revenues divided by sales revenues + other revenues, this criterion is either met or stricter than Schuh's criterion, as it is not known whether the latter includes other revenues in the equation or not);
- no financial services, energy or commodity businesses (this criterion is exactly met in the selection);
- being profitable during the last 3 years (this criterion could not be exactly calculated from the database, therefore it was assumed that retained earning had to be positive and each company had to show positive net earnings for a given year; hence, this criterion can be stricter or softer than that of Schuh depending on a given firm's actual data);
- having more than 100 employees (this criterion is exactly met);

Table 1 Population of Hungarian firms in the private sector and number of Local Heroes

	2009	2010	2011	2012	2013
Private sector (N)	385,723	392,670	409,007	424,815	425,739
Local Heroes (n)	183	187	212	234	240
	0.047 %	0.048 %	0.052 %	0.055 %	0.056 %

Source: Author's calculation

- the foundation and management base is located in the CEE region (these criteria could not be analysed in the database, but it is likely to be met as those companies who have at least 50 % Hungarian private ownership are founded and managed in the CEE region. According to these criteria, the Hungarian Local Heroes can be described as successful, profitable in the long-term, medium-sized or large private companies whose export intensity is more than 25 %. These criteria were met by around 0.04–0.05 % of the Hungarian private sector. The exact number of companies in the private sector and the selected Local Heroes are presented in Table 1.

According to the Local Heroes database, a series of significant financial variables were calculated, including revenues, employment size, personnel expenses, value added, depreciation and amortisation, export intensity, return on equity, long-term debt financing etc. The Hungarian Tax Database and therefore the Hungarian Local Heroes Database consists mostly of HUF measures, although these were also recalculated in euros using each year an average EUR/HUF rate (average of first and last trading day of the year).[1] Because of different exchange rates, compound annual growth rate measures are different in EUR and HUF (usually around 1–3 % less in EUR than in HUF).

Discussion

While it could be suggested in line with the previous research that a very limited number of Local Heroes are present in Hungary, this was falsified as 234 companies met the criteria in 2012 and 240 in 2013, which corresponds to more than 200 highly successful firms which could be identified in this analysis. According to the aforementioned criteria, it could be supposed that LH's should come from a lot of different industries (or the ones revealed in Schuh's research). This is, however, not the case in Hungary. The industry distribution of Hungarian Local Heroes is presented in Table 2.

Around 73–78 % of Hungarian Local Heroes are active in manufacturing sectors. In each year companies operating in the *manufacture of fabricated metal*

---

[1] Average of first and last trading day of the year was calculated to obtain an annual average as significant fluctuation happened in some years of analysis.

Table 2 Industry distribution of Local Heroes in Hungary

Industry distribution of Local Heroes in Hungary	2009	2010	2011	2012	2013
No. of Local Heroes	183	187	212	234	240
Agriculture, forestry and fishing	8	4	4	6	8
Mining and quarrying	1	0	0	1	1
Manufacturing	142	146	163	172	181
Electricity, gas, steam and air-conditioning supply	0	0	0	0	0
Water supply, sewerage, waste management and remediation	1	1	1	1	1
Construction	4	6	6	10	8
Wholesale and retail trade, repair of motor vehicles and motorcycles	13	12	14	17	14
Transportation and storage	6	8	13	17	17
Accommodation and food service activities	1	1	0	0	0
Information and communication	1	0	3	3	3
Financial and insurance activities	0	0	0	0	0
Real estate activities	0	2	1	2	1
Professional, scientific and technical activities	4	2	4	1	1
Administrative and support service activities	1	3	2	3	5
Public administration and defence; compulsory social security	0	0	0	0	0
Education	0	0	0	0	0
Human health and social work activities	0	0	0	0	0
Arts, entertainment and recreation	0	0	0	0	0
Other services	1	2	1	1	0
Activities of households as employers; undifferentiated goods and services	0	0	0	0	0
Activities of extra-territorial organisations and bodies	0	0	0	0	0

Source: Author's calculation

products, except machinery and equipment were the most numerous, closely followed by *manufacture of machinery and equipment n.e.c.*, or *manufacture of food products* (as it can be seen in Table 3).

Hungarian Local Heroes are mostly manufacturing, wholesale, retail or repair, transportation and storage or agricultural companies. A significant number of manufacturing companies seems to be tier 1 or tier 2 suppliers of the large automotive companies operating in Hungary (Audi, Mercedes, Opel, Suzuki, etc.). Manufacturing food products companies are increasing their share in the sample almost year by year, with the manufacture of computer, electronic and optical products and manufacture of electrical equipment firms also gaining a significant share. Firms active in the manufacturing of wearing apparel are the

Table 3 Distribution of manufacturing Local Heroes in Hungary

	2009	2010	2011	2012	2013
Manufacture of food products	20	23	23	22	31
Manufacture of beverages	0	0	0	0	1
Manufacture of tobacco products	0	0	1	0	0
Manufacture of textiles, wearing apparel and leather product	3	2	1	2	2
Manufacture of wearing apparel	12	12	9	9	4
Manufacture of leather products	3	0	3	1	5
Manufacture of paper and paper products	2	1	0	1	1
Printing and reproduction of recorded media	0	1	2	2	2
Manufacture of chemicals and chemical products	5	7	7	6	9
Manufacture of basic pharmaceutical products and pharmaceutical preparations	1	1	1	2	1
Manufacture of rubber and plastic products	8	7	10	9	8
Manufacture of other non-metallic mineral products	3	5	7	8	7
Manufacture of basic metals	6	8	8	9	8
Manufacture of fabricated metal products, except machinery and equipment	24	30	35	37	42
Manufacture of computer, electronic and optical products	10	8	9	10	8
Manufacture of electrical equipment	8	7	7	8	9
Manufacture of machinery and equipment n.e.c.	20	16	19	21	19
Manufacture of motor vehicles, trailers and semi-trailers	8	10	11	15	12
Manufacture of furniture	2	2	2	3	2
Other manufacturing	6	6	6	6	8
Repair and installation of machinery and equipment	1	0	2	1	2

Source: Author's calculation

only manufacturing industry which decreased significantly throughout the period of analysis.

The year 2010 was the worst for Hungarian Local Heroes in the period of analysis, in which almost all data were less favourable than in other years. Hungarian Local Heroes employed 59,564 people in 2009 and 76,088 in 2013. The number of employees displayed a compound annual growth rate of 5.02 % in the period of analysis (but the "growth" in 2010/2009 amounted to −27.6 %; see Table 4).

The total revenues amounted to 1353 billion HUF (5043 million euros) in 2009 and 5492 billion HUF (18,621 million euros), which means that the compound annual growth rate of Hungarian Local Heroes reached 32.33 %, which is a strikingly high value. Although one should bear in mind that each year an increasing number of companies qualified as Local Heroes, the annual growth rate of the number of companies was only 5.85 %. This suggests that Hungarian Local Heroes had a very significant intensive revenue growth in the period of analysis.

Table 4 Basic characteristics of Hungarian Local Heroes

Local Heroes in Hungary	2009	2010	2011	2012	2013	CAGR
No. of firms	183	187	212	234	240	5.57 %
No. of employees (person)	59,564	43,113	52,071	66,349	76,088	5.02 %
Total revenues (billion HUF)	1353	1169	1613	3436	5492	32.33 %
Value added (billion HUF)	350	278	386	662	1040	24.36 %
Personnel expenses (billion HUF)	168	149	195	309	365	16.75 %
Depreciation and amortisation (billion HUF)	42	35	47	141	240	41.89 %
Total revenues (million euros)	5043	4263	5469	11,328	18,621	29.85 %
Value added (million euros)	1303	1013	1308	2183	3527	22.03 %
Personnel expenses (million euros)	626	542	662	1019	1236	14.56 %
Depreciation and amortisation (million euros)	156	128	158	463	814	39.24 %

Source: Author's calculation

Value added (which was calculated as EBIT + depreciation & amortisation + personnel expenses) reached 350 billion HUF (1303 million euros) in 2009 and 1040 billion HUF (3527 million euros) in 2013, which corresponds to a CAGR of 24.36 %, which is also a remarkable result. The fact that revenues of Hungarian Local Heroes are growing faster than added value, suggests that *Hungarian Local Heroes are in their growth period*, where they make investments. This will be reinforced by additional data shown later.

The personnel expenses of Hungarian Local Heroes were 168 billion HUF (626 million euros) in 2009 and 365 billion HUF (1236 million euros) in 2013, which stands for a CAGR of 16.75 %. Compared with the CAGR of 5.02 % for the number of employees, this clearly shows that personnel expenses are increasing intensively, in a much greater way than the inflation or GDP growth of the country. This indicates that *Hungarian Local Heroes are increasing the compensation of their employees to a much larger extent than other companies*. Comparing the revenue growth and the growth of added value, it can be seen however that *Hungarian Local Heroes are not labour intensive*. It means that although the intensive growth of Local Heroes is positive for the economy, *existing Local Heroes will not solve employment problems*. Employment in this logic can only be increased significantly with the emergence of new Local Heroes, which should be a major aim of the economic policy decisions.

Depreciation and amortisation amounted to 42 billion HUF (156 million euros) in 2009 and 240 billion HUF (814 million euros) in 2013, which corresponds to a high CAGR of 41.89 %. This high measure compared with the lower revenue growth, and the even lower added value growth means that *Hungarian Local Heroes invested heavily in the past years, and built up capacities which can be hopefully utilised more intensively in the future*. Based on the present study,

Table 5 Additional characteristics of Hungarian Local Heroes

Local Heroes in Hungary	2009	2010	2011	2012	2013	CAGR
Average revenue per firm (billion HUF)	7	6	8	15	23	25.35 %
Average no. of employees per firm	325	231	246	284	317	−0.52 %
Total revenues per employee (thousand HUF)	22,720	27,107	30,983	51,780	72,178	26.01 %
Value added per employee (thousand HUF)	5872	6438	7412	9978	13,671	18.42 %
Personnel expenses per employee (thousand HUF)	2822	3446	3752	4656	4791	11.17 %
Depreciation and amortisation per employee (thousand HUF)	701	812	895	2118	3156	35.11 %
Value added/total revenue	25.84 %	23.75 %	23.92 %	19.27 %	18.94 %	−6.03 %
Personnel expenses/total revenue	12.42 %	12.71 %	12.11 %	8.99 %	6.64 %	−11.78 %
Depreciation and amortisation/total revenue	3.08 %	3.00 %	2.89 %	4.09 %	4.37 %	7.23 %
Average revenue per firm (million euros)	28	23	26	48	78	23.00 %
Average no. of employees per firm	325	231	246	284	317	−0.52 %
Total revenues per employee (thousand euros)	85	99	105	171	245	23.65 %
Value added per employee (thousand euros)	22	23	25	33	46	16.20 %
Personnel expenses per employee (thousand euros)	11	13	13	15	16	9.09 %
Depreciation and amortisation per employee (thousand euros)	3	3	3	7	11	32.58 %

Source: Author's calculation

it cannot be stated when Hungarian Local Heroes can become fully mature. Currently, they seem to be in the growth period, but the longer they grow, the more significant the externalities will be for the home country, their owners, as well as managers and employees. Employee-based average characteristics of Hungarian Local Heroes can be seen in Table 5.

The average revenue per firm was 7 billion HUF (28 million euros) in 2009 and 23 billion HUF (78 million euros) in 2013, which stands for a steady growth rate of 25.35 % CAGR by company on average. The average number of employees decreased slightly in the period of analysis with a CAGR of −0.52 %, which reduces the already low labour intensity of the Hungarian Local Heroes even further.

Total revenues per employee were 22,720 thousand HUF (85 thousand euros) in 2009 and 72,178 thousand HUF (245 thousand euros) in 2013 which is also extremely good not only in absolute numbers, but with its 26.01 % CAGR as well. One can only hope that this growth rate will be sustained for a longer period of time.

Value added per employee amounted to 5872 thousand HUF (22 thousand euros) in 2009 and increased to 13,671 thousand HUF (46 thousand euros) in 2013. In this sense, the value added per employee was average in 2009, but its 16.2 % CAGR can be regarded as substantial. Its absolute number in 2013 is large enough to cover personnel expenses, depreciation and amortisation, interests and profit. The CAGR of 16.2 % has to be compared with the CAGR of the GDP of Hungary in the period of analysis, which was 0.5 %. Hence, *Hungarian Local Heroes are major contributors to GDP growth* (apart from foreign multinationals).

Personnel expenses per employee reached 2822 thousand HUF (11 thousand euros) in 2009, which is low, but increased to 4791 thousand HUF (16 thousand euros) in 2013. With taxes deducted this demonstrates that *Hungarian Local Heroes pay around 40 % more than the average wage in Hungary.* Bearing in mind that these companies are mostly manufacturing companies, where most employees are either unskilled trained labour, or low-skilled labour, these personnel expenses numbers are apparently encouraging. Depreciation and amortisation per employee amounted to 701 thousand HUF (3 thousand euros) in 2009 and 3156 thousand HUF (11 thousand euros) in 2013, which corresponds to a CAGR of 35.11 %.

Although the value added per employee and personnel expenses per employee are impressive and growing, their revenue proportions are increasingly shrinking. Value added per total revenue was 25.84 % in 2009 and shrunk to 18.94 % in 2013 at a CAGR of −6.03 %, but personnel expenses per total revenue shrunk even more (from 12.42 % to 6.64 %) at a CAGR of −11.78 %. These negative growth rates with a CAGR of depreciation and amortisation of 7.23 % of the reinforces the *increasing trend related to capital (tangible assets) intensity of Hungarian Local Heroes.* If these companies are importing materials, the EUR/HUF changes could be a major factor behind the decrease in the value added per revenue. However, in this case the increasing exposure of local suppliers would have a positive effect on the value added per revenue. Less efficient new Hungarian Local Heroes could be another explanation, while the decrease in capacity utilisation could be another. Based on the depreciation and amortisation per revenue measure, one can nonetheless hope that the decrease in the value added per revenue is mostly the decrease in the capacity utilisation and hence the increase in capacity utilisation could result in an even higher growth of the value added of Hungarian Local Heroes.

All the aforementioned measures suggest a high profitability of the Hungarian Local Heroes. Table 6 illustrates this case. *The Hungarian Local Heroes are very profitable companies,* as their mean return on equity reached 21.68 % in 2009 and 20.87 % in 2013. Although it shows a CAGR of −0.75 %, a RoE of more than 20 % is a sign of good performance.

Table 6 Complex measures of Hungarian Local Heroes

Local Heroes in Hungary	2009	2010	2011	2012	2013	CAGR
Export intensity (%)	61.94	64.24	64.18	64.83	64.33	0.76
Return on equity (%)	21.68	18.75	30.66	32.16	20.87	−0.75
Long term debt by total assets (%)	6.70	7.82	7.80	7.55	8.87	5.79

Source: Author's calculation

Export intensity of at least 25 % was a selection criterion, but it was not expected that average export intensity would be as high as 61.94 % (in 2009) or even higher as 64.83 (in 2012). The mean export intensity was very close to 64 % in each and every year and it had a very low standard deviation, as well. Based on these numbers it can be noted that Hungarian Local Heroes are selling their goods and services mostly in foreign markets.

The long-term debt was only 6.7 % of total assets in 2009 and increased to 8.87 % in 2013, but these numbers remain low and show that Hungarian Local Heroes are still very underleveraged companies with a high cost of capital. Their enterprise value could be significantly increased with more leverage, but it also suggests that some psychological effect could be in place against using debt financing. In fact, after the credit crunch such behaviour could be understandable, but successful companies of this type could be expected to use leverage to a larger extent as part of their entrepreneurial growth.

Hungarian Local Heroes are highly profitable, very underleveraged companies with around 64 % of Export Intensity. Stocker (2014) found that learning by exporting can be observed in Hungarian companies, as companies with higher export intensity create higher added value per employee. This is not true, however, for Hungarian Local Heroes, as there was no correlation at all between value added and export intensity in the period of analysis (see Fig. 1).

The Hungarian Local Heroes are a small group of Hungarian exporters (around 0.5 %), which is homogenous in terms of export intensity, thus export intensity cannot explain value added. Interestingly, export intensity only shows a significant correlation with personnel expenses per employee in each year of the analysis, but the value of correlation remains weak. Value added per employee and personnel expenses per employee have a significant, strong correlation, since by definition personnel expenses are included in the value added. It is interesting, however, that the correlation between value added and the number of employees is increasing year by year, ending with a strong significant correlation in 2013 (Table 7).

This means that those companies *that employ more employees are creating even more added value*, which remains in harmony with the scale economies or the efficiency gains postulated by size-related theoretical explanations. It is, however, even more interesting that the return on equity does not have any significant reasonable correlation with export intensity, Value added per employee, number of employees or personnel expenses per employees. Moreover, studying industry-related measures could also be important. One could suggest from the industry

Fig. 1 Value added per employee and export intensity in 2013. *Source*: Author's calculation

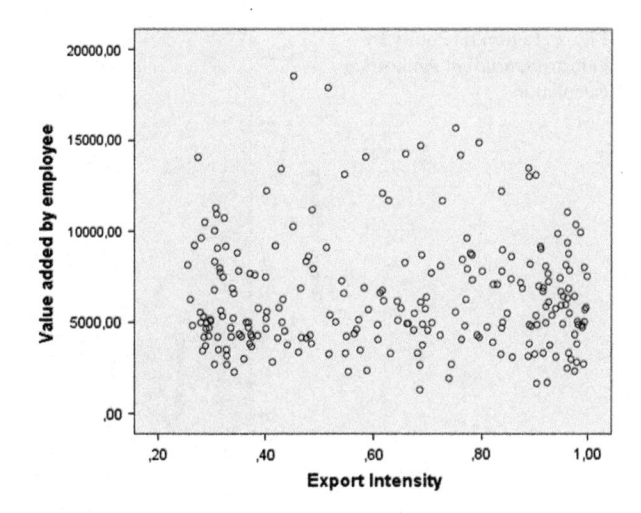

Table 7 Correlation between value added per employee and no. of employees

		2009		2010	
		Value added per employee	No. of employees	Value added per employee	No. of employees
Value added by employee	Pearson correlation	1	.007	1	**.148**[*]
	Sig. (2-tailed)		.927		**.043**
	N	183	183	187	187
		2011		2012	
		Value added per employee	No. of Employees	Value added per employee	No. of Employees
Value added by employee	Pearson correlation	1	**.155**[*]	1	**.363**[**]
	Sig. (2-tailed)		**.024**		**.000**
	N	212	212	234	234
		2013			
		Value added per employee		No. of Employees	
Value added by employee	Pearson correlation	1		**.530**[**]	
	Sig. (2-tailed)			**.000**	
	N	240		240	

Source: Author's calculation
*Correlation is significant at the 0.05 level (2-tailed)
**Correlation is significant at the 0.01 level (2-tailed)

Fig. 2 Return on equity by industries. *Source*: Author's calculation

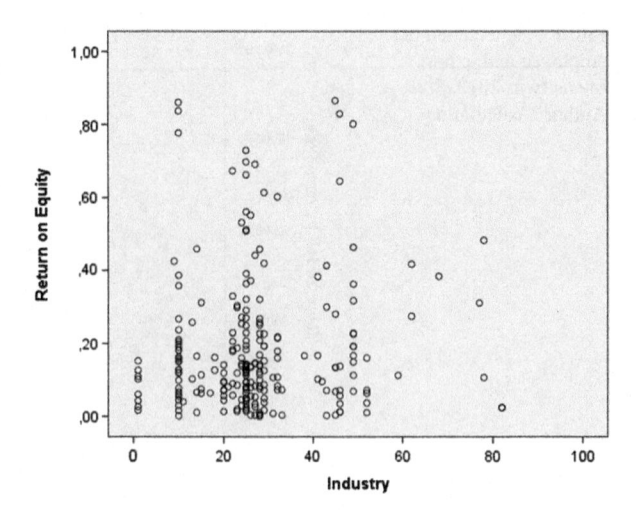

perspective that industries can have a significant effect on profitability, but his seems not to be the case of Hungarian Local Heroes (see Fig. 2).

It is apparent that industry does not have any significant effect on profitability of Hungarian Local Heroes. In each and every industry covered by the Hungarian Local Heroes, very heterogeneous return on equity measures can be observed. This finding is also completely in harmony with the Resource-Based View, *as Hungarian Local Heroes business performance is mostly affected by company characteristics (resources and capabilities), rather than by industry factors.*

Conclusion

Hungarian Local Heroes are a very well-defined group of companies consisting of around 200 companies. Although the number of companies is only slightly increasing, their revenues and added value are increasing to a significant extent (with CAGR of 32 % and 24 %, respectively, from 2009 to 2013). Hungarian Local Heroes are locally-owned, medium-sized or large, very successful, but highly underleveraged, mostly based in manufacturing sectors and showing an average of 64 % export intensity.

Hungarian Local Heroes are clearly in their growth period, thus they are increasing the compensation of their employees at a much higher than other companies. However, they are not labour-intensive. Hungarian Local Heroes invested heavily in the past years, they built up capacities, and hopefully these capacities can be utilised even more in the future. It can be stated that Hungarian Local Heroes are major contributors to the GDP growth, hence they should attract more attention of decision-makers dealing with economic policy. Hungarian Local Heroes pay around 40 % more than the average wage in Hungary. These companies are very profitable with a mean of about 20 % return on equity. The business performance of Hungarian Local Heroes is mostly based on their own company characteristics (resources and capabilities), and not mainly by industry factors and those companies who employ more employees are creating even more added value per employee.

Local Heroes should be cultivated by economic policy makers as their contribution to the GDP, their export revenues and their wage contributions are all important elements in any economy which want to close up to the most developed economies. It would be even more interesting which economic policy decisions could help potential companies to become Local Heroes and therefore increase their contribution as well.

References

Békés, G., & Muraközy, B. (2011). *Magyar gazellák: gyors növekedésű vállalatok jellemzői és kialakulásuk elemzése Magyarországon*. Műhelytanulmány. MTA Közgazdaságtudományi Intézet.

Czakó, E. (2009). A hazai exportot adó vállalatok néhány sajátossága a 2000-es évek elején. In Gy. Kocziszky & A. Gubik (Eds.), *VII. Nemzeközi konferencia kiadványa* (pp. 63–70). Miskolci Egyetem. Gazdaságtudományi Kar. Miskolc.

Kazainé Ónodi, A. (2013). Hazai kutatási eredmények exportáló vállalatainkról. In I. Ábel & E. Czakó (Eds.), *Az exportsiker nyomában* (pp. 55–80). Budapest: Alinea Kiadó.

McKiernan, P., & Purg, D. (Eds.). (2013). *Hidden champions in CEE and Turkey, carving out a global niche*. Berlin: Springer.

Reszegi, L., & Juhász, P. (2014). *A vállalati teljesítmény nyomában*. Budapest: Alinea Kiadó.

Schuh, A. (2014, October 23). Local Heroes – A new breed of competitors in Central & Eastern Europe. In 6. Grow East Congress, WU Vienna.

Simon, H. (2009). *Hidden Champions of the 21st century*. New York: Springer.

Stocker, M. (2014, October 10). Business performance of Hungarian exporting companies. In *Competitiveness of the CEE region in the global economy*. First AIB-CEE Chapter Conference, Budapest.

Stocker, M., & Szlávik, P. (2013). Hidden Champions of Hungary. In P. McKiernan & D. Purg (Eds.), *Hidden Champions in CEE and Turkey, carving out a global niche* (pp. 201–217). Berlin: Springer.

Printed by Printforce, the Netherlands